ANCIENT TEXTILES SERIES VOL. 7

FROM MINOS TO MIDAS
Ancient Cloth Production
in the Aegean and in Anatolia

FROM MINOS TO MIDAS
Ancient Cloth Production
in the Aegean and in Anatolia

Brendan Burke

Oxbow Books
Oxford and Oakville

ANCIENT TEXTILES SERIES VOL. 7

Published by
Oxbow Books, Oxford, UK

© Brendan Burke 2010

ISBN 978-1-84217-406-7

This book is available direct from

Oxbow Books, Oxford, UK
(Phone: 01865-241249; Fax: 01865-794449)

and

The David Brown Book Company
PO Box 511, Oakville, CT 06779, USA
(Phone: 860-945-9329; Fax: 860-945-9468)

or from our website
www.oxbowbooks.com

A CIP for this book record is available from the British Library

Library of Congress Cataloging-in-Publication Data

Burke, B. (Brendan)
  From Minos to Midas : ancient cloth production in the Aegean and in Anatolia / Brendan Burke.
    p. cm. -- (Ancient textiles series ; v. 7)
  Includes bibliographical references and index.
  ISBN 978-1-84217-406-7
 1. Textile industry--Aegean Sea Region--History--To 1500. 2. Textile industry--Turkey--History--To 1500. 3. Textile fabrics, Ancient--Aegean Sea Region--History--To 1500. 4. Textile fabrics, Ancient--Turkey--History--To 1500. 5. Aegean Sea Region--Antiquities. 6. Turkey--Antiquities. 7. Aegean Sea Region--Economic conditions 8. Turkey--Economic conditions I. Title.
  HD9868.A34B87 2010
  338.4'76770093809013--dc22

*Front cover: Boeotian black-figure skyphos. Circe and Odysseus with loom
(Ashmolean AN1896–1908, G249, with permission, Ashmolean Museum, University of Oxford).*

Back cover: Odysseus and Circe (Walters 1892–93, plate 4)

Ancient Textiles Series Editorial Commitee:
Eva Andersson, Margarita Gleba, Ulla Mannering
and Marie-Louise Nosch

Printed in Great Britain by
Short Run Press, Exeter

…from inside he took out twelve robes surpassingly lovely
and twelve mantles to be worn single, as many blankets,
as many great white cloaks, also the same number of tunics.
He weighed and carried out ten full talents of gold, and brought forth
two shining tripods, and four caldrons, and brought out a goblet
of surpassing loveliness that the men of Thrace had given him
when he went to them with a message, but now the old man spared not
even this in his halls, so much was it his heart's desire
to ransom back his beloved son.

(*Iliad* 24.229–236, Lattimore trans.)

CONTENTS

PREFACE

The field of textile studies, taking wide account of numerous types and uses of cloth in societies around the world, is multifaceted. As two organizers of a conference on textiles stated, 'On a world-wide scale, complex moral and ethical issues related to dominance and autonomy, opulence and poverty, political legitimacy and succession, and gender and sexuality, find ready expression through cloth' (Weiner and Schneider 1989, xi). This book, however, is more narrow in focus and, before I describe what it is, I believe it is necessary to make mention of what this book is not. Although I consider myself a field archaeologist, in no way does this book present a comprehensive catalogue of textile tools for archaeological seriation and stratigraphy. I hope that it is a useful tool for excavators in the Mediterranean but it is not meant to be a field-guide. This book does not focus on costume and adornment, and is not an 'archaeology of the body', where textiles express various negotiations of individual and group identities in specific social contexts, such as gender, age, social rank, and ethnicity (Chapin 2008; Colburn 2008; Joyce 2005). It does not profess any replication experiments based on depictions in art, nor does it try to recreate the 'fashion' of peoples in the past (Marinatos 1967; Jones 2001, 2005, 2007, 2009; Lillethun 2003; Marcar 2005). I should also stress that I am not a fiber specialist, and have no significant background in chemistry or even the intricacies of hand-weaving. I acknowledge that some of the material presented here should be studied in much more depth, in particular the textile remains from Gordion. Although my knowledge is limited on the subject of textile science, there is much left to be learned.

Admittedly I am not particularly concerned with *what* people wore, but rather, I look at how people in the past mobilized resources, organized labor, and produced cloth for exchange. I am particularly interested in what the organization of production tells us about individual societies and prehistoric economies. My objective is to assemble as much evidence as possible, disparate though it may be, and to present a coherent picture for organized cloth production on a scale beyond the household level at regional economic centers in the Aegean and in Anatolia. This book covers over 2000 years of evidence. Although it may seem to elide geographical boundaries and chronological periods, I am well aware of the distances between Early Minoan Crete and Iron Age Gordion. And in defense, my efforts to study the materials at hand are limited by the nature of the data itself: textiles are generally ephemeral, and the tools of production are rarely considered aesthetically pleasing, nor are they a prime object of study in archaeological publications.

The unifying feature of this work is that the included data show some evidence for standardization and centralized production. The investigation here confines itself to three main sources of information: excavated craft residues (artifacts), administrative documents (seals, sealings, tablets), and, to a much lesser degree, visual and literary culture, to illustrate the complex nature of cloth production, exchange, and consumption, and how developments in these reflect larger aspects of social organization.

This book takes an explicitly economic approach to textile production, a social craft activity that was of greater value and importance to people in the past than the production of painted clay pots, metal tools, and objects carved from precious materials: everyone depended on cloth. As with other craft goods, such as pottery, metal objects, and ivory carving, the large-scale production and exchange of textiles required specialization and some degree of centralization. Therefore, the focus of my study is on regional centers, most often referred to as palaces, to understand the means by which a state financed itself with cloth industries. From this we can look for evidence of social stratification, inter-regional exchange, and organized bureaucracies. A working hypothesis is that aspects of the textile industry are particularly suited to centralized, palatial control. Textile production is labor intensive and involves many different processes, including the mobilization of agricultural resources, the preparation of raw materials, skilled manufacturing, storage, and distribution, all of which are best administered under the direct control of a regional economic center or palace.

ACKNOWLEDGEMENTS

Two institutions are credited with help in the conception, research, and completion of this book: the Cotsen Institute of Archaeology at the University of California, Los Angeles, and the American School of Classical Studies at Athens. At UCLA, I became a much better archaeologist for having studied with Jim Hill, Tim Earle, and Richard Leventhal. At the American School, Willie Coulson, John Camp, and Charles Williams made me a more thorough and competent classicist. Sarah Morris was consistently guiding and directing me at both institutions and her influence on my scholarship is pronounced. I value greatly her thoughtful mentoring and, now, her collegial friendship. I warmly thank Elizabeth Barber, whose expertise on textile production and cloth deeply informs this work: my hope is that this book makes some addition to the major advances in textile research she has spearheaded throughout her career. Elizabeth Carter and Brent Vine, as original committee members, were also helpful in preventing me from making major errors. Any that remain belong, of course, to me. Since completion of the dissertation on which this work is based, new sources of evidence have come to light and several ideas have been rethought.

For logistical and financial assistance studying in Greece and Turkey I am grateful to UCLA, the 1984 Foundation, the Doreen Canaday Spitzer Fellowship from the American School of Classical Studies at Athens, and the Loeb Classical Library Foundation. Maria Pilali of the American School is thanked for her help securing necessary permissions from the British School at Athens and Knossos, and from the Greek Ministry of Culture. John Killen and John Bennet gave freely their time and advice in the early stages of this project. On Crete I would sincerely like to thank Penelope Mountjoy, Yannis Sakelarakis, Metaxia Tsipopoulou, and Joe and Maria Shaw. Permission to include material in this book is gratefully acknowledged from Peter and Elizabeth Warren, Ingo Pini, Patty Anawalt, and Deborah Ruscillo. The British Museum, the Ashmolean Museum, Oxford University, the Machteld Mellink Slide Collection at Bryn Mawr College, and the University of Pennsylvania Gordion Archives are warmly thanked for providing illustrations. Art Resource also supplied necessary images.

I am truly fortunate to be a part of the research at Gordion since 1994, sponsored by the University Museum of Archaeology and Anthropology at the University of Pennsylvania. I am grateful to the Project Director, G. Kenneth Sams, and former Director of Excavations, Mary Voigt, for their help and permission to study Phrygian material. The generous contributions of Keith DeVries and Ellen Kohler are especially acknowledged. Their extensive knowledge about Gordion, on-site and in the archives, are sorely missed. I thank the General Directorate of Cultural Property and Museums in Turkey, and especially the successive representatives from the Museum of Anatolian Civilizations in Ankara for their vital assistance in the conduct of my research.

While on a half-year sabbatical from the University of Victoria I was fortunate to spend time as a Visiting Scholar at the Danish National Research Council's Centre for Textile Research at the Saxo Institute of the University of Copenhagen, where major revisions of this work took place in 2006. I thank Marie Louise Nosch, Ulla Mannering, Margarita Gleba and Eva Andersson for their friendship, hospitality, and scholarship. I also gratefully acknowledge a publication subvention from the Centre for Textile Research and the 1984 Foundation. Useful comments and criticisms by Marie Louise Nosch and an anonymous reader have been most helpful.

Illustrations were improved upon by Kim Lehmann Insuwa, Genevieve Hill, Kicker Conlin, and Tina Ross. Bibliographical research and editorial corrections were done by Caitlin Smith Bingham and Sara Davis, to whom I am very grateful. Significant contributions to the work were made by Trevor Van Damme who is also thanked most sincerely. Other friends have helped me with this project perhaps without even knowing it and that is why I'd like to thank them here: Judith Binder, Bob Bridges, Wendy Closterman, Ernestine Elster, Jessie Johnson, Ann-Marie Knoblauch, Susan Lupack, Nate Marsh, John Papadopoulos, Steve Pigman, Karen Stamm and Zekeriya Utğu. Finally I happily acknowledge the friendship and thoughtful advice I received over the years from Bryan Burns, Camilla MacKay, Molly Richardson, and my sister Maryellen Burke. Other family members contributed to the project indirectly, numerous brothers and sisters-in-law, and our mother, and to them I dedicate this with my heartfelt gratitude.

Brendan Burke
Athens, August 2009

ABBREVIATIONS

Abbreviations of ancient sources

Arist. *Hist. an.*	Aristotle *Historia animalium*
Arist. *Pol.*	Aristotle *Politica*
Ar. *Plut.*	Aristophanes *Plutus*
Ar. *Lys.*	Aristophanes *Lysistrata*
Arr. *Anab.*	Arrian *Anabasis*
Ath.	Athenaios
Curt.	Quintus Curtius Rufus
Dsc.	Dioscorides *de Materia Medica*
Dsc. *Eup.*	Dioscorides περὶ Εὐπορίστων
Euseb. *Chron.*	Euscbius *Chronica*
Hes. *Theog.*	Hesiod *Theogony*
Hdt.	Herodotus
Il.	Homer *Iliad*
Od.	Homer *Odyssey*
Just. *Epit.*	Justinus *Epitome* (of Trogus)
Pind. *Ol.*	Pindar *Olympian Odes*
Pliny *HN*	Pliny the Elder *Historia Naturalis*
Plut. *Vit. Alex.*	Plutarch *Vitae Alexander*
Ovid *ad Liv.*	Ovid *ad Livia*
Ovid *Fast.*	Ovid *Fasti*
Ovid *Metam.*	Ovid *Metamorphoses*
Thuc.	Thucydides
Xen. *An.*	Xenophon *Anabasis*
Xen. *Mem.*	Xenophon *Memorabilia*
Xen. *Oec.*	Xenophon *Oeconomikos*
Vitr. *De arch.*	Vitruvius *De architectura*
Zen.	Zenobios

Abbreviations of periodicals, series, and books

AA	*Archäologischer Anzeiger*
Aegaeum	*Aegaeum: Annales d'archéologie égéenne de l'Université de Liège*
AJA	*American Journal of Archaeology*

AmerAnt	*American Antiquity*
AnatSt	*Anatolian Studies. Journal of the British Institute of Archaeology at Ankara*
ASAtene	*Annuario della Scuola archeologica di Atene e delle Missioni italiane in Oriente*
BAR	*British Archaeological Reports*
BASOR	*Bulletin of the American Schools of Oriental Research*
BCH	*Bulletin de correspondance hellénique*
BCH Suppl.	*Bulletin de correspondance hellénique. Supplément*
BSA	*Annual of the British School at Athens*
CAH	*Cambridge Ancient History*
CANE	*Civilizations of the Ancient Near East, ed. J. Sasson, 1995. New York*
CHIC	*Corpus Hieroglyphicarum Inscriptionum Cretae, Études Crétoises 31, J.-P. Olivier, L. Godard, in collaboration with J.-C. Poursat, 1996. Paris*
CMS	*Corpus der minoischen und mykenischen Siegel, Akademie der Wissenschaften und der Literatur, Mainz and Berlin.*
CMS II.6	*Corpus der minoischen und mykenischen Siegel. Iraklion, Archäologisches Museum, die Siegelabdrücke von Aj. Triada und Anderen Zentral- und Ostkretischen Fundorten, Bd II.6. ed. W. Müller and I. Pini. Akademie der Wissenschaften und der Literatur, Mainz and Berlin.*
CMS V. Suppl.1A	*Corpus der minoischen und mykenischen Siegel. Kleinere Griechische Sammlungen. Agina-Korinth, Bd. V. Suppl. 1A. ed. I. Pini. Akademie der Wissenschaften und der Literatur, Mainz and Berlin.*
CoMIK	*Corpus of Mycenaean Inscriptions from Knossos, Chadwick, J., Godart, L., Killen, J., Olivier, J.-P., Sacconi, A., Sakellarakis, I. Vol. I, 1–1063 (1986), Vol. II, 1064–4495 (1990), Vol. III 5000–7999 (1997), Vol. IV 8000–9947 and index to Vols. I-IV (1998), Rome and Cambridge.*
CurrAnthr	*Current Anthropology*
Docs¹	*Documents in Mycenaean Greek, M. Ventris and J. Chadwick, 1956. Cambridge*
Docs²	*Documents in Mycenaean Greek, 2nd Edition. M. Ventris and J. Chadwick, 1973. Cambridge*
Emporia	*EMPORIA: Aegeans in the Central and Eastern Mediterranean. Proceedgins of the 10th International Aegean Conference, Athens, Italian School of Archaeology, 14–18 April 2004 (Aegaeum 25), ed. R. Laffineur and E. Greco, 2005. Liège and Austin.*

Floreant Studia Mycenaea	*Floreant Studia Mycenaea: Akten des X. internationalen mykenologischen Colloquiums in Salzburg vom 1.–5 Mai 1995, (Österreichischen Akademie der Wissenschaften), ed. S. Deger-Jalkotzy, S. Hiller, and O. Panagl, 1999. Vienna.*
Function of the Minoan Palace	*The Function of the Minoan Palaces: Proceedings of the Fourth International Symposium at the Swedish Institute in Athens, 10–16 June, 1984, ed. R. Hägg and N. Marinatos, 1987. Stockholm.*
GORILA	*Recueil des inscriptions en Linéaire A. Études Crétoises 21, vols. 1–5. L. Godart and J.-P. Olivier, 1976–1985. Paris*
JAS	*Journal of Archaeological Science*
JMA	*Journal of Mediterranean Archaeology*
JNES	*Journal of Near Eastern Studies*
JHS	*Journal of Hellenic Studies*
Knossos: Palace, City, State	*Knossos: Palace, City, State. Proceedings of the Conference in Herakleion organised by the British School at Athens and the 23rd Ephoreia of Prehistoric and Classical Antiquities of Herakleion, in November 2000, for the Centenary of Sir Arthur Evans' excavations at Knossos 2004, ed. G. Cadogan, E. Hatzaki, and A. Vasilakis, eds. (British School at Athens Studies 12), 2004. London.*
METRON	*METRON: Measuring the Aegean Bronze Age: Proceedings of the 9th International Aegean Conference, Yale University, 18–21 April 2002, (Aegaeum 24), ed. K. Foster and R. Laffineur, 2003. Liège and Austin.*
OpAth	*Opuscula Atheniensia*
Politeia	*Politeia: Society and State in the Aegean Bronze Age. Proceedings of the 5th International Aegean Conference, University of Heidelberg, Archaologisches Institut 10–13 April 1994, (Aegaeum 12), ed. R. Laffineur and W.-D. Niemeier, 1995. Liège and Austin.*
Prakt	*Praktika tes en Athenais Archaiologikes Etaireias*
SMEA	*Studi micenei ed egeo-anatolici*
TEXNH	*TEXNH: Craftsmen, Craftswomen and Craftsmanship in the Aegean Bronze Age Proceedings of the 6th International Aegean, Philadelphia, Temple University, 18–21 April 1996, (Aegaeum 16), ed. R. Laffineur and P. Betancourt, 1997. Liège and Austin.*
WorldArch	*World Archaeology*

1 FRAMING THE DISCUSSION

Metaphors of spinning and weaving in Greek and Latin literature suggest that a basic understanding of cloth production was common knowledge to ancient audiences. The key role of cloth is revealed by the liberal use of textile metaphors in Classical writing. For example, the *Moirai*, or three Fates, are personified as old textile workers (Fig. 1): Clotho spins, Lachesis measures the thread of life to varying lengths, and Atropos cuts the threads of an individual's life (*Il.* 24.525, *Od.* 1.17, 3.208, 4.208; Hes. *Theog.* 217, 904; Pind. *Ol.* 1.40; Ovid *ad Liv.* 164, *Fast.* 6.757). In one famous comedy, (Ar. *Lys.* 568–70) the playwright compares wool processing and weaving to the proper governance of the city of Athens: problematic citizens are likened to the prickly burrs found in wool that need to be picked off one by one. Another indication of the importance of cloth in Greek society is

Figure 1. Relief of Three Fates in Tegel, Berlin, 2nd century AD (Hauser 1903, p. 99, fig. 48).

Figure 2. East frieze of the Parthenon (Block V), presentation of peplos for Athena, 447–432 BC (Inv. 1816.0610.19 ©Trustees of the British Museum).

the *peplos* of Athena, the ceremonial garment which was woven each year for the goddess, and was arguably the most important cult object in Classical Athens (Fig. 2)(Mansfield 1985; Barber 1992).

Cloth manufacture was certainly an important activity throughout antiquity, and it is often studied to highlight the lives of women in the past. The role of men, however, in cloth production, in reality and myth, should not be over-looked or discounted: even in earliest Greek legend the father of the gods had a craftsmen's role with an emphasis on cloth production. In the marriage of Zas (Zeus) and Chthonie (Ge), as described in the *Theologia* by the 6th century Pre-Socratic philosopher Pherekydes of Syros (7, fr. 2, I, p. 48.5 Diels-Krantz), Zeus makes a great and beautiful veil (*pharos*) embroidered with the earth, Ocean, and Ocean's palace on it; he presents it to Chthonie, making her his wife (Svenbro and Scheid 1996; Schibli 1990, 50–1). Similarly, the weavers of the first peplos for the Greater Panathenaic festival were two professional Cypriot men with appropriate textile names, Akesas, whose name is probably related to ἀκεστής 'mender' or 'tailor', and Helikon, perhaps related to ʽελικτός, 'twisted/spun' (Ath. 2.24b; Zen. 1.56, I, p. 22.12 von Leutch-Schneidewin. See also Mansfield 1985, 4, 21–2; Loftus 1998–2000, 13–14; Thompson 1982). Cloth production, contrary to some modern scholarly biases, is not 'just women's work'.

Actual fragments of Greek textiles, unfortunately, have rarely survived in the Mediterranean, but the few extant examples indicate a sophisticated knowledge of diverse weaving technologies that were part of a long-lived tradition. The production of textiles prior to the Archaic period in the eastern Mediterranean is investigated here; in particular, the focus is on organized cloth production in the Aegean and in Anatolia during the Bronze and Early Iron Ages (*c.* 2700–800 BC). Employing a multidisciplinary approach, this study takes into account archaeological remains, visual culture, and textual sources, to look at cloth manufacture, distribution, and consumption. The manufacture of cloth in palace centers is addressed in order to demonstrate that many aspects of craft production reflect social organization. By studying the distribution of tools, the organization of labor, and the means of mobilization, greater insight is gained into social structures of the past. In premonetary economies, finished textiles often functioned as a kind of currency, and were used as a value good for craft specialists, mercenaries, and overseas trading partners. Within the Aegean and the Anatolian spheres elites exercised control of many craft activities, including the many phases of textile production, in order to maintain and finance social, religious, and military institutions. In the following chapters the economic, political, and social implications of well-developed, centrally controlled textile industries are analyzed within three cultural regions and chronological periods: the Minoans of the mid-third to mid-second millennium BC, the Mycenaeans of the Late Bronze Age (*c.* 1600–1150 BC), and the Phrygians of the Anatolian Iron Age (*c.* 1000–800 BC).

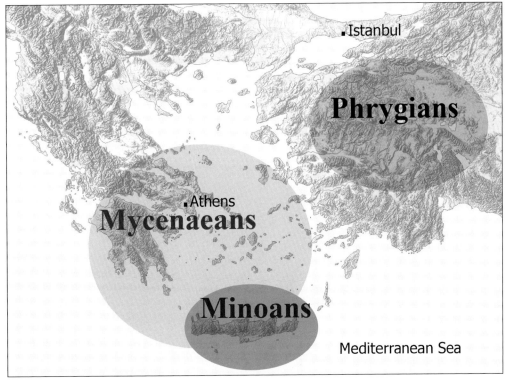

Map 1. Minoan, Mycenaean, and Phrygian regions. Adapted from Interactive Ancient Media.
http://iam.classics.unc.edu/.

Important distinctions are found among Minoan, Mycenaean, and Phrygian social economies, over a wide span of time, from the Early Bronze Age through the Iron Age. This is fully acknowledged. To speak in terms of cultural similarities within each of these modern determinations is difficult: not every 'Minoan', 'Mycenaean' or 'Phrygian' (however these designations are defined, by ethnicity, language, geography, chronology) was the same, of course, and when material from intermediate zones, such as the Cyclades, the Troad, Ionia and western Anatolia are included, the picture gets very murky indeed.

References in later Greek literature, such as the poetry of Homer, help some in reconstructing contexts for cloth consumption and distribution, such as guest-gifts, war prizes, and funerary offerings (Schoenhammer 1993). A large vocabulary of specialized cloth terms is often paired with metals in contexts of Homeric gift exchange. The shroud woven by Penelope for Laertes plays a key role in the *Odyssey*, and the skyphos from Chiusi nicely illustrates the most common weaving technology of Homeric Greece and presumably the Bronze Age, the warp-weighted loom (Fig. 3). Before weaving, however, one would need spun thread, another time consuming activity often referred to in ancient literature and shown in art, such as the spinner on the vase by the Brygos Painter in London (Fig. 4).

While it is acknowledged that the Homeric epics are not reliable guides to the culture and habits of Bronze Age Greeks, archaeological data used critically can be shown to reflect objects and practices in the *Iliad* or the *Odyssey*. For example, while Homer uses at least a dozen different words to refer to cloth (see Table 4) they fall into two basic types: fancy and plain cloth. These categories roughly parallel the two types described by Aegean scribes and fit the basic outline of textiles known from visual representations. They also

Figure 3. Attic red-figure skyphos from Chiusi, showing Penelope at her loom and Telemachos to the left, by the Penelope Painter, 440–430 BC, Museo Archeologico, Chiusi, Italy (left, photo, ©Scala / Art Resource, NY, for permission fee; right, drawing from Fürtwangler, Reichold, and Hauser 1932, pl. 142).

adhere to the two types of economic goods in the staple-wealth finance model (D'Altroy and Earle 1985), which can be applied to economies of the prehistoric Aegean and Anatolia. Finely crafted cloth was often the product of Homeric women and was used to display status (*Il.* 3.125–28; 16.220–224; 22.440–44; *Od.* 3.349–351; 7.95–97) in the contexts of war, marriage, and death. We might imagine these kinds of textiles looking something like the garments shown on Bronze Age wall paintings from Crete and mainland Greece. The other type is the plainer, every-day textile made by slaves and captives (*Il.* 1.29–31; 6.456; *Od.* 7.103–106) for daily use, or produced as an item for tribute or a good to be paid to dependents of the palace, including craftsmen and soldiers. Before pursuing these issues in more detail, an outline of methodology is necessary.

Methodology

The field of textile studies is truly multidisciplinary: some archaeologists have approached the study of textiles as socio-cultural anthropologists, building theoretical models from ethnographic parallels and comparing these observations to

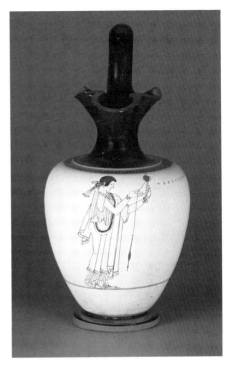

Figure 4. White ground oinochoe by Brygos Painter, from Locri, 490–470 BC, British Museum Vase D13 (Inv. 1873.0820.304 ©Trustees of the British Museum).

the archaeological record (*e.g.*, Parsons 1975; Smith and Hirth 1988; Parsons and Parsons 1990; Brumfiel 1991; Costin 1991; 1993; Anderson and Nosch 2003). Others have focused their examinations on specific classes of textile tools (Carington Smith 1975; 1992; Dabney 1996), including specialized studies of the spindle whorl (*e.g.*, Balfanz 1995; Crewe 1998). Some scholars, particularly those working in the Near East where records are abundant, have looked exclusively at textual documents related to textile production (Jacobsen 1970; Waetzoldt 1972; Dalley 1977; Ribichini and Xella 1985; Sollberger 1986; Szarzynska 1988; Völling 2008), while others have relied on a combination of textual and archaeological evidence for studying cloth manufacture and labor within complex economies (Murra and Morris 1976; Murra 1989; Stein and Blackman 1993; McCorriston 1997). Kemp and Vogelsang-Eastwood (2001) for example, have thoroughly examined aspects of New Kingdom Egyptian textile technology and production methods and found that there was a complex interrelationship between public and private spheres when it came to cloth manufacture.

Ideally, we would like to have archaeological evidence from a well-excavated political and economic center that includes workshop facilities preserving textile equipment *in situ*. In addition, we would like administrative records from this same site that describe the raw materials, their sources, the production targets, the ultimate destination of the finished products, the objects traded in return, and the organization of the labor used to make these goods. In the Aegean and Anatolia, however, a complete picture like this is an archaeological fantasy. As it is, the data sets related to textile production are limited and vary greatly. The primary sources of evidence preserved for us are the tools associated with cloth production, the inscribed documents recording the administration of this industry and its exchange, and the visual arts which depict the finished product in use.

In this book two general questions are addressed: how was textile production within the Minoan, Mycenaean, and Phrygian territories organized, and how does this organization reflect broader aspects of cultural development? The examination of one craft activity in detail will better inform us about the general structure of the production system, from the acquisition of raw materials to the final distribution of finished goods. Although there are differences in time and place between centers in the Aegean and in Anatolia, textiles were a source of wealth for these regional authorities. Once the production of cloth is understood it is possible to place that product within the context of the overall political economy. This information can also be compared to other industries, such as food production, pottery manufacture, and metallurgy, in order to confirm or refute suggestions about social complexity.

As Stein and Blackman (1993, 30–1) state, 'the organizational context of craft production reflects both the institutional structure of the state and the nature of the state's interaction with the broader, more heterogeneous society in which it functions.' To investigate the organization of craft activities, the context, concentration, scale, and intensity of production require examination. Concentrated deposits of craft residues, such as raw materials, tools of manufacture, craft debris, unfinished and finished goods, are all indicative of specialized production. Administrative documents, when they can be deciphered, facilitate this investigation. The consumption of textiles is more difficult to study than the production, but this topic is addressed by examining representations of cloth in art and literature to understand their function and cultural context.

In the eastern Mediterranean, during the Bronze and Iron Ages, generally speaking, regional authorities administered the phases of production, from the acquisition and preparation of raw materials to the subsistence of the personnel and the distribution of the final product. This of course does not exclude independent household production which must have also played an important economic role, but this aspect is nearly invisible in the archaeological record preserved for us in the areas under discussion. The evidence we have from the Bronze and Iron Ages is highly incomplete, but, following Zagarell (1986, 420) who looked at Mesopotamian economies of the third millennium, I would apply his view to the Bronze Age Aegean and Iron Age Anatolia: I believe most of the exchanges were on the community-to-community level rather than on a individual merchant-to-merchant level. Similarly, I believe 'power is seen as an expression and reflection of community/state productive power and administrative control' (Zagarell 1986, 420). Craft specialization is defined as repeated, surplus production of one type of good (in this case, cloth) by attached, dependent specialists for exchange directed by a central authority (the palace).

By quantifying the distribution of certain tools concentrated within a workshop complex of a regional center and assessing evidence for standardization we can locate specialized production. In some cases it is likely that workers were not free laborers but were slaves or prisoners captured in war and employed by the state, in other cases they may be highly skilled and valued craftspeople. Raw materials (primarily wool and flax) and component elements (dyes, perfumed oil, and decorations) are transformed into valuable property at the disposal of the ruling authority. The palace directs consumption of the finished product, for military, ideological and political purposes, and to acquire other prestige goods which serve to maintain power. With this methodological framework in place, the materials under study should be introduced.

Spinning and Weaving

Most textiles in the ancient world were made from plant and animal fibers. The basic element for woven cloth was spun threads or yarns. Felted textiles have been found at Gordion and in Greece, and they were made by applying heat and pressure to make unspun wool. The naturally occurring scales on wool fibers made this possible. Most wool and plant fibers, however, were manually spun together – a time consuming process requiring more energy than actual weaving. Much can be learned from yarn analysis, using the naked eye or under a microscope, including fiber identification, processing methods, and traditions followed. Distinguishing between plant and animal fibers is sometimes very difficult (see Gordion fabrics below). Sometimes the fiber is no longer preserved but a cast, or pseudomorph, will still allow structural and manufacturing analysis. Pseudomorphism is not fully understood but the basic process seems to be that molecules from corroding metal nearby migrate to the interstices of any adjacent organic material, leaving either a negative or positive cast of that material (Unruh 2007, 167). Thread counts, diameters, and spinning direction are other key components. Fibers are either spun clockwise or counter-clockwise, twisting to the left or the right. The general convention for describing the direction of spun thread is to call it S-spun (counter-clockwise) or Z-spun (clockwise), referring to the direction of the slant in the middle of these letters. This descriptive information is useful: for example, most yarn in Egypt was S-spun, while contemporary European thread was Z-spun, so when even small fragments of cloth are found arguments can be made for possible origins.

Plant Fibers

Hardy (2008) has suggested that the earliest textile technology was most likely the production of string or cord, and she notes that binding and attaching things is among one of the cultural universals (see also Brown 1991). String production, it is proposed, leads to developments in looping and weaving, enabling the production of bags and nets – for hunting, fishing, and the collection of small items, and there is support for this in the ethnographic record. Palaeolithic evidence for string is rare, yet, ingeniously, Hardy looks at indirect evidence, including perforated beads, net weights, and cord impressed pottery. Assuming that anything that was perforated was suspended by some string or cord, a perforated bone point and a perforated wolf incisor, both from Repolusthöhle, Austria, dating to *c.* 300,000 years ago, show the earliest evidence for the use of string, and a form of textile technology. By 200,000 years ago, perforated ostrich eggshell beads are known as well (Hardy 2008).

Physical remains of twisted fibers approximately 25,000 years old have been found at the Upper Paleolithic site of Pavlov in the Czech Republic (Adovasio, Soffer and Klíma 1996, 526–34). What the original source for the fibers was is uncertain, but almost certainly it was a plant, probably a bast fiber related to linen and hemp. Linseed remains from pre-farming contexts dating to the Epipalaeolithic (*c.* 9200–8500 BC) have been found in North Syria (Hillman 1975; Zohary and Hopf 2000, 127–31). Domesticated flax (*Linum usitatissimum*), which yields linen, is a highly useful crop since the oily seeds are a good source of nutrition and the long fibers can be used for textiles (Fig. 5). Charred linseeds have been found at Pre-Pottery Neolithic B sites (*c.* 8000 BC), including Ramad, Jericho, and Nahal Hemar (Miller 2006, 48). These do not ensure fiber use, but scraps of linen cloth from Nahal Hemar in the Judean desert conclusively demonstrate the production of linen by the eighth millennium BC (Barber 1991, 11–15; McCorriston 1997, 519; van Zeist and Bakker-Heeres 1975; Schick 1988).

Figure 5. Flax plant (From Köhler 1887).

Not surprisingly, along with the many innovations of the Neolithic period, clay impressions of textiles have been found that are the earliest evidence for loom-woven cloth, most certainly linen, at 7th millennium BC Jarmo in northern Iraq (Adovasio 1983, 425–6). Neolithic linen is also known from Çatal Höyük and Çayönü in Anatolia (McCorriston 1997, 519), and flax is reportedly cultivated widely in Anatolia before the eighth millennium BC (Nesbitt 1995, 75). Evidence for textile production, including stamp seals, has been found at the Neolithic site of Ulucak, near İzmir, Turkey (Çilingiroğlu 2009, 16–7). Linen does not appear in the archaeological record of Egypt until the fifth millennium BC, where pieces of coarse linen were found in the Faiyum oasis along with spindle whorls and flax seeds (Barber 1991, 10, Wetterstrom 1993). By the 19th Dynasty, in the tomb of Sen-Nedjem at Egyptian Thebes, flax harvesting

Figure 6. Book of the Dead of Nakht, papyrus sheet 13, flax-harvesting scene, 1350–1300 BC (Inv. 1888.0512.101.13 ©Trustees of the British Museum).

Figure 7. Hank of flax (1875.0810.283 ©Trustees of the British Museum).

is shown, as it is in the Book of the Dead of Nakht, dating to the 14th century BC (Fig. 6). In the lower panel of the Book of the Dead, tall green flax is shown growing closely together to produce long straight fibers which are pulled up by hand at just the right time for long, fine threads (Fig. 7). More detailed discussion of flax growing in Pharaonic Egypt is discussed in Kemp and Vogelsang-Eastwood (2001, 25–37).

The cultivation of flax is one of the most labor-intensive chores in agriculture. The plant is fairly unaggressive and requires much weeding. With proper timing the harvest of flax can yield several benefits: ripe seeds for linseed oil, stalks with fibers still pliable enough for fine linen cloth, and processing debris which can be used for fuel, fodder, and manure (Salmon-Minotte and Franck 2005). Well-watered, easily drained agricultural land is needed for flax and harvesting requires strong manual labor, first for weeding and then for pulling the stalks of flax out of the ground whole. The process of removing the seed pods from the stalks is called rippling. Pods can be crushed to separate the seeds from the

Table 1. Various phases in flax processing and uses.

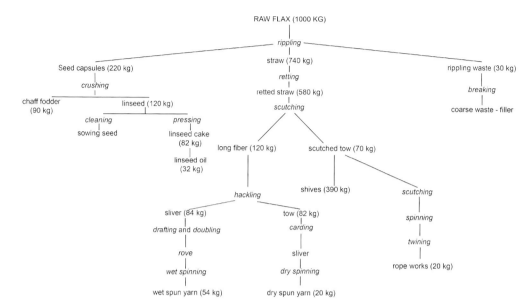

protective cortex and collected for sowing, or the crushed pods and seeds used for chaff fodder. Seeds cleaned further can be pressed for linseed oil. The stalks, on the other hand, are retted, that is, left to rot, either in standing water or spread out on a flat surface to collect dew and decompose (ground retting). Pectins that bind fibers to other parts of the plant are dissolved by enzyme action from bacteria or fungi. The next stage for the fibers is scutching, to remove the line fibers from the retted straw, producing short fibers (tow) and long fibers. The scutched tow will yield shives, woody matter which can then be used for fertilizer, or it can be further processed for spinning and twining coarse fibers into rope. The long fibers are hackled, that is, combed to remove short fibers and to ensure all the long fibers are parallel. The retting process can last 10–14 days, and after the stalks are left to dry and then beaten and combed to break the pith away from the usable fibers in the center. At this stage in the processing the raw linen, or rove, is ready for spinning, which can be either dry or wet spun (Salmon-Minotte and Franck 2005). Treating the rove with boiling water and sodium carbonate or sodium hydroxide will further breakdown the fibers and remove any unwanted color, yielding softer finer threads. Details of flax processing can be followed in the table above. Note that from 1000 kg of raw flax, the yield of useable fibers is less than 100 kg.

Spinning Wool
Wool is a different story (Fig. 8): sheep were first domesticated in the Near East at about 9000 BC, based on molecular dating (Hiendleder, Kaupe, Wassmuth and Janke 2002).

Figure 8. Sample of undyed raw wool (Am1986.07.179.e ©Trustees of the British Museum).

Figure 9. Sarab sheep figurine, Iran, c. 5000 BC (©Oriental Institute of Chicago).

Prior to the fourth millennium BC, most sheep had fairly short hair of coarse fibers not well suited to spinning. The earliest preserved wool dates to the fourth millennium BC from Upper Egypt but animal figurines decorated with woolly backs are found in Mesopotamia along with texts that show sheep were of concern to economic centers (Barber 1991, 25; Waetzoldt 1972; 2007). The clay figurine from Sarab, Iran, dating to 5000 BC shows what appears to be tufts of wool, providing an early appearance for such sheep (Fig. 9). Early on most Neolithic sheep were reared for their meat (Sherratt 1983; Ryder 1969; 1983; 1993; Barber 1991, 20–30). Thousands of years after flax and short-haired sheep were domesticated some species of sheep were selectively bred for their woolly fibers, giving rise to extensive wool-based economies in the eastern Mediterranean. This change is visible in the faunal record: sheep bones appear more robust over time because a heavier musculature develops from carrying a weightier coat of wool (McCorriston 1997, 521; Payne 1973).

Since females yield better wool than males, palaeozoologists studying the age and sex ratios of bones have also been able to identify sheep that were used primarily for meat or primarily for wool. The highest quality wool, however, comes from young neutered males, called wethers. Fleecier sheep purposefully bred for use in textile production show a shift in agricultural patterns that had significant social ramifications: the transition to exploiting wool, which is a fiber more efficiently produced than linen, initiated the development of large textile workshops and an attached labor class (McCorriston 1997).

Weaving

In the eastern Mediterranean the dominant tradition for cloth production was the warp-weighted loom, beginning as early as the Middle Neolithic period. Other methods of working spun thread were of course possible, and even likely, but the warp-weighted loom predominates in the archaeological and textual records (Hoffman 1964; Barber 1991). The

Figure 10. Modern warp-weighted loom from Scandinavia (B. Burke).

basic design is simple and the ancient form no doubt compares well to Scandinavian looms used today: a shed is created by leaning a simple frame against a flat upright face (Fig. 10). Rows of vertical warp threads fall downwards which can be divided into any number of smaller sheds. Weft threads are run horizontally through these sheds, using a shuttle, to create a variety of patterns. The woven design generally starts from the top and is packed upwards, gradually building toward the bottom.

Warp-weighted weaving provided several advantages over the ground looms of Egypt and the Near East primarily in terms different dimensions of cloth and the ease of production (Hoffmann 1964, 21, 314; Crowfoot 1936; Carington Smith 1975, 97–99). That warp-weighted looms from the Mediterranean leave behind archaeological indicators of cloth production is also extremely fortunate: archaeologists are often left with large numbers of clay loom weights, although the wooden frames and the cloth itself have disappeared. From Knossos, for example, in the so-called Loom Weight Basement, 400 loom weights were found by Arthur Evans (1921). They were most likely grouped into sets numbering 20 to 50 weights for each loom. The 450 loom weights from a wealthy town house on the island city of Akrotiri (Room D15 of the West House) also indicate a large number of working looms, and are well dated to the eruption which destroyed the city in the 17th century BC (Tzachili 1990; 2007). The hundreds of preserved loom weights found in the Early Phrygian destruction level at Gordion, dating to 800 BC in central Turkey, similarly locate large-scale, centralized weaving workshops producing massive amounts of cloth (Fig. 11).

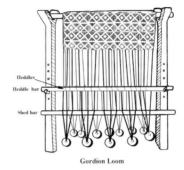

Figure 11. Reconstruction drawing of Early Phrygian warp-weighted loom from Gordion (B. Burke, G. Hill).

Minoan Crete

I begin this study of cloth production by examining the archaeological remains from Crete, the mountainous island equidistant from the Greek mainland and the north coast of Africa. Crete is always seen as a cross-road in the Mediterranean. Although relatively poor in natural resources, the island was home to the mythical King Minos residing in his palatial labyrinth at Knossos and figured heavily in later Greek tradition. The rule of Minos was thought to have been a thalassocracy, when Minoan ships brought foreign goods to Crete and skillfully crafted Minoan products were carried abroad. Our understanding of this distinctive civilization is very much a product of the primary excavator at Knossos, Sir Arthur Evans who worked intensively during the first half of the 20th century AD and whose influence is still felt today in Minoan scholarship. His work and that of others revealed a sophisticated palace system that finds parallels in other centers on Crete (Phaistos, Malia and Kato Zakros). Minoan civilization emerged toward the late third millennium BC, at the end of the Early Minoan period (EM), but the earlier Neolithic period was itself significant and good evidence is preserved at Knossos.

Major questions revolve around the origins of Minoan civilization, in particular the rate of economic and social development during the Bronze Age. Was it a protracted, progressive process, as advocated by gradualists, or was it a swift quantum leap forward brought about by sudden stimuli new to the island (Cherry 1983)? Related to this debate is the issue of contact with pre-existent Near Eastern states that show similar organizational features to the Minoans. Of primary interest to me is the role of cloth in these interactions. As Cherry (1986) has noted, 'what is beyond doubt in terms of Minoan development is that major changes in the scale and nature of socio-political integration on Crete took place in the twentieth century BC (*c.* 1950–1930), signaled by the construction of political, religious, and economic central places, or 'palaces''. The multi-component aspects of emergent complexity cannot be addressed in great detail in this study, but by focusing on cloth production as one of several important palatial features, we will understand a key aspect of economic development on Crete.

The Minoan period is divided between the Old and New Palace periods, marked by destruction and rebuilding. Because the New Palaces were built over the Old, the earliest phases of development are obscured although both have similar architectural features. They are large, multi-storey buildings, with rooms built around open, central, north-facing courts. On their western side is often another courtyard. In terms of construction, all palaces have large, sawn ashlar blocks, downward-tapering columns, pier and door partitions, light wells, lustral basins, monumental stairways, and major public rooms on upper floors. The palaces also functioned as administrative centers complete with archive rooms, containing documents inscribed with Minoan hieroglyphics and Linear A signs, which provide information about early administration, including aspects of textile production.

Chapter two traces the history of cloth production on Crete, from the Neolithic period to the end of the Late Bronze Age. There are several specific examples of textile tool assemblages presented, many of them from Knossos. Various sizes and types of loom weights are described, and a detailed discussion of purple dyeing from murex snails is presented. The early administrative records related to cloth production are presented in Chapter two, but a great deal of information about the Mycenaean age also comes from Crete: the Linear B tablets that were preserved in the fiery destructions of the palace at Knossos are discussed thoroughly in Chapter three.

Mycenaean Greece

At around 1390 BC, destructions are observed at sites throughout Crete and the Mycenaeans of the Greek mainland begin to play a dominant role in the economic history of the Aegean. Clay tablets inscribed in the Linear B script are accidentally fired toward the close of this Mycenaean age, *c.* 1200 BC. The tablets record a variety of transactions at Mycenaean palaces in the earliest form of written Greek. They are our best source for understanding the complex organization of the Mycenaean economy. A large percentage of these tablets refer in some way to a well-organized textile industry. The Linear B studies by John Killen and others describe the many stages of textile production in the Late Bronze Age, primarily at Pylos and Knossos. The tablets are our best source of information for the organization of labor in Bronze Age Greece and from such records we see that Mycenaean textile production, like its Minoan counterpart, was subject to the central authority of the palace. Linear B scholarship clarifies aspects of the organization of the Late Bronze Age economy in general, but often these inquiries do not take full advantage of the material culture and archaeological evidence.

Tablets record large amounts of raw textile material, wool and linen, assessed as a kind of tax from surrounding towns and villages under the administration of the palaces. The documents also provide information about personnel, including food rations for dependent workers involved in the textile industry (Gregersen 1997). All indications are that there was a high degree of specialization for the craftsmen and craftswomen listed, recording specific occupations such as spinners, weavers, and fullers.

Technical aspects of weaving can be inferred from descriptions of work groups and the amounts of cloth that were finished and the amounts that were owed, as recorded in the tablets. Additionally, Mycenaean artistic depictions of clothing can further inform our understanding of Late Bronze Age textile technology. While Mycenaean tools of production are not as plentiful at palace centers as they are in the Minoan and Phrygian centers, there is evidence for cloth production at Mycenaean palaces. Because archaeological evidence related to the production of cloth is relatively scanty, it is possible that certain methods of production left little archaeological trace, such as the horizontal ground loom made of wood. The Mycenaeans may have excelled at band-weaving, for example, which would also leave little archaeological evidence (Barber 1991, 335–7; 1997). Finally, as is the case with Minoan spindle whorls, perhaps the organization of weaving is such that we should not expect loom weights at major Mycenaean centers, where most excavations have been concentrated.

Late Bronze Age Aegean textiles were more probably woven in outlying Mycenaean settlements but the production was administered by palatial centers, such as Pylos and Knossos, as will be discussed in Chapter three. From reading tablets at these centers we learn that many of the women textile workers listed have ethnic descriptions locating their origin in Anatolia, at places such as Knidos (*ki-ni-di-ja*), Miletus (*mi-ra-ti-ja*), and Halikarnassos (Zephyra, *ze-pu$_2$-ra$_3$*) suggesting a shared, continuous tradition of cloth working in the Aegean and Anatolia which allows us to make some inferences about textile working throughout the eastern Mediterranean, and allows us to turn our attention to Anatolia.

Iron Age Gordion

After the Late Bronze Age collapse in the 12th century BC, palace-centered economies are no longer extant in Greece. In Iron Age Anatolia, however, strong regional centers comparable in scale to Bronze Age Aegean palaces are known. Throughout most of the first millennium BC the Phrygian capital of Gordion was one of the strongest economic and political centers on the Anatolian plateau. The Early Phrygian period ends with a destruction level preserving the best archaeological evidence for textile production on a scale comparable to that described in the Linear B tablets and as suggested by finds from Minoan Crete. While the destruction level at Gordion dates approximately 350 years after the Mycenaean age, to the late ninth century BC, the palatial economy of the Phrygians is likely to have been similarly organized to that of the Bronze Age Aegean.

Substantial amounts of cloth are preserved from Phrygian burials around Gordion and from the citadel itself. Some of the fragments have been heavily burnt but they all reveal diverse textile technologies of great sophistication. Descriptions of the weave structure and identifications for the fibers, most probably wool and linen, are possible with microscopic analysis. Rather than attempting a detailed study of the Gordion textile fragments, the analysis in Chapter four focuses on the enormous quantity of tools of cloth manufacture in primary workshop contexts and how this reflects organized production at Gordion.

Artifactual evidence for large-scale textile production at Gordion is systematically presented. The study focuses on the workshop areas of the Terrace Building and Clay Cut structure located within the fortification walls and preserved in a major destruction fire dating to 800 BC. Although no textual records of palace administration from Gordion have yet been found, we can infer from the architecture at Gordion and from historical references to King Midas that Phrygian society was fairly complex, with a well-established economy, heavily dependent on textile production. Thousands of spindle whorls and loom weights have been found in primary depositional contexts within workshop buildings, making the evidence unique within the Mediterranean, and details of these craft residues provide an informative picture of organized cloth manufacture at a major center.

Summary

This study focuses on the economic aspects of textile production, combining textual, artifactual, and theoretical research, in order to understand the significance of cloth manufacture in complex political economies of the Bronze and Iron Ages. The second chapter begins with a survey of textile production on Minoan Crete from the Neolithic through the Late Bronze Age. Aspects of textile production, such as dyeing, administration, and weaving are included to understand the changing nature of the Minoan palatial economy during the second millennium BC. The third chapter focuses on Mycenaean cloth production as revealed by the Linear B documents. The approach to these texts is more archaeological than philological, incorporating contextual data to expand our understanding of Aegean craft production. Chapter four analyzes the large amounts of textile tools preserved in original workshop contexts at the Phrygian capital of Gordion. While the separation in time and space between the Bronze Age Aegean and Iron Age Anatolia is fully acknowledged, both areas use the warp-weighted loom and have centralized redistributive economies. Chapter five attempts to expand the discussion beyond the eastern Mediterranean and looks at cloth production in the Near East, Egypt, and in the New World. Admittedly this is a cursory discussion of only a fraction of the available evidence, but the effort is made to show that cloth figures heavily in economies all over the world, disparate in time and space.

2 PREHISTORIC TEXTILE PRODUCTION ON CRETE

The island of Crete (Map 2), located midway between Egypt and the Greek mainland, is a unique landscape. The land is constantly changing due to tectonic movements that are felt both island-wide and within smaller geological zones. Cretan topography is determined by three major mountain ranges: the White Mountains in the west, the Ida (Psiloritis) massif in the center, and the Lasithi Mountains in the eastern part of the island. In between there are flat, fertile plains many of which have been the subject of intensive surveys, for example, the Lasithi plain in north-eastern Crete (Watrous and Blitzer 1982) and the Mesara plain to the south (Watrous, Hadzi-Vallianou, and Blitzer 2005). These areas have provided agricultural land as well as rich pasture zones for an important Cretan wool industry throughout the island's history.

Crete is relatively poor in natural resources: there are no major deposits of metals on the island, which is remarkable considering that the people of Crete became famous for their crafting skills, so much so that the legend of Daidalos, the 'cunning craftsman', is located on the island (Morris 1992; Muhly 2008). The earliest settlers, who tinkered with a wide variety of materials such as copper, lead, silver, gold and ivory, were working exclusively

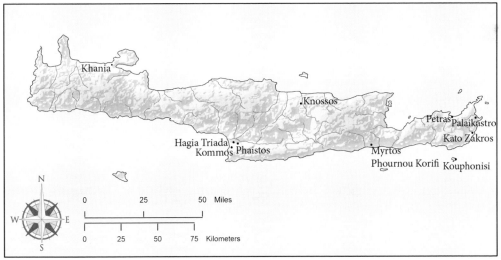

Map 2. Crete. Adapted from Interactive Ancient Media. http://iam.classics.unc.edu/.

with imported materials, mainly from the Cyprus, the Near East, and Egypt. This chapter posits that locally woven textiles provided the necessary commodities of exchange with extra-island trading partners since the beginning of the Bronze Age, and that a centralized economy, for production and exchange, was of key importance for this complex arrangement of acquisition, production and exchange.

Although few textiles are preserved, tools and administrative documents from Bronze Age sites on Crete reveal that the production of cloth was a major factor in the Minoan economy. One aim of this chapter is to show that changes in the organization of production on Crete reflect socio-economic and political developments found in the greater Minoan palatial economy. The history of cloth production is traced from the Neolithic through the beginning of the Mycenaean period on Crete, paying special attention to the site of Knossos since it has been thoroughly investigated and provides so much information on Minoan textile industries and administration. Because the physical remains of wool and linen cloth are not preserved from Crete, the discussion here relies upon a variety of sources including tools of production, like loom weights and spindle whorls, as well as administrative documents such as seals, sealings, and inscribed tablets. While some may question whether loom weights and spindle whorls will explain the 'emergence of civilization' on Crete, it cannot be disputed that organized textile production contributed to the rise of the civilization on Crete we call Minoan (see also Barrett and Halstead 2004).

Cloth and Cultural Complexity

How did the large administrative centers in the Aegean and Anatolia emerge, and what roll does the organization of textile production play in the debate? Agricultural surplus is assumed as a key component of the processual model used to explain the origins of complex society in the Aegean. This idea is based on agricultural specialization, as proposed by Colin Renfrew in his highly influential work, *The Emergence of Civilisation* (1972). The raw materials of cloth production, sheep wool and flax, as agricultural products should also figure into this debate, since they were widely exploited and one of the area's few natural resources.

Renfrew's redistributive model suggests that by the end of the Neolithic period, farmers mainly exploited the 'Mediterranean triad': cereal grains, olives, and grapes. Local specialization in agricultural production was based on the geographical predisposition of different regions and environments. Lower and flatter land was suited to cereals while more mountainous terrain with thinner soil cover was used for cultivating olives and vines. Successful agriculture of this kind led to both increased productivity and an increase in population. With this success, Renfrew posits that 'redistributive chiefs' emerged at the local level to administer the specialized products from different farmers and to coordinate storage facilities prior to redistribution. The production, mobilization and consumption of cloth would be a bi-product of this economic system of increasing complexity. In archaeological theory, the term complexity is often defined as vertical (or centralized) and horizontal (integrated) differentiation, often with an implicit meaning of social hierarchies (Schoep and Knappett 2004, 24–5).

Supporting Renfrew's tenets, Bintliff (1977) states that 'the prehistoric cultures of Greece were fundamentally agricultural, pastoral and piscatorial... Minoan and Mycenaean civilizations were in all essentials constructed upon the redistribution of local foodstuffs rather than commerce and mercenary service.' Under the patronage of these local chiefs, craft specialization is thought to have led to a positive feedback loop wherein the production of prestige goods demanded increased agricultural production and at the same time reinforced the dependence of the specialized farmers on the controlling elites (Renfrew 1972, 340–5, 483–5).

Renfrew argues for an indigenous development of 'civilization' in the Aegean, without any 'diffusion' or influence from the Near East. Unfortunately, however, there is no accounting for the initial stimulus which brought about such a drastic change during the third millennium BC, where the Early Bronze Age societies emerge into the complex, palace-centered societies of the early second millennium BC. It is unlikely that Early Bronze Age farmers would willingly have taken the risk of specializing in one crop with the expectation that trade with their neighbors would supply other essentials. And significantly, architectural and administrative features of large centers in the Near East, such as at Mari and Ebla, show strong similarities to the Old Palaces on Crete, suggesting that there was some inspiration, if not influence, upon the earliest Minoans from the powerful kingdoms to the east (Watrous 1987; Cline 1995; Weingarten 1990). As an adjustment to Renfrew's model, Gamble (1982) has suggested that early farmers were forced by powerful elites to live in large nucleated settlements, removed from their farmsteads and coerced into producing specialized crops, but again this doesn't explain how the elites emerged initially.

Rather than an altruistic or coercive theory, Halstead and O'Shea (1982) propose a 'social storage' model that posits a mutually beneficial approach to explaining surplus and emergent complexity. In Greece, where climate and topography can differ within fairly short distances, stored surplus crops can be shared with another group suffering a short-term deficit. This is a way of ensuring a stable food supply in case the situation should be reversed later. In addition, any unused surplus could be fed to animals, increasing their secondary product output, such as wool, hides, and milk. Evidence in support of this model includes the additional storage areas, such as the magazines and possibly the circular pit structures, known as *kouloures,* added during the Middle Minoan (MM) II period in the West Courts of Knossos and Phaistos. Administrative records and archives focusing primarily on agricultural goods also support this model of agricultural surplus. Perhaps specialized food producers sent their surplus to regional centers where this food was dispersed to non-food producers, such as weaving specialists, and other dependents. An accumulation of wealth is possible in this model if an unused surplus of food accrues over time. Whenever one group experienced a shortage they could 'contribute' some kind of prestige good or craft item to a more stable party, or promise some service, in exchange for food. More often than not, people who had limited access to good agricultural land compensated for it by diverting their attention to craft production, possibly textile manufacture. A labor force of craftspeople, freed from toiling at agriculture, would devise strategies for producing better, more valuable goods, perhaps accruing an even greater advantage over their subsistence-focused neighbors. This would quickly foster an accumulation of wealth and an increase in specialized production for exchange. Specialization in ceramics during the Early Minoan period has been mapped by Whitelaw and Day, who show that there were fairly sophisticated craft technologies during this formative period (Whitelaw, *et al.* 1997 and Day, *et al.* 1997; Whitelaw 2004). It is not unlikely that cloth production showed similar sophistication.

The palaces of the Middle Bronze Age generally functioned as the heads of agricultural states (see Hägg and Marinatos 1987; Pelon 1983). As a critique of the subsistence and storage models discussed above, however, it can be argued that the emphasis on agriculture in terms of the origins of complexity is misplaced and that the production and exchange of prestige goods, such as finely crafted and dyed textiles and valuable metal items, first allowed such centers and their elites to develop. Transport, storage, distribution, and administration are key features for early state formation.

Long distance commercial trade also played a major role in Aegean development (Alexiou 1987, Wiener 1987, Runnels and Van Andel 1988, Sherratt and Sherratt 1991). By the mid-third millennium BC, advances in sailing technology, such as the longboat, shown commonly inscribed on Cycladic pottery, and the invention of the sail in the Aegean, allowed for long-distance exchange along well-established trade networks (Casson 1971, Tiboni 2005). Increases in agricultural productivity are a response to this growing trade. This would in turn lead to a greater emphasis on secondary products like wool and textiles. Relatively contemporary advances in metallurgy also increased the exchange of raw materials for metals and finished goods, which further enhanced the development of trade networks. Exchange centers located along these networks would quickly have accumulated wealth in prestige goods that would have empowered emerging elites. I am, however, getting ahead of myself; to begin, we should look at the Neolithic material on Crete, which is too often overlooked because of the impressive Bronze Age remains throughout the island.

Neolithic Knossos

The history of textile production on Crete begins at Knossos. After excavations by Sir Arthur Evans ceased in the first decade of the 20th century, the British School at Athens maintained a strong research presence at the site, with Sinclair Hood and many others continuing the work begun by Evans. Although Arthur Evans uncovered material of the Neolithic period, including textile production equipment (Fig. 12), John Evans began excavations which concentrated on these strata, and marked an important formative period before the famous Bronze Age 'Palace of Minos'. From 1957–1960 and again in 1969 and 1970, J. Evans recorded the earliest, largest, and longest lived Neolithic settlement known on Crete underneath the Bronze Age palace at Knossos (Fig. 13). 'Knossos has become one of the best known, best defined and best dated Neolithic sequences not just in Crete, but within the entire southern Aegean' (Tomkins, Day, and Kilikoglou 2004, 51).

The early settlement gives us some idea of the topography of the site before the major construction projects of the palatial periods. Built on the promontory junction of the Vlykhia and Kairatos streams, the settlement's earliest levels indicate an aceramic hamlet dating to about 7000 BC, composed of houses made of mud-brick on stone foundations. Radiocarbon samples taken in 1997 corroborate those of J. Evans and present a good

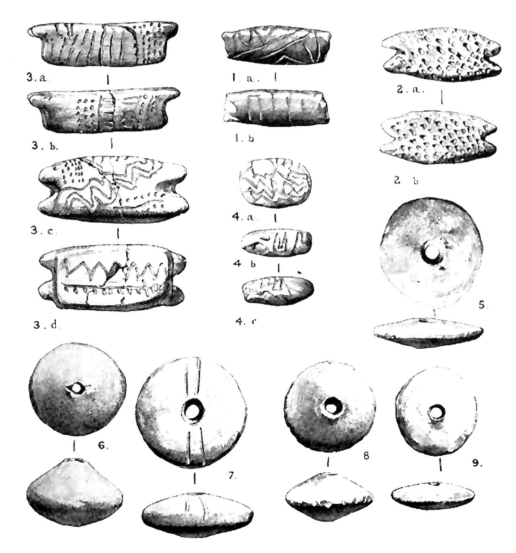

Figure 12. Neolithic weft bobbins and spindle whorls from Knossos (Evans 1921, p. 43, fig. 10, with permission, Ashmolean Museum, University of Oxford).

chronological framework from the eighth millennium BC onwards (Efstratiou, Karetsou, Banou and Margomenou 2004). The houses were used by an estimated 1000 individuals and covered approximately five hectares built atop a rather sloping mound that was later leveled for the MM II West Court. The site was ideally located near the sea, with abundant fresh water and fertile land. Sheep, goat, pigs, dog, and small cattle were domesticates here, as well as legumes, emmer, and einkorn wheat.

The Neolithic settlement at Knossos lasted at least 3700 years, from 7000 to 3300 BC,

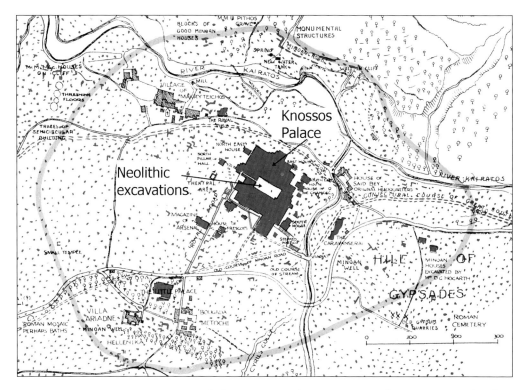

Figure 13. Knossos area, c. 1700 BC (Evans 1928, facing p. 77, with permission, Ashmolean Museum, University of Oxford).

much longer than the palatial Bronze Age (Fig. 13). Evans divided the site into four ceramic phases (Evans 1994): Early Neolithic I (EN I) featured fired mud-brick architecture and was the longest lasting Neolithic period, spanning perhaps 2000 years; EN II lies four meters above EN I and dates to the fifth millennium BC, lasting another several hundred years; Middle Neolithic (MN) was revealed under the Central Court in the form of two large, square multi-room buildings dating to the late fifth millennium. The Late Neolithic (LN) period is also recognized in the Central Court excavations, where three building levels date to the second quarter of the fourth millennium BC.

Steady, uninterrupted growth characterizes the settlement throughout the Neolithic period, and households that pool production and consumption tend toward greater stability and continuity (Perlès 1992, 121, Halstead 1995, 14, 17; Tomkins 2004, 49). By the Late Neolithic periods several changes in the organization of space, storage, and craft production are detected at Knossos: architecture tends to be more substantial and free-standing (Evans 1994, 11); pottery production also tends toward more standardization, with improved preparation and limestone-tempered fabrics; and an increase in the overall scale and intensity of production is seen (Tomkins 2004, 52). Broodbank and others, however, see a less uniform rate of growing complexity and identify a shift in material culture in the transition from Early to Middle Neolithic (Broodbank 1992, Whitelaw 1992). Given the evolving nature of the Neolithic evidence, we might ask, how do changes in the textile equipment map onto other developments at Neolithic Knossos?

Radiocarbon dates suggest that the first appearance of textile equipment at Knossos occurred in the Middle Neolithic, in approximately the first quarter of the fourth millennium BC (Evans 1968, 272; Carington Smith 1975, 182–84). Found within the Middle Neolithic (Stratum III) level were 25 clay whorls; 2 stone whorls; 88 sherd-discs, of which six were pierced, suggesting they functioned as whorls; two possible weft-bobbins, one of clay and the other of bone; and two sets of clay loom weights consisting of 7 and 13 weights respectively (Evans 1964, 180–82, 234–35, figs 56.1 and 61.13, pls 56.1–2, 57.2 no. 1–7, pl. 60, 1, no. 5; Barber 1991, 100 and 387). The loom weights are box-shaped or cuboid, with four holes in each corner, some showing evidence of thread wear. The set of 7 was made of creamy white clay, ranging in weight from 350 to 635 grams (Barber 1991, 100; Carington Smith 1975, 185). The other set of 13 was less well-preserved and lighter, weighing between 200–300 grams. That these weights were used on warp-weighted looms is difficult to say with certainty, although the form of the weight does recur in the Middle Minoan period associated with textile equipment. Stratum II revealed nearly 100 spindle whorls, three of which were decorated (Evans 1964, 182–8). The Late Neolithic (Stratum I) level was greatly disturbed by the later Knossos builders but it revealed a group of loom weights, 36 spindle whorls and 2 weft-bobbins. In total, over 150 clay spindle whorls are reported from the final three Neolithic periods of the Central Court excavations, along with many loom weights. The co-occurrence of weaving and spinning equipment at Neolithic Knossos is remarkable because they are rarely found together on Crete during the Bronze Age.

Since we can be certain that Neolithic people at Knossos were weaving and spinning, it is important to know what fibers were exploited. Because sheep and goat comprise 75% of the earliest animal remains from Knossos (cattle was 7%, pig 18%, and the rest dog: Ryder 1983, 57), one might assume that the Neolithic textiles woven at Knossos were primarily wool. Using sheep and goats for wool is possible by the fifth millennium BC, but this date would be the earliest known exploitation of woolly sheep in the Aegean. Furthermore, preliminary faunal analysis at Knossos runs contrary to what would be expected if there was a growing wool-based industry during the Neolithic (Jarman and Jarman 1968; Strasser 1992, 70–73; Broodbank 1992). 'The appearance of spinning and weaving technology at exactly the time when the sheep and goat component goes into sharpest decline represents a suspicious mismatch between two types of data,' notes Broodbank (1992, 62). This may not be such a puzzle if we consider the possibility that linen, or some other bast fiber, was the primary fiber exploited in the Neolithic period. It is also likely because the evidence for bast fibers is so strong in Anatolia for this same period (Nesbitt 1995).

The Neolithic excavations at Knossos uncovered only a small portion of the settlement and yet the changing pattern of textile equipment found in such a small area suggests a shift in the organization of craft production. Textile equipment first occurs in the Middle Neolithic in wide distribution throughout the site, perhaps illustrating that individual household units were producing cloth for their own needs. By the Late Neolithic, however, cloth equipment is concentrated only in certain areas of the site, suggesting a shift towards specialization, wherein autonomous individuals or household-units aggregated to produce cloth for group consumption and probably exchange. It has recently been shown by Tomkins, Day and Kilikoglou (2004, 57) in their study of Neolithic ceramics from Knossos that 'ceramic vessels were not only being made in a number of locations, but were also being exchanged between communities…' A shift in production, from dispersed to restricted and perhaps specialized can be noted in the ceramics (Tompkins 2004, 53). There may very well have been a similar pattern emerging in textile manufacture at Neolithic Knossos.

Toward the end of the Neolithic period, the cuboid weights seem to have been replaced by taller, heavier weights, pear or pyramidal in shape with one suspension hole at the top. This type appears concurrently in northern Greece (Carington Smith 1975, 154–6). Interestingly, the Neolithic cuboid weight disappears only to re-emerge during the Middle Minoan period, but almost exclusively at the eastern end of the island, appearing only as far west as Malia. It is possible that the cuboid weights are a cultural feature associated with the earliest inhabitants of Crete, and that toward the end of the Neolithic, this group was pushed eastwards by the newly arrived 'Minoans'.

Early Minoan Crete and the Emergence of the Palatial System

The period after the Neolithic marks some dramatic changes on Crete. The third millennium BC, generally speaking, spans the Prepalatial period, also known as the Early Minoan. For the most part, it is a period of marked regionalism across Crete, particularly from EM I–EM II B, lasting up to about 2200 BC (Wilson 2008, 79). One of the major questions occupying scholars of Crete's cultural history is the emergence of the Minoan palace as an economic, political, and religious institution in EM III. The palaces dominate the political economy of the second millennium BC and many have looked to the Prepalatial phases for hints of its origins.

To Arthur Evans, the palace was a gradual development over time, comparable to an organism's natural lifespan of birth, maturity, and eventual decline (Evans 1906). In contrast, J. Cherry has argued that the origins of palatial society on Crete were the result of swift, punctuated changes in social organization (Cherry 1983; 1986). Looking at the foundations for palatial Crete in the late third millennium BC, Cherry sees the development of social complexity as a swift quantum leap forward rather than a protracted process. He also notes the importance of contact with pre-existing Near Eastern states in the formation of what we know as the Minoan palace, an idea also followed by Watrous (1987). The objective in the analysis here is to see if changes in the organization of craft production, especially cloth manufacture, informatively reflect changes in social organization on palatial Crete over time in these early periods.

Archaeological evidence, including textile equipment, indicates that in the EM I and EM II periods (from about 3100–2200 BC), all of Crete had a scattering of fairly simple farmhouses (Watrous 2001). At the conclusion of the EM III period (*c.* 1900 BC) we first see the elemental forms of the Old Palaces, at Knossos and elsewhere on Crete. What caused this change is difficult to say but it is not a satisfactory explanation to simply assert that change merely happens over the course of time for its own sake (Cherry 1983, 1986).

Clearly, something external stimulated the Early Minoan system between EM II and MM IB. So, we might ask, what is the evidence for extra-island contact in the third millennium BC and why did it occur?

Recent work at Poros-Katsambas, the harbor site 5 km from Knossos, has shown a remarkable level of contact with the Cyclades very early in the third millennium BC, *c.* EM I. Craft activity here focused on metallurgy, and it has been suggested that copper was imported from the Cyclades to north-central Crete and the east, near Siteia, during this time (Dimopoulou 1997; Wilson 2008, 82). Most Early Minoan metal items were probably cast on the island in the EM I and IIA periods, although the smelted ores themselves likely came from outside: Laurion, near Attica was a source of silver, lead and copper; Siphnos for lead; and Kythnos for copper (Wilson 2008, 90). What was given in exchange for these raw materials is archaeologically invisible and therefore untraceable.

During the Early Minoan IIA period more Cycladic imports to Crete are found at Knossos than in the earlier periods, and the first Minoan colony is established on Kythera (Coldstream and Huxley 1984, Wilson 1994). Over 30 Early Cycladic II jars and sauceboats, an obsidian bowl, and several examples of Urfirnis ware ceramics, possibly from the mainland via Keos and Melos, appear at Knossos. Also, in EM IIA levels a hippopotamus tusk is found at Knossos, suggesting early contact between Minoans and Egyptians. Long distance trade is also indicated by the form of the longboat, designed for fast overseas expeditions of short distances, connecting the islands of the Aegean with distant places. By the later Prepalatial period (MM IA) Egyptian stone vessels, scarabs, cylinder seals and ivory, all from the Near East and Egypt, are imported to Crete (Whitelaw 2004, 241). As Watrous notes, 'In contrast [to the imports] the list of EM II exports in the Aegean is relatively short' (2001). This early evidence shows that the Minoans were acquiring a wide variety of exotic goods from abroad: the most likely item given in exchange is cloth.

Knossos

At Knossos, Wilson reports that in the West Court Houses, excavated in 1969–70, spindle whorls and loom weights of the EM IIA period were found (1984, 214–9). The fabric of the whorls was fine clay, gray to grayish brown, usually smoothed, not burnished, and with a brown to black surface. The clay was not well-fired and crumbled once the whorls broke. All but one of the spindle whorls was plain; one had four rows of punctuated single or double dots dividing the upper surface into four equal parts. The biconical whorl was the most common at Knossos, ranging from 3.2 to 4.9 cm in diameter. In contrast are examples from Myrtos Fournou Koriphi, discussed below, where the most common form of spindle whorl was the cylindrical type. Comparative examples of other early whorls on Crete are found at Kastellos (Pendlebury and Money-Coutts 1937–1938); at EM I Arkalochori (Hazzidakis 1912–1913, 42, fig. 4m); at Debla, Phase I, EM I (Warren and Tzedakis 1974, 330, fig. 21). The loom weights at EM II Knossos were dome shaped or cylindrical and made of unbaked or poorly fired coarse clay. Based on this evidence, we can say with confidence that, as with their predecessors of the Neolithic period, the Prepalatial Minoans were spinning and weaving throughout the settlement at Knossos.

From Minos to Midas

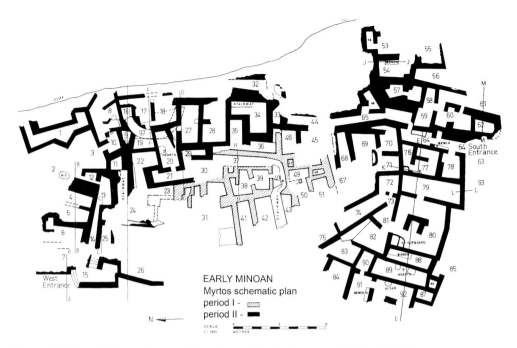

Figure 14. Plan of Myrtos Fournou Koriphi, mid 3rd millennium BC (modified from Warren Myrtos 1972, facing p. 11, with permission).

Myrtos Fournou Korifi and Vasiliki

Elsewhere on Crete we find a few Prepalatial settlements contemporary with the sparse remains from Knossos, and they are of key importance to the question of emergent complexity on Crete. Driessen has recently noted that 'Early Minoan II really was the moment when Minoan society took off' (2004, 77). One site of key importance in these arguments was Myrtos Fournou Korifi, excavated in 1967 by Peter Warren and located on the southeastern coast between Ierapetra and Arvi, dating to about 2600–2170 BC (Fig. 14). Warren identified two periods of occupation at the site: Period I, which corresponds to EM IIA and is unburnt; and Period II, which corresponds to Early Minoan IIB and is marked by a burnt destruction level. Most of the remains at the site date to Period II, which is significant because of the site's central role in debates regarding the origins of social complexity on Crete.

The complete excavation and thorough publication of Myrtos by Warren provides a great deal of evidence for competing interpretations of Prepalatial Crete. Originally, Warren interpreted Myrtos as a single, integrated community with specialized areas for economic, political, and ritual purposes (Warren 1972, 267; 1987). Branigan, however, interpreted the one hundred-room site as an integrated whole: a mansion, or proto-palace, for a local chief (Branigan 1970, 47–8). The reinvestigation of Myrtos Fournou Korifi by Whitelaw (1983) concludes that there are no signs of complexity beyond that of a large nuclear

E Spindle Stand 142.

F Spindle Whorls. Above, Room 81, Room 90, 154. Below, 156, 149, 150.

D Spindle Stand 141.

A Spindle Whorls 158, 157, 151.

Figure 15. Spinning equipment from Myrtos, mid-3rd millennium BC (Warren Myrtos 1972, pl. 77 d, e, f and 78 a, with permission Elizabeth Warren).

family, or a hamlet, comprised of perhaps six separate households. More recently Whitelaw states, based on studies of ceramic production at the site, that even though the ceramics were specialized and exchange relations were extensive, there is no evidence for centralized production and distribution (Whitelaw 2004, 236). Given such varying interpretations of the same evidence, we might look specifically at the textile production material from Myrtos to see if this presents a clearer picture of Early Minoan social organization.

The textile equipment from Myrtos has been well-published by Warren, with cautionary remarks about over-interpretation (Warren 1968; 1972, 262–3; Evely 2000, 494–6). Taking full account of the equipment, we find that Myrtos yielded four spindle whorls from EM IIA levels (Period I), and 28 from EM IIB (Period II). The majority of the whorls were cylindrical in shape and fifteen of them were painted. There were also portable stone slabs that had depressions drilled in them, presumably from resting a spindle on them while in use, and these are called spindle stands (Fig. 15). Discoid loom weights numbered about thirty, many of them were fragmentary, but they had one to three suspension holes pierced through the top and a grooved top edge: twenty-two came from Period I and eight from Period II (cat. numbers 74 through 100)(Fig. 16). Some of these clay weights show thread-wear marks on the suspension holes.

Warren identifies certain areas of the site in connection with textile manufacture. Several tubs and channels were located in rooms 8, 59, and 81, suggesting textile dyeing

E Above, disk **163**, whorl **26**, disk **161**. Below, loomweights **77**, **7**, **78**.

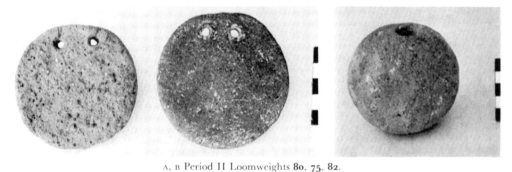

A, B Period II Loomweights **80**, **75**, **82**.

Figure 16. Loom weights from Myrtos, mid-3rd millennium BC (Warren Myrtos 1972, pl. 73 e and 74 a, b, with permission Elizabeth Warren).

installations. Room 8 was located near a hearth that could have been used to heat certain dyes. Burnt pieces of oak may have been used as fuel or may indicate the remains of a loom. Residue analysis of the tub in room 59 showed animal lipids, which would be expected if the tub was used for washing and dyeing wool (Bowyer, in Warren 1972, Appendix X, 330–1; Barber 1991, 240). Rooms 4 and 8 may have been used for wool washing, processing, and possibly dyeing. Warp-weighted looms were indicated by loom weights, perhaps fallen from above, from rooms 58 and 74. The presence of both loom weights and spindle whorls in the same area, some in the same room, parallels the distribution of finds at the contemporary Early Minoan settlement of Knossos.

Additional evidence for sophisticated cloth production at Myrtos includes fired clay vessels known as Minoan spinning bowls found in areas associated with textile production

Figure 17. Spinning bowl from Myrtos, mid-3rd millennium BC (Warren Myrtos 1972, fig. 96, pl. 68, P701 with permission Elizabeth Warren).

(Fig. 17). Wear-marks under the internal loop-handle of these vessels suggest that they were used for thread making. Spinning bowls dating to the Early and Middle Minoan periods have been found elsewhere on Crete, at Drakones (Xanthoudides 1924, 78), Phaistos, Palaikastro (Bosanquet and Dawkins 1923, pl. 6c), Kommos, and Archanes (Λεμβεσσι 1970, 269, pl. 378d), while examples outside of Crete are known from Messenia, Palestine and Egypt (Fig. 18)(Dothan 1963). Spinning bowls are known as διμιτεῖς in modern Greek and have been discussed by many Minoan archaeologists (see Marinatos 1964; Carington Smith 1992, 686–7, pl. 11–34; Barber 1991, 74–6; Τζαχίλη 1997, 124–5; Soles, Bending and Davaris 2004, 28). The examples from Myrtos are the earliest known spinning bowls, and Barber has suggested the possibility that the Egyptians and other spinners in the Near East adopted the idea of fiber-wetting bowls from the Minoans (1991, 74–6). She also suggests that since 10th Dynasty wall paintings in Egypt show a Minoan double-heart spiral pattern, probably inspired by Cretan textiles, some of the textiles produced at Myrtos could have been elaborate, patterned textiles created for export to Egypt (Fig. 19)(1994, 109; 1997, 516 and pl. CXCIIIa and b). Warren noted in 1972: 'It also remains unknown whether textiles were produced at Myrtos for home use only, or were exported. We may feel that the latter is possible, in view of the numbers of finds connected with textile manufacture in so small a settlement' (1972, 263). The proximity of Myrtos to Egypt, the absence of local wool in Egypt, the growing number of goods originating from the East on Crete dating to the Early Minoan period, and the long history of international textile trade all suggest a Minoan origin for both the double heart spiral and the spinning bowl in Egypt, confirming, in my mind, Warren's speculation.

Another settlement, contemporary with Myrtos and having an important EM IIB phase, is Vasiliki, located near the modern city of Ierapetra on the western side of the long valley that runs from Pacheia Ammos south to the Libyan Sea. The site was excavated by Richard Seager in 1904 and 1906 and reinvestigated by Antonios Zois in 1970 (Seager 1908; Zois

Figure 18 (above). Egyptian spinning and weaving scene, in Tomb of Chnem-hotep, 12th Dynasty, 2000–1785 BC (Roth 1913, fig. 2).

Figure 19 (left). Egyptian patterns inspired by Minoan textiles: a) from Tomb Chapel of Ukh-Hotep; b) on kilt of Keftiu ambassador, Rekhmire Tomb, c. mid-15th century BC (Evans 1928, fig. 480, with permission, Ashmolean Museum, University of Oxford).

1995; Betancourt 2000). The settlement is made up of several buildings clustered together. Along with the distinctive pottery known as Vasiliki ware (Fig. 20), deposits of loom weights and spinning equipment were noted in some of the rooms. The textile equipment is not published in detail, but the co-occurrence of tools for cloth making and materials of foreign origin, including copper and obsidian, suggest that textiles could have been an item of exchange (Watrous 2001). As at Myrtos, the craft residues indicate that production at Vasiliki was aggregated within household units, possibly for exchange overseas or with other centers on Crete.

Figure 20. Vasiliki ware pitcher, c. *2200 BC (Inv. 1921.0515.32 ©Trustees of the British Museum).*

From the evidence presented above, we can be confident that spinning and weaving crafts were practiced at Myrtos Fournou Korifi, Vasiliki, and Early Minoan Knossos. The co-occurrence of weaving and spinning at these Early Minoan sites is significant since it indicates that there was not any degree of specialization but rather independent, household production. Presumably individuals participated in all aspects of cloth production, from spinning raw thread to weaving finished textiles.

After the Early Minoan period, with the rise of the Minoan palaces, the archaeological distribution of textile equipment changes: no longer are spinning and weaving tools found together as they were at Prepalatial sites. The textile equipment at the EM II sites suggests that these settlements were not major economic centers but that people here may have been producing a small surplus of cloth for some kind of exchange. The presence of Melian obsidian and other raw materials from the Near East and Egypt, the increasing amounts of metals imported to Crete, and the beginning of specialized pottery production, all suggest developing complexity which contributed to the emergence of the palace system. During the Early Bronze Age on Crete, it seems most feasible that foreign trade increased the wealth of emerging elites and brought about the first palaces in the Aegean. The appearance of mountain shrines built just at the end of the Prepalatial period on Crete demonstrates the importance of pastoralism to the power base of these elites during this period (Cadogan 1986, 161; Branigan 1988; 1995). At these sites the main dedications are informal figurines of women and sheep, strongly supporting the idea that a wool-based economy was thriving. Long distance trade supplied by textile exports and abundantly fertile land contributed to the rise of social complexity on Crete, as evidenced by the Old Palaces at Knossos, Phaistos, Malia, and Zakros.

The First Palaces on Crete

After thousands of years, just after the turn of the second millennium BC, the Neolithic and ensuing Early Minoan settlements at Knossos are leveled and replaced by a new building form, the Minoan palace (Fig. 21). Large-scale structures are also built over Early Minoan remains at Phaistos, Malia, and Zakros. Polychrome pottery of MM IA found in the destruction debris predates these first palaces. It is therefore the MM IB period, *c.* 1930 BC,

1 N. Entrance & Portico   8 Great Staircase
2 Bastion & Guard House   9 Hall of the Colonnades
3 Anteroom to Throne Room   10 Hall of the Double Axes
4 Throne Room with Tank   11 Queen's Megaron
5 W. Portico   12 Built Drains
6 Storage Magazines   13 Loom Weight Basement
7 Northern bath

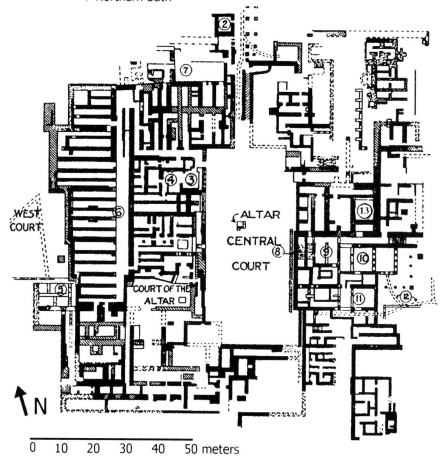

Figure 21. Knossos plan, c. 1700 BC (modified from B. Fletcher 1921, fig. 69b).

which marks a fairly sudden and dramatic shift in the way in which people were organized into communities on Crete. The Old Palace period is marked by a cycle of destruction and rebuilding activities, until a series of fires at sites throughout Crete, including Knossos, Phaistos, Malia, Monastiraki, Apolodoulou, and Galatas, destroy the Old Palaces in the MM IIB period, *c.* 1750 BC. The causes of these calamities are not completely understood and the true consequences are yet to be fully determined (Watrous 2001).

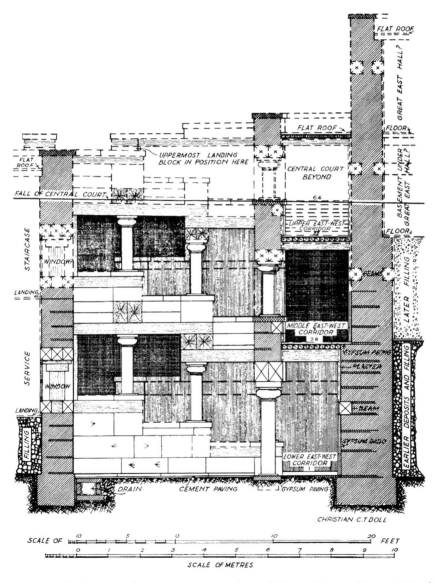

Figure 22. Restored elevation of Grand Staircase, Palace of Minos, Knossos (Evans 1921, fig. 247, with permission, Ashmolean Museum, University of Oxford).

What we can say is that the Minoan palace, as a monumental building complex within a settlement, shows specific architectural features and specialized functions. The most prominent feature of all Minoan palaces is an open, rectangular court with rooms radiating off of all sides. This central court has an orientation within 15 degrees of North, allowing light into the western cult rooms. In addition, most Minoan palaces have a west court in which there are storage facilities and raised walkways leading into the central court; perhaps this was the location of processions and ceremonies. Workshops, ritual areas, archives, and public reception spaces are also found in the palaces. Minoan palatial architecture is multi-storied, with large sawn ashlar blocks, downward-tapering columns, pier and door partitions, light wells, lustral basins, and monumental stairways (Fig. 22). Broadly speaking, three functions, not mutually exclusive, are suggested for the Minoan palace: an elite residence, a redistributive center, and a religious complex.

The main economic function of these centers was to facilitate the production of valuable trade goods and to coordinate the redistribution of agricultural goods, such as wine, oil, and textiles (Burke 1997; Militello 2007). The term 'redistribution' is potent and often misunderstood as it is applied to the Bronze Age palaces of the Aegean. A better term, perhaps, is mobilization, as it seems that palaces served to mobilize raw materials and products from producers to consumers. Goods, such as livestock, grain, wine, oil, and textiles, were collected by the state as a share of commoner produce and housed in large store-houses at the palaces. They were then transported to non-food producers who were employed by and dependent upon the center.

Inventing Purple

As we have seen, explaining the emergence of the first Minoan palaces is difficult given the evidence from Prepalatial and Protopalatial Crete. One contributing factor to this major social, political and economic change is the increasing exploitation of natural resources on Crete for the production of Minoan commodities desired by foreign trading partners. A new development in cloth production technology, which was contemporary with the early palaces of Crete and may have had a profound impact on the incipient Minoan economy, was the emergence of purple-dye industries from murex snails. Archaeological evidence and textual sources tell us that the shell species *Murex brandaris, Murex trunculus,* and *Purpura* (a.k.a. *Thais*) *haemostoma* were used for purple production, earlier than anywhere else in the Mediterranean (Fig. 23).

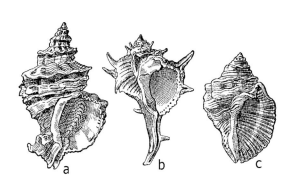

The Roman historian Pliny (*HN* 22.2–3) is clear that the shade of

Figure 23. Three types of Murex snails which yield purple dye: a) M. trunculus, b) M. brandaris, c) Purpura haemostoma.

Figure 24. Hypobranchial gland of a Murex trunculus, Crete (Ruscillo 2005, p. 103, fig. 2, used with permission).

Figure 25. Archaeological Murex from Kommos, Crete (B. Burke).

purple itself can vary depending on the species and the technique, ranging from black to purple to red. In reference to purple, Pliny (*HN* 9.125–42) extols that 'Its highest glory consists of the color of congealed blood, blackish at first glance when held up to the light; …this is the origin of Homer's phrase, 'blood of purple hue''.

Purple dyeing was an arduous, odorous, and labor-intensive process lasting several days. The production of purple-dyed cloth has been studied in some detail by archaeologists and is described by several ancient writers, most notably Aristotle (*Hist. an.* 5.15.22–25), Pliny (*HN* 9.62.133), and Vitruvius (*De arch.* 7.13.1–3). While these sources post-date by more than a millennium the earliest Cretan purple dyeing, the technology described is unlikely to differ very much: baited baskets in shallow coastal waters were used to collect the voracious snails. Once harvested, the shells are crushed to access the hypobranchial gland containing the clear mucous which, upon exposure to sunlight, turns purple (Fig. 24). As Pliny (*HN* 9.62.126) describes the snail: 'It has the famous flower of purple, sought after for dyeing robes, in the middle of its throat: here there is a white vein of very scanty fluid from which that precious dye, suffused with a dark rose color, is drained, but the rest of the body produces nothing. People strive to catch this fish alive, because it discharges this juice with its life.' After harvesting, the snail remains are mixed with salt as a preservative; Pliny recommends one pint of salt for every hundred pounds of flesh. This liquid stew should steep for three days and then gently boil for nine more. With oxidation and exposure to sunlight the pot and its contents turn a deep purple. The addition of sugar or honey slows the chemical reactions and helps to produce a deeper dye. Honey was also said to be a great preservative of textiles, as evidenced by the five thousand talents' worth of purple cloth from Hermione, in the Argolid, taken to Susa and seen in 331 BC. It was said they were in storage for 190 years and had been treated with honey (Jameson et al. 1994, 316–9).

Many archaeological examples of murex show punctured holes in the shells and scholars have interpreted these holes as the marks left by someone manually piercing the shell to extract the dye (Fig. 25). This interpretation, however, seems highly unlikely given the very tough hard shell of the murex and what we know of their eating habits. The holes are most likely caused by other snails cannibalizing their neighbors, rather than the manual extraction of dye (Spanier and Karmon 1987, 183). In Mediterranean harbors, where dead fish and other edible refuse are plentiful, murex species are observed as voracious omnivores. If they are denied other sources of food, they will start to cannibalize each other. The murex snails bore a hole through the shell using two organs, one of which secretes an acidic substance to soften the surface crystals of the calcium carbonate shell so that the second organ, the radula, can penetrate and extract the food (Spanier and Karmon 1987, 184–5, fig. 12). This feeding method is significant because of the distinctive bore holes found on excavated murex shells. In their natural environment, along the Levantine coast, researchers from Haifa University found no such examples of bored *M. trunculus*. Yet when snails were kept in captivity they would start to eat each other by boring holes in the shells. The prevalence of pierced shells from archaeological contexts, then, strongly suggests that murex snails with pierced shells were from artificial holding tanks, as part of a dye industry, and then harvested for their purple.

To dye a significant amount of wool purple required liquid dye from a great many snails, a fact often cited in the archaeological literature. E. Schunck in 1870 first isolated 7 mg of pure purple from 400 snails, building on the scientific study of murex purple by W. Cole in 1684 and R. Reaumur in 1711. Some scholars have continued to work with these early studies and exaggerate the miniscule quantity of dye yield from a snail. Evely (2000, 504) repeats citations to Reese (1979–80), and Doumet (1980), both of whom cite Bruin (1970, 82) in noting that there is 0.1 mg of dye yield per 'shell' (although of course the dye comes from the snail itself, rather than the shell). Jensen and Jensen (1965, 17) say 100 *M. brandaris* snails yield 6.8–12 mg of dye. According to Fouqet and Bielig (1971) one *M. trunculus* will produce 1.2 mg of dye, and one *M. brandaris* 0.6 mg. What must be remembered about these descriptions is that they are referring to the pure dye extract in its chemical form, rather than the practical solution described by Pliny which is readily usable for coloring spun fibers and woven textiles. Recent examples of experimental archaeology have changed our understanding of purple dyeing (Koren 2005). The labor and technology required to acquire the sea purple from snails was highly specialized, and this contributed greatly to the high cost of purple and made it a highly sought-after product.

D. Ruscillo (1998; 2005; 2006) has shown that murex snails were actively exploited in the MM I/II B period at Kommos, most probably to dye purple yarn for textiles early in the second millennium BC. A slab-paved stone floor with drainage channels running westwards toward the sea was packed with murex debris and the area just to the west of the room was covered with murex remains as well, all clearly dated to the MM IB period. Ruscillo concluded that murex debris from purple dye production consistently dates to the early Protopalatial period at Kommos, suggesting that during the formative period of the Minoan palace, purple dye production became concentrated at certain centers. Interestingly, after this period there is a noticeable absence of murex snails throughout the archaeological record on Crete.

A similar pattern is observed at the site of Petras in eastern Crete: early in the sites history there is evidence for the exploitation of murex purple, dating to the Old Palace period, and then very little evidence for purple dyeing afterwards. The earliest material related to cloth production at Petras is a large deposit of murex shells from the MM I period (Burke 2006). Stratigraphic excavations between Sectors I and III found nearly 200 crushed shells, making it the earliest reported evidence for purple dyeing not only on Crete, but from anywhere else in the Mediterranean.

We are fortunate that the components of the purple dye industry can be located archaeologically. Often in older publications one finds references to 'heaps,' or the mere presence of certain shells is noted. Systematic counts, however, of crushed murex shells based on a thorough understanding of the particulars of dye extraction have been only a recent development in Mediterranean archaeology. A recent discovery on the coast of Turkey, dating to the late Roman period, shows an extensive murex dye facility (Forstenpointner, Quatember, Galik, Weissengruber, and Konecny 2007). This survey noted a high proportion of very young murex snails in massive deposit of snail shells, and also demonstrated that not all purple dye facilities are located far removed from other buildings, since a storage complex was close by.

For a dye industry, the snails need to be living, and therefore any locus of production had to be close to the sea, probably within a few kilometers. The earliest known deposits of murex shells on Crete in quantities substantial enough to indicate dye-extraction are found on the small island of Kouphonisi, at Petras, Palaikastro (Bosanquet 1904 and 1939–40), and Kommos (Reese 1995; Ruscillo 1998; 2005; 2006). Pottery found at these sites suggests a date within the early to middle MM period, *c.* 20th–18th century BC, which is earlier than any dyeing facilities in the Levant. Work in Apulia, Italy has suggested a starting date for purple dye there possibly as early as the Early Bronze Age (Minniti 2005).

Dye facilities including water channels and spouted tubs were found at Kato Zakros in Hogarth's House I. Platon (1985) reports that House J also contained a dye vat and numerous loom weights. Nine rectangular troughs were found coated with plaster in an industrial annex of the palace at Zakros and the 'cistern' in the eastern wing might also be related to wool washing and dyeing (Hogarth 1900–01, 138–141; Platon 1964, 146, pl. 144a; 1967, 167; 1985, 29; Carington Smith 1977, 63–64; Barber 1991, 241).

The only parallel for this round hydraulic feature elsewhere on Crete is the 'Caravansarai' at Knossos (Fig. 26). Rather than see the Caravansarai as a rest stop or a place for travelers to wash their feet, as suggested by Evans (1928) and Schofield (1996), a more likely interpretation is that it is a place for washing, and perhaps even dyeing, special palace cloth. The evidence for heated water and the numerous basins and other containers found in this area further suggests a craft production (Fig. 27). The elegant architecture and the painted frescos should not preclude this area at Knossos from being viewed as a workshop area, since storage facilities, within the palace at Knossos itself, and on the mainland at Gla, for

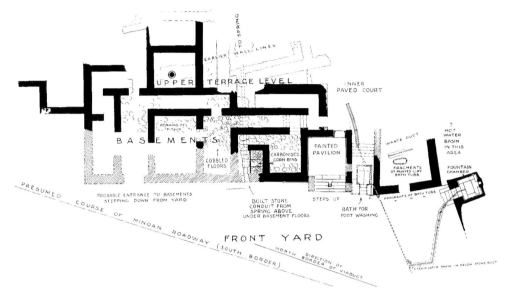

Figure 26. Plan of front section of 'Caravanserai', facing north, showing Spring-Chamber to Right, by Piet De Jong. (Evans 1928, p. 106, fig. 48, with permission, Ashmolean Museum, University of Oxford).

Figure 27. Interior water tank or dyeing installation, at 'Caravanserai', Knossos (B. Burke).

example, show painted frescoed walls in rooms used for seemingly mundane purposes like grain storage. Evidence from Vathypetro near Knossos has also yielded dye installations: a spouted tub and spherical loom weights were found along with burnt wood that might be the remains of a standing loom in Room 13 (Marinatos 1951, 269; Carington Smith 1975, 63; Driessen and Sakellarakis 1997, 75). The sophisticated drainage system discussed by MacDonald and Driessen (1988) found throughout the palace at Knossos might also be related to textile dyeing and fulling.

Minoan Purple in the Levant and Egypt

Although it is argued here that murex purple dyeing first occurred in the Mediterranean region on Crete, the best purple dye according to ancient sources (Pausanias 3.21.6; Pliny *HN* 9.127), is found along the Levantine coast, in the areas around Tyre, Sarepta, and Byblos. This region was the homeland of the Canaanites in the Bronze Age, and the Phoenicians in the subsequent Iron Age (Albright 1965). Both ethnic names, 'Canaan' and 'Phoenicia', seem originally to refer to the same concept, a purple-red color designation associated with both the name of this region and the people therein (Morris 1992, 98). Did the Levantines adopt this dyeing technology as a result of contact with Middle Minoan Crete or was it an independent invention? Did the red-purple dye give the name to the ethnic group, or was the dye color named for the people who excelled at this technology? It is difficult to answer whether the Minoans influenced the development of murex dyeing in the Levant, but no evidence for extensive purple dyeing has been found earlier than the material from Petras, Kouphonisi and Kommos on Crete.

The earliest textual reference to trade in purple dye comes from Nuzi, dating to the mid-second millennium BC, recording the transfer of dye from Syro-Phoenicia to the eastern Tigris (Reinhold 1970, Speiser 1935–6). The earliest archaeological evidence for purple in the Levant is found at Minet el-Beidha, the harbor of ancient Ugarit, and is tentatively dated to the fifteenth century BC based on textual evidence (Reese 1987, 205). The earliest purple dye, based on scientific analysis of dye residues found at Sarepta, dates to the thirteenth century BC (McGovern and Michel 1984; Michel and McGovern 1990). Dalley infers purple dyeing from murex snails at Mari from the later Ugaritic evidence, although the term for purple-dyed fabrics in the Mari tablets cannot yet be isolated and there is no archaeological evidence for such textiles there (1984, 54). M. Dothan notes that the earliest evidence for purple workshops in southern Canaan dates to the 13th–12th centuries BC at Akko and suggests that new settlers, the Sherdana, brought purple dyeing to the Levant, beginning the intensified purple-dye production for which the region became so well known (1988). Itamar Singer (2008) has recently analyzed purple-dyeing in Hittite and Ugaritic sources, building on the work of Lackenbacher (2002) and van Soldt (1990; 1997). He focuses in particular on the island of Lesbos (Hittite Lazpas) and demonstrates how terms for 'making tribute' can in some cases actually mean 'make purple wool'. Singer's comprehensive study further demonstrates the great value of purple, and that the name itself is synonymous with tribute.

Woolen textiles, the most valuable of which would have been purple-dyed, were probably among the first goods exchanged by Minoans to the Near East and Egypt. Overseas trade in goods does not explain all aspects of emergent Minoan culture, and Whitelaw makes an important critique, stressing a multi-lineal approach to the available data. Certain trading communities (Poros-Katsambas, Mochlos) seem to be eclipsed by larger-scale, expansionist polities rooted in agricultural production and surplus (Whitelaw 2004, 244). Yet we also know that the Minoans throughout the Palatial periods were active merchants. References to Aegean products in international exchange first occur in the eighteenth century BC, on a tablet from Mari (Durand 1983, 432) which lists clothes and leather shoes sent from Kaptara (Ugaritic *kptr*, also known as Caphtor), which most likely refers to Crete (Knapp 1991, 42; Cline 1995; Kitchen 1966, 191).

During the 12th Dynasty in Egypt we see on seated sculpted figures, a new, heavier cloak possibly made of Minoan wool since there is little evidence for woolly sheep in Egypt this early. Sir Flinders Petrie describes 12th Dynasty 'weaver's waste' at Kahun, '...mainly made up of blue worsted ends, and blue wool, with some red and some green ends' and a 'lump of red dyed wool, not yet spun' (Petrie, Griffith, and Newberry 1890, 28). As Barber (1991, 224, 351) points out, what is so significant about this find is that at this time there is no reason to believe that the Egyptians were dyeing and weaving wool. The workers of the wool were possibly immigrants from Crete, or they may have been working with Aegean-imported materials. The wool itself is almost certainly non-Egyptian since representations of sheep in contemporary art show that the hairy species, rather than the woolly kind, was prevalent.

Wall paintings at Tell el-Dab'a, Tel Kabri, and Alalakh demonstrate the transfer of ideas and artistic skills from Crete throughout the Eastern Mediterranean, and techniques of cloth manufacture would not be out of place in such transactions (Niemeier 1998; Shaw 1997). While evidence for purple dyeing might someday be revealed in the Levant in contexts earlier than those on Crete, it is equally possible that earlier Minoan evidence for purple dyeing will be found in the Aegean. Perhaps the Early Minoan colony on Kythera, known as '*Porphyroussa*' ('the purple-island') to Aristotle, was settled to acquire more sources of murex purple along with valuable mineral resources. Phoenician colonies, such as D'Jerba, ancient Meninx cited by Strabo (17.3.18) and Pliny (*HN* 9.127) as the best source of purple dye in Africa, were founded for similar reasons in the Iron Age.

Minoan venturers (possibly from east Crete, Kommos, or Myrtos) were very likely trading patterned textiles overseas in exchange for raw materials, like bronze, tin, and gold in the late third and early second millennia BC. Egyptian wall paintings offer the best evidence for the exchange of Aegean cloth with overseas partners and, in line with what Mary Helms (1988; 1993) has argued, the foreign origin of Minoan textiles, purple or not, only increased the value of this prestige good overseas.

By the Late Bronze Age, international gift-exchange among elites was common. In Amarna letter 34, lines 16–24, we read that the King of Alashiya (possibly Cyprus) sent 100 talents of copper to his 'brother' the Egyptian pharaoh expecting in return a gold decorated bed, a chariot with gold, two horses, 14 (pieces?) of ebony, 17 jars of good oil, 54 items of linen, and, finally, eight pieces of 'the royal linen' (Knapp 1991, 21, 38). It is highly significant that half of all the elaborate goods listed in this letter refer to some kind of textile. Another el-Amarna letter records an official of Byblos complaining to an official in Egypt that there were no blue-purple or red-purple woolen garments to give as tribute, implying that the Egyptians had requested some from the Levantines. Knapp refers to an unpublished document from Mari that lists a variety of goods from Crete, including 'elaborately-decorated weapons, a *katappu*-container, a large vase, and perhaps some fabric.' Hittite and Amarna documents also refer to trade in linen and wool, the latter occasionally dyed purple (Knapp 1991).

Exchange between the Aegean and Egypt continued in the second half of the fifteenth century, during the reigns of Hatshepsut, Thutmose III and Amenhotep II. Several representations of tribute bearers were painted along the walls of tombs belonging to Egyptian nobles at Thebes. Figures labeled as 'Keftiu', identified as princes 'from the isles in the midst of the Great Green (sea)', are recognized today as Minoan and Mycenaean ambassadors (Vercoutter 1956; Schachermeyer 1960, 44–60; Sapouna-Sakellaraki 1971, 224–35; Wachsmann 1987; Heltzer 1988, 167–8; Barber 1991, 330–51; Sherratt and Sherratt 1991, 368; Morris 1992, 94; Rehak 1996; 1998; Matthäus 1995; Panagiotopoulos 2002). These individuals bear gifts and wear garments that are characteristic of the Middle and Late Bronze Age Aegean, although their representation is clearly Egyptian in style and execution. This evidence has been well studied over the last hundred years, most often in terms of the tribute bearers' ethnic identity and their chronology, *i.e.*, which figures are Minoan and which Mycenaean. The traditional view is that three earliest tomb paintings show Minoan figures wearing breechcloths, cinch belts and codpieces in the typical red, white, and blue Minoan color scheme (tombs of Senenmut, Puiumre, and Useramun). The fourth tomb was built for the Vizier Rekhmire and shows 16 Aegean figures bearing gifts (Fig. 28). At some point in the mid-fifteenth century Rekhmire had the costumes of only these figures repainted, changing the Minoan-style breechcloths with codpieces and backflaps into Mycenaean-style kilts. This was first noticed by Davies (1926, 46) and highlighted by several scholars since (Vercoutter 1956, Barber 1991, 333–6) who remark on the chronological significance of this change: this period coincides with major destructions on Neopalatial Crete in Late Minoan (LM) IB and marks the beginning of Mycenaean participation in overseas trade. Does the change from a 'Minoan' loin cloth to a more 'Mycenaean' kilt on the Theban tomb document a change in economic influence in the Aegean? Rehak (1996, 1998) has shown that the style of clothing worn by the figures in the tomb of Rekhmire should not be taken as strict chronological markers since examples of the types are found from MM II times onwards and that representations of the Mycenaean kilt are quite late. Rehak suggests that the types of individuals coming to Egyptian Thebes may have changed, perhaps of a different status or age and that this is indicated by the change in dress.

While the origin of the 'Aegeans' (or Keftiu) in the Theban tombs is a debated issue, the ambassadors from 'the isles in the midst of the Great Green sea' most likely traded with the Egyptians for resources they lacked, in particular precious metals. We might assume that higher status was achieved and greater wealth acquired by the Aegean elites controlling these ventures. The Minoans were, most likely, in regular contact with the rulers at Mari and other metal traders of the Near East by the early second millennium BC, and trading agricultural goods, manufactured metal tools, vessels (with oil, wine, and possibly perfume),

Figure 28. Cretans Bringing Gifts, Tomb of Rekhmire, facsimile, (TT 100), c. 1479–1425 BC (Garis Davies, Nina de (1881–1965). ©The Metropolitan Museum of Art / Art Resource, NY, for permission fee).

and dyed textiles. There is a fairly clear reference at Mari to a Kaptorite merchant receiving tin in exchange for western-made goods at Ugarit. In addition to the material exchange between the Aegean and the Near East, we can surely assume an exchange of ideas involving concepts of rulership, economic administration, and craft technologies, including methods of textile manufacture such as purple dyeing. While none of the textiles shown is purple, we do know that the most valuable textiles were colored since Near Eastern records tell us that purple-dyed cloth equaled if not exceeded that of gold and silver, acting as nearly a kind of currency itself (Wiener 1987, 264).

Administration of Cloth Production

The major Minoan centers of the Old Palace period became increasingly complex economic systems and required some method for recording the flow of goods and services in and out of the palace. Much has been written about the Bronze Age administration of the palaces on Crete and of the later Mycenaean period because so many extensive records are preserved to us, although not all of them can be read. Evidence for early administration and archives on Crete are found in three different scripts: Cretan Hieroglyphic, dating primarily to MM IA–III; the script of the Phaistos disc, dating to MM II or MM III; and Linear A, dating to MM IB–LM IB; plus a system of ideographic signs and symbols on seal stones.

Minoan Seal Stones

Minoan seals and sealings offer information on the early control of activities in the palaces (Palaima 1990; Krzyszkowska 2005), and some of the earliest seal uses on Crete date to the Prepalatial period, perhaps foreshadowing the later, extensive use of seals for administration of craft activities (Schoep and Knappett 2004, 26). Some cut seal stones, it is argued here, show that textile production was one of the first craft activities administered by the Minoan palaces. Exactly when seal stones take on an administrative and organizational function is a debated point. Two specialists in the field seem to be divided on this point: Pini maintains that Minoan seals always had a sphragistic, or documentary function, while Weingarten believes Minoan seals did not take on an administrative role until the end of the Old Palace period, in MM II (Pini 1990; Weingarten 1990). From my analysis of seal stones related to cloth production, I would agree with Pini that the stones are administrative from the beginning.

Seal impressions on loom weights and spindle whorls from the Old Palace period and into the New Palace period may suggest the early administration and organization of the production of cloth (Fig. 29)(Vlasaki and Hallager 1995, 253–4; Aruz 1994, 215–8; *CMS* II.6, 380–9). Examples include stamped disc-weights from Palaikastro (Dawkins 1903–04, 202; Hutchinson 1939/40; *CMS* II.6) and Monastiraki; stamped cuboid weights from Malia (Poursat 1980, fig. 275), Chamaizi, and Palaikastro (Hutchinson 1939/40; *CMS* II.6); and a stamped spindle whorl from Chamalevri (Vlasaki and Hallager 1995, 253, 259). Disc weights with seal impressions and graffiti continue from the Middle Minoan period at Amnisos (Guarducci 1935), Zakro (Hogarth 1900–01), and Quartier Mu at Malia (Poursat 1980).

Seventeen stamped pyramidal weights were found in LM I B destructions at Palaikastro, weighing an average of 113 grams (Weingarten 2000, 485; *CMS* II.6). This shape of weight is unusual for Crete, and these examples are highly standardized. Similar weights are known from Gournia, Malia, and Zakros, where 16 pyramidal stone weights were found in Room XLIV of the palace (Weingarten 2000, n. 4). From Enkomi on Cyprus there are similar examples of stamped pyramidal weights (Smith 1995, 217). Further investigation of these stamped weights is warranted and one wonders if the same stamp design recurs on other loom weights, in other media, and at other sites. Do these stamps signify owner, product, or weight? One suggestion by Weingarten is that the pyramidal and cuboid weights, both concentrated in eastern Crete, may have been mimicked in wooden form which no longer

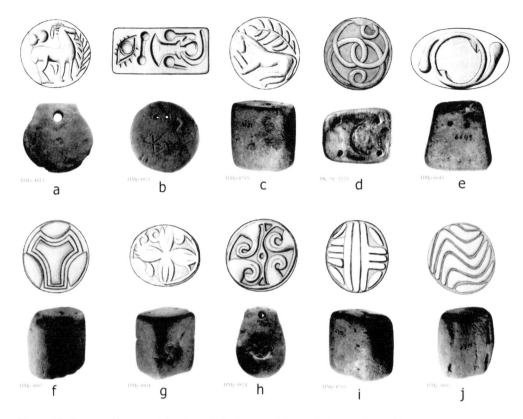

Figure 29. Stamped loom weights from Palaikastro: a) Nr. 248/HMp 4813; b) Nr. 245/HMp 4815; c) Nr. 244/HMp 4793; d) Nr. 243/PK/91/3223; e) Nr. 242/HMp 6643; f) Nr. 241/HMp 4807; g) Nr. 240/HMp 4804; h) Nr. 239/HMp 4814; i) Nr. 238/HMp 4792; j) Nr. 237/HMp 4806 (from CMS II.6, with permission, I. Pini).

survives, and that they were not used for textile production but rather served as tags attached to bags. Their stamps could have indicated ownership, contents, or destination (Weingarten 2000). This idea is explored more fully below under cuboid weights.

A new source of evidence about textile production comes, not from stamped textile tools, but from prism seal stones which I believe depict loom weights (Fig. 30). This type of seal stone is three-sided, made of steatite, and is the largest surviving group of Old Palace seal stones, dating from the MM IB–MM II contexts (Kenna 1960; Yule 1980; Krzyszkowska 2005). I suggest that a certain variety of prism seal stone depicts three to five loom weights attached to bars at the bottom of a warp-weighted loom. If this suggestion is correct, the seals indicate the administration of textile production in the earliest palaces.

In total, there are over twenty-five different seal stones published in the *CMS* volumes with this motif, many of which are chance finds, or were purchased by early collectors with unknown provenance (Table 2). Seven of the one hundred seals found in the Seal

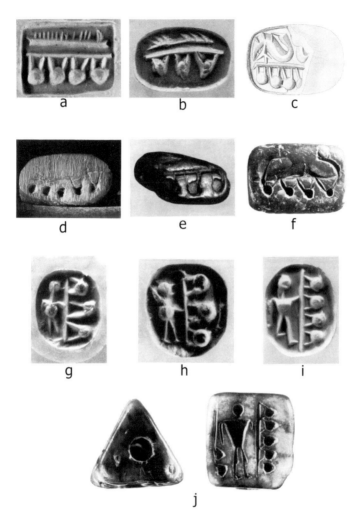

Figure 30. Prism seal stones: a) Nr. 151/Mallia inv. 1823; b) Nr. 125/Mallia inv. 1797; c) Nr. 124/Mallia inv. 1795; d) Nr. 107/Mallia inv. 1777; e) Nr. 297/unknown provenance inv. 1475; f) Nr. 225/Krassi inv. 1458; g) Nr. 214/Artsa inv. 333; h) Nr. 302/unknown provenance inv. 114; i) Nr. 224/Gonies 80; j) Nr. 306 uknown provenance, inv. 1298 (from CMS II.2, with permission, I. Pini).

Engraver's Workshop of Quartier Mu, Malia, show these suspended weights, while other seals from this area show potters and other craftspeople, indicating the administration of these craft activities (Xenaki-Sakellariou 1958, Poursat 1990; Younger 1988, 1995).

The round objects suspended from poles shown on some of the seals are very similar to the circular and discoid loom weights found throughout Crete and the Aegean. Wear-marks on discoid loom weights indicate that the one- and two-holed weights were attached by

Table 2. Minoan prism seal stones showing motifs related to cloth production.

	CMS	Inv. No.	Provenance	Color	Side A	Side B	Side C
1	II.2 107	Iraklion 1777	Mallia Workshop A	yellow-green	5 loom-weights		
2	II.2 124	Iraklion 1795	Mallia Workshop A	brown-yellow	at least 4 loom-weights (frag.)	2 spiders	two-handled jug
3	II.2 125	Iraklion 1797	Mallia Workshop A	green with black veins	3 loom-weights	crouching animal	3 goat heads
4	II.2 151	Iraklion 1823	Mallia Workshop D	green	4 loom-weights	2 water birds	four-legged animal
5	II.2 214	Iraklion 333	Artsa - chance find		standing figure w/ 3 loom-weights	whirl	horned animal & birds
6	II.2 224	Iraklion 80	Gonies - chance find		standing figure w/ 4 loom-weights	framed spider	horned animal
7	II.2 225	Iraklion 1458	Krassi - chance find	deep olive green	4 loom-weights on frame	insect	2 standing figures
8	II.2 297	Iraklion 1475	unprovenanced	olive green	at least 3 loom-weights (frag.)	line & puncture design	not decipherable
9	II.2 302	Iraklion 114	unprovenanced	light olive	figure w/ 3 loom-weights	figure w/ tool(s)	2 water birds
10	II.2 306	Iraklion 1298	unprovenanced		figure w/ 5 loom-weights tool	animal	2 copulating animals
11	IV 10	Iraklion 1255	Mallia	brown	4 loom-weights & 2 jugs	goat	figure w/ 2 vases
12	IV 11	Iraklion 184	Mallia	grey & brown	figure w/ 3 loom-weights	scorpion	bird & fish
13	VII 17	BM1934. 11–20.3	unprovenanced	black	figure w/ 5 loom-weights	dog	2 arrows, 2 branches
14	VII 206	Cambr, F. 78.1901	Sitanos		6 loom-weights	dog	2 two-handled jars sheep head
15	VII 212	Cambr, F. 73.1901	Anavlochos	green-grey	3 loom-weights	bucranium	toothed quadrilateral
16	VII 216	Cambr, F. 72.1901	Epano Zakro	grey & black	3 loom-weights	dog	fish
17	VIII 13	SLG. Dawkins Paris, CdM. N	unprovenanced	brown & cream	3 loom-weights on toothed rod	bucranium	ant
18	IX 13	3437 Zürich	unprovenanced	yellow	5 loom-weights w/ tool	goat	spirals
19	X 272	Bollmann Berlin St. M.	unprovenanced	yellow buff	4 loom-weights w/ line above	bucranium	
20	XI 7	FG 62 Wien Mus. IX	unprovenanced	yellow-green	figure w/ 4 loom-weights	3 fish	2 figures, 2 insects
21	XI 298	1979 NY, Met. Museum	unprovenanced	light brown	2 figures w/ 9 loom-weights	2 animals (?)	4 figures in line
22	XII 29	46.111.3 NY, Met. Museum	unprovenanced		3 loom-weights	5 bird heads	2 joined birds
23	XII 43	26.31.90 NY, Met. Museum	unprovenanced		3 loom-weights w/ fish (or tool?)	2 joined Hs	figure
24	XII 47	26.31.139 NY, Met. Museum	unprovenanced		4 loom-weights w/ tools	hound	S-spiral w/ flower bud
25	XII 48	26.31.140 NY, Met. Museum	unprovenanced	dark	5 loom-weights w/ fish (or tool?)	4 goat heads	hound
26	XII 64	26.31.134 NY, Met. Museum	unprovenanced		4 loom-weights w/ tool	dog	bucranium w/ leaves

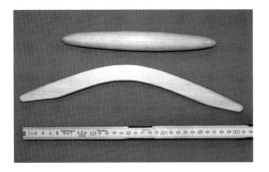

Figure 31 (above). Modern wooden tools for textile work, Centre for Textile Research, Copenhagen (B. Burke).

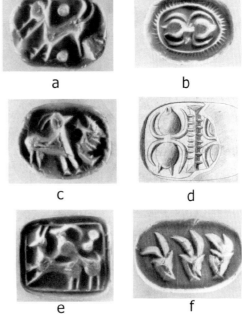

Figure 32 (right). Prism seal stones with loom weights showing obverse sides with goats or spiders: a) Nr. 224; b) Nr. 224; c) Nr. 214; d) Nr. 124; e) Nr. 306; f) Nr. 125 (from CMS II.2, with permission, I. Pini).

straps to some horizontal object to which was attached warp threads. The grooves found on the upper edges of the loom weights are most likely where small poles would be attached to the weights, just as we see depicted on the seals. This placement would give equal tension to all the warp threads, reducing the need for large numbers. Many of the seal images show tassels or fringes running upward, perpendicular to the bar and the weights, which may be the warp threads of the loom, wooden beaters, or combs used in weaving.

On the seal stones the image of the warp-weighted loom is only one of three cut sides. The other sides often depict some combination of a human figure (or two), occasionally with a long tool that may be a sword beater used for beating the weft threads up the warp (Fig. 31). Also carved are horned animals (perhaps indicating the source of the wool), spirals, bucrania, birds, and spiders (Fig. 32). The spider motif may even indicate an early association of the spider with the craft of weaving.

Evans initially suggested that the round images on these seal stones showed vessels attached to poles for transport (Evans 1909, 131–32 figs 69a, 70b, 71a). Publications of similar seals since have followed Evans' identification: Yule, for example, classifies these seals along with others displaying vessel motifs (Fig. 33)(1980, 166–7, pl. 29, motif 53); Younger calls them 'Vertical Supports with Globular Attachments' (1995, 336). There are prism seals which clearly show vessels with lips, handles and rims clearly delineated by the glyptic artist. To my mind, the seals under discussion here seem to be showing something completely different from suspended globular vessels: I believe that they are the one- or two-holed Minoan disc loom weight attached to the bottom of a warp-weighted loom, indicating weaving.

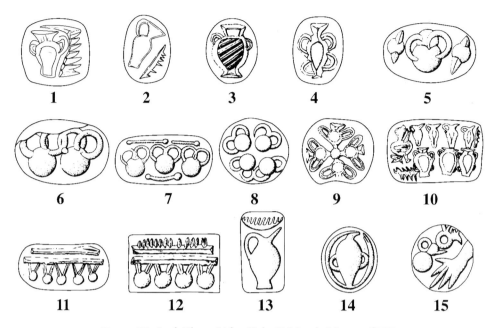

Figure 33. Seal Chart (After Yule 1980, pl. 29, motif 53).

Linear A and Minoan Cloth Production

The Linear A script seems to have developed along with the first palaces on Crete, although it should be noted that developments were not concomitant and that traces of the first palaces pre-date the earliest use of either Hieroglyphic Minoan or Linear A. The Linear A script recorded, among other things, economic transactions during the Old and New Palace periods on Crete and in other parts of the Aegean. Examples of this Minoan script used for administrative purposes are found at eleven different palaces and villa sites on the island, from Chania in the west to Zakros in the East. Inscriptions on non-administrative objects also occur at seventeen sites on the island and at three places outside of Crete.

A well-established Minoan administration system heavily based on a textile industry was most likely adopted by newly arrived Mycenaeans in the Late Bronze Age. As Killen notes, 'One possibility is ...that the greater decentralization at Knossos reflects the fact that the incoming mainland Greeks found centrally-controlled textile industries already established at a number of the Minoan centers, and decided to keep these in being, merely subordinating them to overall central direction' (Killen 1984, 60–1). Killen acknowledges that this hypothesis of an earlier Minoan textile industry is tenuous because of insufficient textual evidence from Minoan Crete and, while Minoan and Mycenaean Greek are completely different languages, it is revealing that Linear A records documenting textile administration often foreshadow tendencies found in the later Mycenaean record-keeping system. For example, a clay roundel from Hagia Triada (HT Wc 3019, *GORILA* II, p. 78), is inscribed with the Linear A sign that is unmistakably a LOOM, as noted by Evans (1921, 253), Brice (1961, pl. xiv, IV.7.a) and Barber (1991, 92, fig. 3.12). Roundels are defined as free-standing, roughly circular pieces of clay that are impressed by seal stones, inscribed, or left blank, but not pressed up against any other document or material, in contrast to a clay sealing (Hallager 1996). The ideogram is a schematic representation of a warp-weighted loom with suspended weights attached to warp threads, likely derived from earlier Minoan seal stones also showing the bottom of a warp-weighted loom. Large quantities of loom weights found in the so-called servants quarters' of Villa A, along with 45 clay sealings (in room 27), indicate that textiles were being produced and stored at Hagia Triada and this sealing appears to be one record of the administration of such craft activity.

A published Linear A sherd not found on Crete but from Akrotiri also contains interesting signs possibly related to textile administration (Michailidou 1992–93). The incised sherd is local Theran pottery, slightly curved, and reused as an inscribed document. The very sketchy inscription was likely made sometime after the pot had been broken, making the sherd a true ostrakon. Horizontal strokes indicate a unit of ten, which is a late characteristic in Linear A also occurring in Linear B, suggesting a date of LM IA for the inscription. Michalaidou applies a Linear B reading for these Minoan signs and their units: 40 units of MA, 5 PU, 7 TE, 9 ZO, and 4 TA (1992–3). The MA, for example, could be an abbreviated form of MA+RU, standing for the Linear A ligature, ideogram ('wool', see HT 12.4–5, HT 24a.1–4, *GORILA* I). More than likely, it is related to Greek μαλλός, a somewhat rare word without an accepted etymology, meaning 'wool'. The other signs on this sherd possibly indicate textile commodities, such as the *te-pa*, *pu-ka-ta-ri-ja*, and *zo-ta* that also occur in Linear B and are discussed in the next chapter.

Finally, another relatively recent discovery in Linear A is of particular interest in terms of the question of Minoans overseas: a Minoan graffito found at the Middle Bronze Age site of Tel Haror, in the western Negev, Israel, shows Linear A signs inscribed before firing (Olivier 1996). Here also we find a Linear A sign taken to mean TELA + *TE*, a type of cloth common in later Mycenaean texts. The other two ideograms seem to indicate figs and a bull's head rhyton.

The three texts discussed above are selected examples related to Minoan cloth production. Many more could be included and further research into the use of Linear A will better inform us about the early administration of craft activities like textile production. By applying our knowledge of Mycenaean administrative features we may also clarify the earlier Minoan material.

Minoan Textile Tools

The purple dyeing and the early seal use may seem like disparate topics but they are key pieces of evidence for explaining a sophisticated social phenomenon which occurred right around the turn of the second millennium BC: the emergence of the Minoan palace system. What now can we say about the physical evidence for the production of cloth on the island that played such an important economic role in this system? Loom weights and spindle whorls from Crete, along with other artifacts such as weft bobbins, needles, dye vats, fiber-wetting bowls, and decks of pierced cards for tablet weaving, are among the evidence. Some evidence for textile manufacture could be located at nearly every Minoan excavation so the material discussed below is meant to highlight case studies, showing distinctive distribution patterns and aspects of standardization. The primary interest here is how palatially controlled cloth production reflects various hierarchies of social organization.

Spindle Whorls

All weaving technologies depend upon some system of tension-spun thread, and in the Aegean this was most often achieved with the dropped, whorl-weighted spindle. Unfortunately all that survives in the archaeological record is the clay whorl, and remarkably it appears infrequently on Crete. Spindle whorls are usually small, fired clay objects of various shapes and weights. In order to spin thread, the whorls are attached at the bottom of a long, slender rod called a spindle, to create tension and torsion. Raw wool is drawn out and hooked around a small notch at the top of the spindle, and the whorl is spun manually so that the spun thread winds itself around the rod.

Minoan spindle whorls have been a source of quiet consternation among Aegean prehistorians for some time. On Crete, the proportion of excavated spindle whorls to loom weights is very low from palatial contexts. In fact, excavations at the Palace of Knossos, excluding the Prepalatial settlement, report no spindle whorls at all. This absence is striking in comparison to the thousands of whorls reported from various contemporary levels at Troy (Schliemann 1880b, 327 and 361; Dörpfeld 1902, 340; Blegen 1950; Balfanz 1995) and Aphrodisias (Joukowsky 1986, 372–81). The sites that yield spinning equipment are usually small, isolated settlements such as Debla, Kastellos, Sklavokampos and Myrtos. Tzachili gives a total count of whorls from Crete: 48 from the Early Minoan period, 15 from Middle Minoan sites, and 11 dating to the Late Minoan period (1997, 126). The number of whorls grows each year with new excavations and better record keeping, however the small numbers demonstrate the scarcity of spindle whorls from Crete which would not have been adequate to supply threads for all the looms on the island, as indicated by the numbers of loom weights. Barber estimates that it takes seven to eight hours to spin thread that could be woven in approximately one hour (Barber 1997, 515); we should therefore expect a greater number of whorls than loom weights, rather than fewer.

The absence of spindle whorls from Crete can be explained by at least three possibilities: the first is that most Minoan whorls were made of a perishable material such as wood; the second, that fibers may have been spun by a different technique from the whorl-weighted drop-spindle, perhaps using an object not recognized in the archaeological record, such as a stone of a certain weight; and the third, that tasks such as spinning might have become highly specialized in an organized Minoan textile industry and occurred far away from excavated centers, perhaps in scattered settlements yet undetected in the archaeological record (Tzachili 1997, 125–9).

Minoan Loom Weights

For weaving, in contrast to spinning, we have very good evidence from Crete. Based on pictograms in Aegean scripts and on significant deposits of loom weights we can say that

Figure 34. Minoan loom weights: a) spherical weight from Knossos; b) discoid loom weight from Loom Weight Basement, Knossos; c) cuboid weight from Petras (B. Burke).

Figure 35. Spherical weights from South House Basement (B. Burke).

in the second millennium BC a great deal of cloth was made on a warp-weighted loom. Suspended clay loom weights gave tension to the warp threads hanging vertically at the bottom of a standing loom. The weights were attached in a variety of ways: they could be tied directly to warp threads, attached to a cord that was fastened to the warp, or tied to a thin bar that had warp threads connected to it. There are three basic shapes for Minoan loom weights: spherical, discoid, and cubic (Fig. 34).

Spherical Loom Weights

Spherical weights occur exclusively on Crete during the late MM to LM II period, primarily associated with the Neopalatial period. These weights are fairly large, approximately the size of an orange (Fig. 35). They often have grooves running parallel to the suspension hole across the entire surface of the weight. The number varies but most often the grooves quarter the sphere. These can be fairly broad grooves, 0.5 cm in width and depth, or they can be very faint and worn, perhaps indicating thread wear. Both the grooves and the interior of the central suspension hole were sometimes painted with the same dark red-brown iron-based paint used on fine wares, perhaps in order to prevent snagging when the weights were threaded. In addition, while these weights appear fairly spherical, close analysis shows that some have slightly flattened sides or 'resting surfaces', as if they were placed on a flat surface to dry while the clay was still soft. The suspension hole is often at a 45-degree angle to this flat surface, perhaps indicating that the malleable clay ball was resting when the suspension hole was pierced through with a stick or finger at a 45-degree angle. Wear marks found at both ends of the suspension holes indicate that the weights were suspended with the hole on the horizontal plane, parallel to the ground.

Spherical or melon-shaped Minoan loom weights have been found on Crete in New Palace period contexts, but not at any of the prominent Neopalatial sites off-island, such as Akrotiri, Kythera, Kea and Rhodes, all of which display a great deal of Minoan material culture and contact (Popham *et al.* 1984, 249; MacDonald 2005, 67). Most of the Cretan examples seem to be concentrated in the northern and eastern parts of the island, especially around the area of Knossos and Archanes. Examples of spherical weights have also been found at Malia (Deshayes and Dessene 1959, pl. xxii 2.3; Pelon 1970, pl. xxvi.3), Vathypetro (Marinatos 1951), Archanes Phourni Building 4 (Sakellarakis and Sapouna-Sakellaraki 1991, 87, fig. 62), the North Building of the Stratigraphical Museum excavations at Knossos (Warren 1980–1, figs 42–3), the Houses by the Acropolis at Knossos (Catling, *et al.* 1979, figs 43–4), the South House at Knossos (Burke 2003), and the Unexplored Mansion (Popham *et al.* 1984, 247–9). The context of these finds, only on Crete, within palatially associated workrooms – suggests that, as with the Loom Weight Basement deposit, these weights indicate textile production for the ruling elites at Knossos. The weights vary in size, from 86 to 710 grams.

Minoan Unexplored Mansion (MUM)
The spherical loom weights from the Minoan Unexplored Mansion (MUM) are probably the best published of the known examples. The chronological context for the loom weights seems to be the end of the Neopalatial period, probably during LM IB. The MUM was initially constructed in LM IA, after completion of the Little Palace immediately to the east and was occupied for a time, damaged in LM II and then reused until LM IIIB2 (Popham *et al.* 1984, 2–3). According to Hitchcock and Preziosi's analysis, the Minoan Unexplored Mansion should be identified as the 'annex' to the 'villa' that is the Little Palace (1997). This villa-annex building system is also found at Tylissos (Villa A and 'Annex' B) and Hagia Triada (Villa A and 'Annex' B). The more regular, rectangular annexes are seen as functional complements to the more sophisticated villas. The remains of buttresses found on the eastern side of the MUM probably once supported a bridge connecting the two structures, as at Tylissos (Hitchcock and Preziosi 1997, 51). Even though there are elite furnishings like floral frescos in them, annexed structures like the MUM were most likely workshop and storage areas rather than any kind of elite residence, dining or ritual area (Graham 1975; Popham, *et al.* 1984).

This new interpretation of the Minoan Unexplored Mansion fits very well with the evidence of textile equipment found therein. In the Stratigraphical Museum, 147 spherical loomweights were examined. Most of these (87) came from room N 31, identified as a storage cupboard under a set of stairs in the southwest corner of the building. Other deposits were found in the four-pillared hall, H (22 weights), in corridor L (8), and under the other set of stairs, J/K (1). Unprovenanced weights from within the Unexplored Mansion numbered 29, including two discoid types and one probable biconical spindle whorl weighing 64 grams. Most of the spheres were made of fired beige-red clay, with small pieces of white, gray and black stones used as grog. Some of the loom weights showed evidence of burning. All had a single suspension hole, ranging from 0.5 to 2 cm in diameter, with some examples showing string wear-marks.

From the 87 loom weights that were found under the stairway N, 58% (50) of the weights had traces of grooves, sometimes painted, along the exterior surface. Some of the interiors of the suspension holes were also painted. Six of the weights showed the same, deliberate cross marking scratched on the surface of the loom weight as was found on the discoid examples from the Loom Weight Basement at Knossos. Eleven percent (10 weights) weighed between 86 and 130 grams and comprised the 'small' group; the majority of weights, 55% (48), ranged between 150 and 250 grams and made up the 'medium' variety; and 21% (19) were between 270 and 350 grams and formed the 'large' group. The remaining ten weights varied greatly, from 370 to 710 grams. These outliers may have added tension to the selvedges. Unfortunately, there did not seem to be any clear correlation between the grooved and the ungrooved weights.

Popham's interpretation of the Unexplored Mansion deposit assumes that all 90 weights found in Room N were intended for a single loom (Popham *et al.* 1984, 248). It is more likely, however, that this assemblage of loom weights was used for several different looms: perhaps one light-weight loom with weights of the first cluster, five looms of the medium size weights, and two of the large set, assuming that each loom used about ten weights. Alternatively, the weight groups could each represent one loom, with the three looms producing textiles of different widths. If this interpretation were correct, the medium weight group (of 48 weights) would make a fairly wide textile.

As Hitchcock and Preziosi demonstrate, the identification by Popham of the Pillar Hall H as a Pillar Crypt, a domestic shrine and/or living area, seems unfounded (1997, 53–4). The abundance of metalworking remains, cast trimmings, bellows nozzles, crucibles, and scrap metal, clearly indicates that this area was used for manufacturing metal. The 22 loom weights found in the same area give a general impression of an industrial quarter. The weights here averaged 280 grams, giving a total of 61 kilograms of textile making equipment in this hall. These weights cluster into two groups, light and heavy. Thirteen weighed between 150 and 300 grams, while eight were between 400 and 500 grams. These may have been used on the same loom, with the heavier weights providing tension along the sides to keep the selvedges straight, or they may indicate the presence of two separate, smaller looms.

'Cult Basement' of the North Building at Knossos

Comparing the weights from the Unexplored Mansion to the nearby Cult Room Basement of the North Building excavated by P. Warren, one finds a similar distribution of spherical weights:

> Measurements of the 79 weights, kindly provided to me by Professor Warren, range from 100 to 670 grams. Eighteen percent (14) weighed between 100 and 150 grams, within the small range. The majority (64% or 51 weights), as at the Unexplored Mansion, were medium size, between 150 and 250 grams. Five were considered large, weighing 270–310 grams, and the rest were outliers at more than 420 grams.

Buildings Near the Acropolis

Another set of loom weights was not available for study but is well published (Catling *et al.* 1979, especially 2, 15, 61, and 78). The main deposit of the LM IA building, Deposit F, contained substantial finds of spherical and cylindrical terra-cotta loom weights that had originally been stored in a clay tub. The range of weights for the spherical loom weights is well within what we find in other examples in the area of Knossos, 200–750 grams. Other finds included LM IA vases and stone vessels, and at the edge of the group of loom weights was a small bronze implement, a rod that was square in section with flattened ends, like a spatula. Perhaps this was a sword beater for pushing up the warp threads (cf. Hoffmann 1964, 279–82). Also found with the loom weight group here were 6 conical cups, all of which had a hole knocked in their bases, doubtless so that they too could be used as loom weights.

South House at Knossos

There is only slight evidence for spinning (2 spindle whorls) at the South House at Knossos, and weaving is suggested by eleven loom weights (Burke 2003). All were of the spherical, or melon-shaped variety, and all were of similar red-brown clay; three were grooved across the body, with the grooves radiating from the suspension hole. They tended to cluster into two groups, medium-size and large-size weights. One set of six ranged from 137 to 214 grams, while the remaining five weighed between 252 and 336 grams. These weights seem well in-line with other comparable examples of spherical loom weights found at Knossos and elsewhere. One of the more remarkable weights is the heaviest, number 11, which is decorated with three fairly large cross markings, a mark that we have seen on other loom weights from Minoan Crete. These marks are not incised, however, but firmly impressed into the soft clay prior to firing. Their meaning is lost to us.

Unprovenanced Knossos Weights

There is one other collection of spherical loom weights in the Stratigraphical Museum, for which there is no context provided other than that they were found somewhere at Knossos. Based on a similar distribution in weights to the examples from the Unexplored Mansion and the North Building, we can be reasonably certain that these 47 spherical loom weights also date to the New Palace period. Only two examples weighed less than 150 grams (these are considered small). Meanwhile, 38% weighed between 150 and 260 grams (medium) and 25% were between 260 and 340 grams (large). The remaining weights (23%) were outliers, between 350 and 600 grams. While we cannot be certain that these weaving tools came from a single deposit, the distribution of their measured weights is thoroughly in line with what we would expect for this type of deposit.

Archanes (Phourni, Building 4) and Vathypetro

The spherical loom weights found farthest from Knossos are those from the Villa at Vathypetro and those from Building 4 at the cemetery of Archanes-Phourni, dating to the LM IA period (Sakellarakis and Sapouna-Sakellaraki 1991, 87, fig. 62; Sakellarakis 1974, 209). These two sites, however, are less than 20 km away from Knossos and may have had significant connections with the palace (Marinatos 1951, 269; Driessen and Sakellarakis 1997, 75). Among the remarkable finds from Vathypetro, Marinatos reports several spherical loom weights and a wine press. The mostly spherical loom weights are still in storage at the site, and have not been studied in detail as far as can be determined. It is thought that wine and textiles were stored in areas 40 and 41 at Vathypetro.

Building 4 at Archanes, excavated between 1974 and 1977, is an unusual Minoan structure, in that it is a workshop located in the center of the Phourni cemetery, between Tholos tombs A and B. The rectangular building is divided into separate wings on the east and west, possibly indicating two phases of construction. In the southern half of the east wing are two rooms (Rooms 1 and 2), which contained between them 46 spherical loom weights. Also found in these rooms were some personal items, perhaps belonging to the weavers: a steatite seal-stone with lions, a monkey amulet, and a bead. Other craft activities are also indicated from the finds nearby: a bronze ingot, other metal-working tools, and debris from stone working. The weights of all studied spherical loom weights are summarized below (Table 3):

Table 3. Spherical loom weights from Knossos and Archanes.

Knossos/Archanes deposit:	*period/date*	*number*	*percentage*	*weight (grams)*
MUM	LM IB/1500	10	11%	small 86–130
		48	55%	medium 150–250
		19	21%	large 270–350
		10	11%	very large 370–710
"Cult Room Basement" of North Building	LM IB	14	18%	small 100–150
		51	64%	medium 150–250
		5	6%	large 270–310
		9	11%	very large 420–670
South House	MMIII-LM IA/1550	1	5%	small 137
		5	45%	medium 156–214
		5	45%	large 252–336
unprovenanced	Neopalatial	2	4%	small 119–130
		18	38%	medium 150–260
		12	25%	large 260–340
		11	23%	very large 350–600
Archanes Building 4	LM IA	2	5%	small 106–121
		22	56%	medium173–238
		10	25%	large 254–327
		5	13%	very large 367–438

Figure 36. Discoid loom weights from Loom Weight Basement, Knossos (B. Burke).

Discoid Weights

The second type of weight is the discoid, which is the most typical Minoan loom weight and was in use on Crete from EM II through LM III (Fig. 36). Carington Smith suggests, in fact, that the Minoan discoid weight is just as culturally distinctive of the Minoans as is the Double Ax or the Horns of Consecration (1975, 275). In Early Bronze Age Anatolia, at Troy I, II, and IV and at Aphrodisias, a similar disc-shaped loom weight is common, suggesting that both types are derived from a common source. The weights have holes in the upper half and often the topside is flattened and grooved. In the Old Palace at Knossos, discussed in more detail below, Evans found over 400 of these discoid loom weights in the Loom Weight Basement of the East Wing (Fig. 37).

    One of the largest single deposits of Minoan discoid loom weights was found by Sir

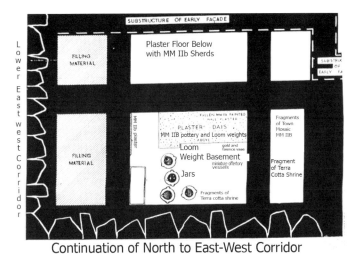

SUBSTRUCTURE OF EARLY FAÇADE

Plaster Floor Below
with MM IIb Sherds

L
o
w
e
r

E
a
s
t

w
e
s
t

C
o
r
r
i
d
o
r

FILLING
MATERIAL

FILLING
MATERIAL

MM IIb plaster

FALLEN MMIII PAINTED
WALL PLASTER
'PLASTER' DAIS
MM IIB pottery and Loom weights
ABOVE
Loom
Weight Basement
miniature offertory
vessels
Jars
Fragments of
Terra cotta shrine

gold and
faience vase

SUBSTRUC
OF
EARLY FA

Fragments
of Town
Mosaic
MM IIB

Fragment
of Terra
Cotta Shrine

Continuation of North to East-West Corridor

Figure 37. Loom Weight Basement plan, Knossos (Evans 1921, p. 250, fig. 187a, with permission, Ashmolean Museum, Oxford University).

Arthur Evans at Knossos in 1902, below the East Wing of the palace (Evans 1921, 253). MacDonald has recently published that these weights were the spherical kind, *i.e.* the so-called melon weights (2005, 67) yet Evans' publication of the weights makes it clear:

> That this chamber belonged to the women's apartments may be inferred by the large stores of loom-weights that it had contained. Over four hundred of these had been precipitated below from its floor-level and were found above the relics belonging to the basement proper. These are pear-shaped in outline and flatter than the oval Late Minoan type. It may be mentioned that looms with pendant weights supply a recurring sign of the Linear Script A. (Evans 1921, 253)

In May of 1997, I was permitted to weigh, draw and catalogue the same 45 loom weights from the Loom Weight Basement. Most of the loom weights were complete and for those that were not, the percentage preserved was calculated in estimating the complete weight. The 45 weights, representing perhaps 10% of the total found by Evans, were striking in their uniformity, especially in comparison to other deposits of weights elsewhere on Crete. All were flat, fired, discoid weights with a single suspension hole. They measured between 9 and 10 cm in height and about 7.5 to 8.5 cm in width. The pronounced, flattened top ranged from 2.5 to 4.5 cm in length. Three of the weights showed incisions of a faint but deliberate cross or X. Interestingly, this same cross mark appears on the other two types of Minoan loom weight.

The weights varied little in comparison to the spherical types, from 127 to 205 grams. This suggests that in the Old Palace (Protopalatial) period, there was some attempt at regularized textile tools. The assemblage of loom weights is rather homogeneous and the total deposit of at least 400 loom weights within the Old Palace at Knossos suggests perhaps 40 working looms, if we assume that each loom used about 10 weights for plain weave. The uniformity of the weights with their single suspension holes, similar fabric and shape, as well as their concentrated numbers, suggest that these weights were part of a regulated textile industry administered by the Old Palace at Knossos. The cross mark incised on some of the weights may also have been used to indicate sets of weights. This deposit is good evidence for retainer workshops with full-time weavers working for the Minoan state, centered at the Palace of Knossos.

Large deposits of disc loom weights like the Loom Weight Basement deposit are also known at other centers, including Minoanized sites off-island such as Akrotiri (1990, 407–19; 1997, 183–93; 2007), Ialysos (Benzi 1984), Iasos (Laviosa 1987) and Ayia Irini (Davis 1984; Cummer and Schofield 1984). J. Davis' 1984 study of the distribution of these discoid weights throughout the settlement of Ayia Irini on Keos is a very good exposition of the cultural implications suggested by large quantities of excavated textile equipment. Middle Bronze Age discoid loom weights found on Keos may have closer parallels in Anatolia than on Crete, although both types may be descended from the same original source.

During the Middle Bronze Age, terracotta spools are also prevalent on Keos. These objects are about five to seven centimeters in height with a pinched waist and are catalogued with other textile equipment at many sites throughout the Aegean, such as Zygouries and Eutresis (Blegen 1928, 190–1, fig. 179.4–5; Goldman 1931, 193; Davis 1984, 162–3). The function of these objects has long puzzled scholars. Barber suggests that they may have been used to give tension to threads while being twisted into a belt or cord (1997, 515–9). Carington Smith associates them with a warping creel or spool rack, used to warp a horizontal loom (1975, 400–4). If they are associated with a horizontal loom, it is interesting that two fundamentally different weaving technologies are present at Ayia Irini in the Middle Bronze Age, the warp-weighted loom and the horizontal loom (Davis 1984, 163).

By the LC I period on Keos, it is the Minoan discoid type of loom weight that dominates the textile equipment assemblage, indicating a shift to the sole use of the warp-weighted loom. This type of loom had an advantage over the others; it provided increased control over warp thread tension and permitted cloths of greater width. Over 185 clay loom weights are found in LC I levels at Ayia Irini, heavily concentrated in the north central part of the site. Davis speculates that this concentration of standardized clay weights indicates the production of specialized textiles woven with Minoan technology for trade within the Aegean sphere.

Cuboid Weights

The third major type of Minoan loom weight is the rectangular prism or cuboid form; most often with four small suspension holes, one in each corner, which are placed along the longitudinal axes and show thread wear. The earliest examples have been found in the Neolithic period at Knossos and a variant of this cuboid type occurs in the Middle Minoan period concentrated in Eastern Crete.

Over one hundred of these 'block' shaped weights were found at Palaikastro, including several that were stamped (Hutchinson 1939–40; *CMS* V Suppl. 1A, nos. 61; *CMS* II.6, 382–4; Weingarten 1999, 491). Stamped disc loom weights of MM III–LM I date were also found (*CMS* V Suppl. 1A, nos. 64). Both types are on display in the Hagios Nikolaos

Figure 38. Cuboid loom weights from Petras (B. Burke).

Museum, room 3. Dating to the LM II period, seventy-one weights from Palaikastro were from one deposit in House E 36. Fifteen of these weights had seal impressions or graffiti on them, suggesting organization, if not administration, of production. Many of the seals depicted goats or horned sheep, strongly connecting the textile tools with wool. It could be argued that these objects were not at all connected with weaving, since it is difficult to reconstruct the use of the four holes in each corner. Weingarten has suggested that these weights, along with stamped pyramidal 'weights' might be tags attached to sacks or bags. While I wouldn't discount this idea, only some of the weights are stamped and when they are it is in a similar manner to other known loom weights, like the discoid types. They do appear fairly standardized in form and weight, suggesting that they were used as textile tools. The few outliers in terms of weight noted by Weingarten (500+ grams) is not unheard of for loom weights, especially in view of the hundreds found at Gordion (see Chapter 4 below).

The cuboid weight is a type which seems to occur exclusively in eastern Crete, only as far west as Malia. Carington Smith suggests that these weights may be related to the much earlier Middle Neolithic cuboid weights found at Knossos (1975, 296). This would suggest that the first Minoans displaced the original Neolithic settlers and pushed them into eastern Crete, where they retained one of their cultural traits, the cuboid loom weight.

I was able to study cuboid weights from Palaikastro that were stored at the Stratigraphical Museum at Knossos, presumably found during the 1962–63 seasons, before proper storage facilities were built Palaikastro. There were twelve four-holed clay cuboid weights (labeled PK 62/3, SMT 826–837). One of them, the lightest, measuring only 67 grams, had a cross or X inscribed on one side. The holes were all fairly uniform in their placement in the four corners and the clay was a similar pinkish-orange color to that of the discoid weights, but generally with less grit. The range of weights was from 67 to 284 grams, without any obvious clustering. There was evidence of wear marks on the string holes, so it is probable that these weights were suspended, possibly for making textiles. The idea that these blocks were used in tablet weaving would fit with the four-holed corners, yet the blocky nature and uneven size of the weights makes this seem unlikely if not impossible. The similar fabric and the cross marking of these block weights, along with the fact that their measured weights fall within the range of other known loom weights, does suggest a weaving function.

Case Studies

Praisos

Many Minoan palaces were built in relatively densely populated areas, as evidenced by buildings such as the Unexplored Mansion at Knossos and the houses associated with the palace at Zakros (Popham, *et al.* 1984; Hogarth 1900–1; Platon 1985, 24–33, 247–9). Excavations on Crete, however, have also uncovered non-palatial settlements that seem to have had mixed economies like the palaces, dependent upon agriculture, craft production and sea-faring; these similarities suggest that there should be evidence of textile production located in these centers as well. The LM IA–B 'villa' in eastern Crete at Prophitis Elias (Praisos) provides such evidence for organized textile production, not in a palatial context, but still at a regional center (Platon 1997). Twenty loom weights were found in the fill above rooms M, N, X, O and P, suggesting to Platon the 'women's quarters' of the Villa (L. Platon 1997, 198–200). A potter's wheel, grape press (or perhaps dye vat?) and millstones were also nearby, adding to the impression that this was an industrial quarter.

Petras

Near to Platon's 'villa' at Praisos, certain features uncovered in the 'palatial building' of Petras, Siteia, fit the criteria for a Minoan palace: storage magazines, ashlar masonry, a central court, masons' marks, and evidence for administration (Tsipopoulou and Papacostopoulou 1997). A true archive in Minoan Hieroglyphic, the first hieroglyphic archive on Crete to have been excavated in its primary context, dates to the MM IIB period at Petras, and suggests a long history of organized administration at the site (Tsipopoulou and Hallager 1996). Four-sided clay bars, medallions, crescents, noduli, and chest sealings, some in an unfinished state, suggest that the archive was in use at the time this building was destroyed in MM IIB.

Neopalatial House II at Petras shows evidence for textile production, yet is located away from the palace building (Tsipopoulou and Papacostopoulou 1997, Burke 2006). Textile equipment from this house is comparable to the loom weights found at Praisos: in three areas of House II (areas A, B, and N) there were dye vats, water channels, discoid loom weights, and a large number of tripod vessels placed on hearths which the excavator associated with dyeing. The ideogram for cloth appears on two conical cups and on some of the loom weights. As at Praisos, these installations and equipment suggest that there was a nucleated textile industry within the community of Petras. Production at Praisos might be contrasted usefully with that from the palatial building at Petras, which will be studied in more detail in the future.

Palaikastro

Other settlements in Eastern Crete, such as Gournia, Mochlos, Pseira, and Palaikastro, are large towns located near the sea that experienced destructions and rebuilding during the Old and New Palace periods. Eastern sites dating to the Late Minoan period are especially interesting because in many ways they lie outside of the reach of the dominating palatial center at Knossos (Kanta 1980, 125–98; Bennet 1987c). Palaikastro, for example, would provide a good opportunity to examine textile production in an urban settlement in Eastern Crete except that no complete publication of the textile equipment has yet appeared. From preliminary reports it is clear that evidence for cloth production occurs in even the earliest levels of the site: stamped disc-weights dating to the EM II period were found in House D 32, and the presence of spinning bowls and murex deposits was noted as well (Bosanquet 1904, 1939–1940; Bosanquet and Dawkins 1923, pl. 6c).

Kommos

Kommos undoubtedly had strong connections to the nearby palatial structures at Phaistos and Hagia Triada, only 7 km away (Shaw and Shaw 1985). Kommos also shows evidence for contacts with the Near East, beginning in the Middle Bronze Age and continuing throughout the Iron Age. There is also a sizable amount of textile equipment from all Bronze Age levels of the site, published in great detail by Dabney (Dabney 1996). Reference has already been made, for instance, to the evidence for purple dyeing at MM I/II B Kommos (Ruscillo 1998, 2005, 2006). In June of 1997, with the help of Professor J. Shaw, I analyzed examples of loom weights and spindle whorls at the site that had not been published by Dabney and were of particular stratigraphic significance. Deposits from Building T were of especial interest, as this monumental structure is the most palatial feature at Kommos, with four wings surrounding a large central court, and evidence for storage facilities, craft production, and perhaps administration (Shaw and Shaw 1993; 1995; 1996; Shaw, Van de Moortel, Day, and Kilikoglou 1997). Of the available data, three assemblages are examined here for how they reflect economic organization at Kommos. These date to the Protopalatial period, the Neopalatial period, and the Final Palatial period.

The earliest loom weights from Kommos date to the MM II period and were found in the fill of the Protopalatial Building AA. These 10 weights were first uncovered in 1993 in trenches 80B, 86D, and 88B. They are all very fragmentary, but seem to be of similar type: the two-holed discoid. Estimated restorations of their weights also show them to be fairly uniform, around 140 grams each.

Excavations during 1995 revealed 16 loom weights in the Eastern part of Room E in Building T, trench 97 E. Since Building T was built in early LM IA and the ceramic evidence gives a date of MM IIB–early LM I for these loom weights, it is probable that they should be associated with the leveling operations for the construction of Building T. In view of the finds from the earlier Protopalatial Building AA underneath Neopalatial T, we can already begin to see a long history of centralized textile production at Kommos. The equipment includes two double-perforated half discoid weights that may be net-weights. The remaining fourteen weights are typical single and double pierced discoid weights weighing an average of 116 grams.

According to Dabney, the majority of loom weights at Kommos were found in mixed deposits, described as fill or dump. A substantial number of loom weights from Room 29 of Building T, however, was found in primary contexts and provided the best evidence for textile production at Neopalatial Kommos during the LM IA period. The weights were fairly uniform: discoid types with one or two holes, and grooves along their flattened tops; they were unpainted, and weighed an average of about 70 grams (Dabney 1995, 245). The lightness of these weights suggests the weaving of finer textiles, perhaps for export.

Some other discoid loom weights were found in the Hilltop House X, dating to LM IIIA1. These weights clustered into two groups, one around 90 grams, the other at 170 grams, as well as a few outliers in the 260-gram range. Dabney makes the ingenious suggestion that since the first two weight-groups equal in total the average weight of the outliers (90 + 170 = 260), the weaving of three different types of fabrics would have been possible by using the lighter weights alone or in combination (Dabney 1995, 246–8).

While textile production is found in LM III houses at Kommos, such as House X, centralized production does not continue in the LM III buildings overlying Building T (Buildings N and P). This period is a time at which many other sites on Crete are severely destroyed, marking the end of the New Palace period. Again, Kommos and Knossos are unusual sites on Crete in that they do not have the same severe LM IB destruction levels that are found at administrative centers elsewhere. If this period marks the arrival of mainland Mycenaeans to the island, they may have centered their operations at Knossos and preserved the port town of Kommos for trade. This evidence fits very well with the pattern we would expect for a Mycenaean system of cloth production as seen on the Greek mainland, which will be examined in Chapter three. There is very little archaeological evidence other than the extensive records in Linear B at Knossos for weaving and spinning in the LM/LH III periods.

Summary

The New Palace period is over by LM IIIA1. Some of the destructions may have been related to social unrest, climatic changes, and shifting political and economic fortunes, all of which could have served to weaken the indigenous Minoan power structure for the arrival of Mycenaeans from the mainland. While this is probably the most intriguing period of inter-regional exchange and influence within Crete and beyond, the LM IIIA–B transition remains the most complicated phase of Minoan history (Hallager 1977, Kanta 1980, Niemeier 1982, Bennet 1985, 1987a; Driessen 1990).

After the New Palace period innovative features, such as chamber tombs, tholos tombs, warrior burials, and mainland Greek pottery forms, appear on the island of Crete. This evidence has suggested to some that Mycenaeans either caused the LM IB destructions or that they supported a stratum of ruling elite Minoans at Knossos who established control over the island, well summarized in Rehak and Younger (2001, 440–1). Whatever the cause of the destructions, after LM IB we can safely say that the Minoan Palace period is over. Knossos continues to function as a major administrative center in the Mycenaean period, evidenced most clearly by the Mycenaean Linear B tablets.

In terms of loom weights and spindle whorls, the evidence in LM IIIA2–B Crete is unfortunately scanty. The Late Minoan site of Kephala-Chondrou in eastern Crete provides some archaeological evidence for textile production on Crete after the New Palace period (Platon 1957, 143). Dating to LM IIIA2, this settlement provides useful information on the material remains of cloth production that is otherwise lacking in the archaeological record of LM III Crete. It would be interesting to see if these weights are representative of an emergent tradition of household weaving that continues into the archaic and classical periods, or if they indicate any organized production under the dominant Mycenaeans. We will revisit Crete in the next chapter in discussion of the detailed records in Linear B, many of which account for an active wool industry controlled by the Mycenaean center at Knossos. As we will see in the next chapter, fragmentary, and sometimes frustrating, archaeological evidence is not unexpected for the Late Bronze Age Aegean.

3 CLOTH PRODUCTION
IN THE MYCENAEAN WORLD

Evidence for textile production on mainland Greece during the Late Bronze Age derives from four sources. The first of these is artifactual remains of textile tools, primarily loom weights and spindle whorls. In contrast to the Minoan and Phrygian material discussed in other chapters, archaeological evidence in terms of tools of production for Mycenaean cloth is much less plentiful: we simply do not have concentrations of loom weights and spindle whorls in workshop contexts from Mycenaean sites. Our second source of evidence is figural representations of garments in Mycenaean art, primarily wall paintings but also in three dimensional sculpture, which attest to the qualities and varieties of Mycenaean cloth. These representations, such as the procession scene from Tiryns (Fig. 39), primarily come from palace and/or ritual settings and may not be representative of the textiles that played a major role in economic transactions (Fig. 40). Our third source of evidence is also problematic: later Greek literature makes reference to textiles, and in particular, the Homeric tradition preserves, however faintly, remnants of Bronze Age economic and social organization. There is, however, great distance in time and space between the Homeric epics and the Mycenaean palaces and therefore, literary evidence should be used cautiously. This chapter examines tools, art and later literature, but focuses most attention on the fourth and final source of evidence for Mycenaean textiles, inscribed clay documents in the Linear B script which record the many stages of production, from the acquisition of raw materials to the final distribution and consumption of the finished cloth (Fig. 41).

Figure 39. Woman with Pyxis, Tiryns Procession fresco, c. 13th century BC, as restored by Gilliéron (Rodenwaldt 1912, pl. 8).

As our best source of evidence for an understanding of the role of textiles in Mycenaean society, Linear B texts must be viewed as primarily temporary accounts written in a kind of scribal shorthand to record transactions of concern to the palatial centers. Nearly 3400 clay tablets or fragments of tablets written in Linear B (Mycenaean Greek) are reported from Knossos (*CoMIK*; Killen and Olivier 1989) and 1,100 from Pylos (Bennett and Olivier 1973; 1976);

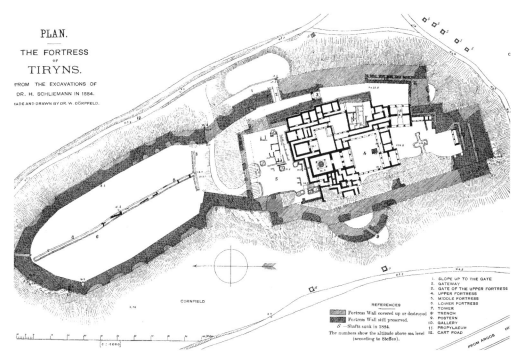

Figure 40. Plan of the Mycenaean palace at Tiryns, 1884. Designed and drawn by Dr. W. Dörpfeld (Schliemann 1886, pl. 1).

Figure 41. Linear B tablets from Knossos, c. 1300 BC (©Trustees of the British Museum).

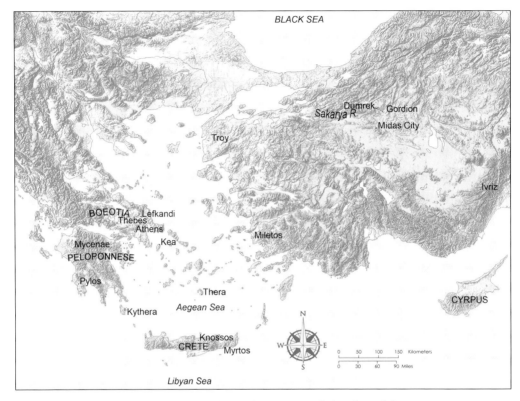

Map 3. General Map of sites mentioned in Chapters 3 and 4. Adapted from Interactive Ancient Media. http://iam.classics.unc.edu/.

Thebes has approximately 400 tablets, many of them recently discovered (Aravantinos, Godart, and Sacconi 2002, 2005); and there is a smaller number reported from the centers at Tiryns and Mycenae (Melena and Olivier 1991) as well as at Chania (Hallager, Vlasaki, and Hallager 1992). References to Mycenaean sheep rearing strategies, wool evaluation, textile administrators and 'collectors', and a wide variety of types of textiles are found in the documents and will be discussed in this chapter. Attention is focused on the archives at Pylos and Knossos because they have the largest number of tablets from any of the Mycenaean citadels and it is cloth production that is most frequently discussed in their texts.

Textiles in the Mycenaean Economy

To understand the role of textiles in the Mycenaean economy we need a general framework. Much discussion about the Mycenaean economy results from the nature of the evidence. The documents in Linear B are much less detailed when compared to economic texts of the Near East. They are, however, extremely important for reconstructing many aspects of

Bronze Age life and they are our only first-hand account of the workings of the palaces of mainland Greece and the island of Crete. The major debate in characterizing the Mycenaean economy revolves around scale: how much involvement did the palace have in the overall economy of Late Bronze Age people in Greece? Some see 'state control' as monolithic and pervasive; others suggest that the palace was just one part of the whole economy and that various crafts and other activities took place well beyond the palaces' purview.

Clearly the Mycenaean economy was complex business. Craftspeople and agricultural producers were tied palace industries, contributing and receiving raw materials and foodstuffs. Some craft activities were more heavily controlled by the center, or, the center showed more interest in administering certain products, as evidenced by the tablets. Ceramics, for example, were not of great concern to palace scribed, whereas textiles, in contrast, were the major activity recorded in the palace bureaucracy.

By viewing the economic system as operating within a staple-wealth finance system we might be in a better place to conceptualize its workings. Wealth finance involves the production of goods that have some standard of value and are used by the state, possibly as some form of payment to craft specialists, administrators, or elites (D'Altroy and Earle 1985; Levine 1992). Specialists and second-order administrators are able to draw from palatial centers their own rations and are granted access to provincial land, labor, and tribute. These goods of standard value may be converted into staples or exchanged for other wealth goods. Cloth and the constituent raw materials play a particularly prominent role in the Mycenaean economy as wealth and staple finance goods, sometimes even taking on the function of a kind of currency.

The Linear B tablets allow us to reconstruct separate, localized, redistributive economies centered at major palaces of the Aegean, namely Knossos, Pylos, Mycenae, Thebes, Tiryns, and possibly Chania. The records provide information on the raw materials used in the cloth industry and they describe the phases of production by a specialized labor force under the administration of the Mycenaean palaces. Less explicit in the tablets are references to the final use and consumption of textiles in Mycenaean society. For this, we can look to visual evidence for garments and textiles in Aegean Bronze Age art and perhaps even later Greek literature.

Linear B documents record five basic types of transactions: the mobilization of goods and services, agricultural production, personnel maintenance, distribution of offerings for cult purposes, and craft production. In all of these transactions cloth plays a substantial role. From the taxation documents, one commodity, prevalent in the Pylos Ma-series represented by sign *146, is most likely a type of cloth produced in villages that was received as payment by the palace along with other commodities (Fig. 42). Other products which have been suggested as tithed goods include ox-hides, honey, and sheep and goats (Duhoux 1974; Chadwick 1964; Shelmerdine 1973; *Docs*² 289–90; Killen 1984, 61–62, 1985, 2008b; and Perna 2004). With reference to agricultural goods, the scribes at Pylos, Knossos, Mycenae, and Thebes record flax and wool as the primary raw materials for textiles. Personnel records describe a variety of laborers, general textile workers and specialists such as spinners, weavers, fullers and decorators, all under the administration of the palace (Hiller 1988; Chadwick 1988). Finally, in terms of craft production, the records describe various

*Figure 42. Fragments of undyed linen cloth, perhaps like Mycenaean textile ideogram *146. Rectangular with knotted warp fringe and series of self-bands (AN125564001 ©Trustees of the British Museum).*

kinds of cloth produced by specialists at Mycenaean centers mostly under a system called *ta-ra-si-ja*, whereby workers receive raw materials from the palace with the expectation that targets of production will be met (Killen 2001; Nosch 2001a).

Although the tablets tell us a great deal about the Mycenaean economy, it is possible, perhaps even likely, that our picture of the textile industry based on the Linear B sources is incomplete. We know that there is economic and subsistence activity beyond the purview of the palace scribes (Bennet 1988a; H. Morris 1986). For example, ceramic production lay largely beyond the scope of the palace bureaucracy. Only a handful of references to individuals thought to be potters (*ke-ra-me-we/wo* and *ke-ra-me-ja*) at Pylos, Mycenae, and Knossos exist and nothing in the texts seems to refer to palatial administration of this craft (Whitelaw 2001). The collection of certain commodities, such as pulses and some livestock, are known from archaeological sources yet they are not mentioned in the texts (Halstead 1992a, 1992b, 1999a). Most of the plant species that have been found in paleobotanical studies are not recorded in the archives, including pulses which must have figured heavily in the Mycenaean diet. Similarly, the faunal remains of livestock do not correspond to the species recorded in the Linear B tablets (Halstead 1992b; Bennet 1988a, 26; Rougemont 2004). Industries, and products in which the palace labor force was self-sufficient, *i.e.* not in need of raw materials from outside the immediate palace vicinity, do not seem to have been recorded in the archives (Halstead 1992b, 64, 1999a). In addition, some distant geographical regions of the Mycenaean world also may have been beyond the administration of the palaces. Textual and archaeological evidence suggests that sites within the separate regions of the Mycenaean world had some degree of economic autonomy in the Late Bronze Age period (Kanta 1980, 318–21; Palaima 1984, 1987, 302).

Pylos and Knossos

The two most informative and most complete Mycenaean archives were found at Knossos and Pylos. In terms of textile production, the tablets from Pylos show a greater interest by the palace scribes in flax and linen production compared to those from Knossos (Robkin 1979; Shelmerdine 1981, 320–25; Killen 1984; Carington Smith 1992; Perna 2005; Rougemont 2007). Most likely this can be attributed to the geographic predisposition of the Pylian kingdom to growing flax: well-watered, loamy soil in the moderate climate of Messenia is well-suited for flax cultivation (Foster 1981). Halstead notes that 'the ecological potential for growing and processing flax existed more or less throughout the Pylian kingdom' (Halstead 2001, 45). At Knossos, the multitude of sheep figurines in peak sanctuaries from the Minoan period discussed in the previous chapter and the Linear B texts show that the island of Crete was heavily focused on sheep rearing and wool production.

The timing of the respective destructions at Pylos (late spring) and Knossos (early autumn) may be partly responsible for the emphasis on either linen or wool (Godart 1977, 39–40), but the tablets also indicate that the kingdoms themselves were organized differently. Shelmerdine notes that differences between Pylos and Knossos might be explained by different economic conditions prevailing at the time when the archives at each palace were burnt. The Pylos tablets may reflect a greater state of emergency in LH IIIB2 than those at Knossos, destroyed in LM/LH IIIA2 (Shelmerdine 1987b). Evidence for regional variation at Mycenaean centers has been found (Olivier 1984; Killen 1984; Hooker 1987; Shelmerdine 1999b). The archives from Pylos reflect a highly centralized economy distributed between two provinces, known as the Hither and the Further provinces, which were made up of sixteen lower-order sites (Chadwick 1963; 1973). The administrative center for the Hither province was the palace at Pylos itself, while Leuktron was the center for the Further province (Bennet 1999a; 1999b). More work groups and more workers were concentrated at the two provincial centers than in any of the outlying towns throughout the kingdom, although it is puzzling in the case of Pylos because the palace was well excavated and yet so few tools of textile production have been found.

Documents from Knossos, on the other hand, suggest a decentralized economic system, with many second-order sites distributed throughout the central and western parts of the island. These second-order places collaborate with the palace at Knossos, giving and receiving raw materials and finished goods (Palaima 1987, 301–6; Bennet 1985). Almost certainly the Mycenaeans adopted an already decentralized Minoan system of administration on Crete and retained aspects of this older system in the organization and administration of the new Mycenaean cloth industry at Knossos.

At both palaces, Knossos and Pylos, we find documents related to wool and linen procurement, processing, and finishing. The evidence is fragmentary and information from one set of tablets informs our understanding of the others to various degrees. Below I outline the ways palace scribes refer to textiles, and the many stages of production, beginning with sheep and wool. The organization of labor, the *ta-ra-si-ja* system, including the so-called collectors and non-collectors, are examined next, primarily on Crete but with some examples from Pylos when relevant. After this discussion, flax and linen textiles are discussed.

Sheep

Of all the Linear B tablets from Knossos the largest group is the D-series, recording an estimated 100,000 sheep under the administration of Knossos, on over 1,100 separate tablets (Killen *passim*; Olivier 1967a; 1967b; Halstead 1991; Rougemont 2004). Most of these tablets were found in the upper east-west corridor at Knossos in the East Wing of the

sheep   goat

ram   he-goat

ewe   she goat

sheep + TA   special kind of sheep?

Figure 43. Linear B signs for varieties of sheep and goat.

Palace, conventionally known as the Domestic Quarter. The number of sheep is very large and suggests that flocks of Knossos-administered sheep grazed over one-fourth to one-third of the total land area of Crete (Halstead 1981b, 204). Most likely these pastures were located in the central and western parts of the island, since these were the areas reflected in the place names recorded in the palace archives and thus controlled by Knossos during the LM III period (Bennet 1987b).

Six different animals appear as ideograms in the Linear B tablets: deer, horse, pig, oxen, sheep and goat. Most were easily recognized by their naturalistic representations even before the Linear B script was deciphered, but distinguishing sheep and goat were more difficult. It has been deduced that the sign which occurs frequently, and often with the wool sign, refers to sheep. We not only have large counts of flocks of sheep but we are able to discern whether they are rams (males), ewes (females), or wethers (neutered males)(Fig. 43). Evans correctly distinguished the marking for sex among the animal signs: two horizontal bars indicating males and a bifurcated stem distinguishing females. This marker is used on the sheep sign to indicate RAMS and EWES as it is also found on signs for MAN and WOMAN, OX and BULL. Kober was the first to demonstrate conclusively the sex differences when she read totals for sheep with grammatical inflections, *to-so,* 'so many', for RAMS and *to-sa* for EWES (Kober 1949), a discovery that contributed greatly to the ultimate decipherment of the script.

Eight variations of the signs for sheep and goat exist in Mycenaean Greek: two generic signs that only distinguish between sheep and goat, but do not indicate sex; a third sign for the male sheep; a fourth for the male goat. A fifth sign indicates female sheep, or ewes; a sixth shows the female goat. The seventh and eighth signs are ligatured sheep signs, one with the sign *TA* added, and the other, which is quite rare, with Linear B *WE* (*75) added. Ewes generally produce better wool than rams, yet the highest quality of wool comes from neutered males, wethers, which are the ligatured *we*-sheep. This is an abbreviation of *we-ka-ta*, which is also occasionally found in association with the BULL ideogram. This designation is also found on records of oxen. Sign *23 has been identified as OX based on a tablet at Pylos where it occurs along with the word *qo-o* heading the list of animals, almost certainly equivalent to Greek ὁ βοῦς, 'ox, cattle'. The ox is qualified by the term *we-ka-ta*, taken to mean 'working' (eg, βοῦς ἐργάτες in Archilochus, 39). Killen (1964) identifies bulls described as *we-ka-ta* (ἐργατικός) to mean that they were 'working', or castrated. Sheep from Nuzi are also similarly described in terms of practical animal husbandry (Morrison 1981, 277). Uncastrated livestock would be unworkable with other animals.

The WOOL Unit

The wool unit, sign *145, is conventionally noted by the Latin word LANA in Linear B scholarship, and it is a unique measurement, used only for quantifying wool. Measuring commodities such as metals, spices, and grain in terms of this unit of weight would be possible but from the extant Linear B tablets this sign was used only in connection with the textile industry. It would also have been possible to measure wool with the more common unit of weight measurement in the Mycenaean period, the double mina which equals a little less than one kilogram. The special wool sign appears to be a monogram of two syllabograms clustered together into one sign, MA + RE, probably inherited from two Linear A signs (See *Docs²* 52; Linear A tablets HT 12, PH 3a, and KH 43 all have the sign representing wool in Minoan, Melena 1987, 400–1). Evans first connected the sign with wool when he suggested that it depicted a pair of shears attached to a syllabogram *RE*. A major problem with this interpretation, however, is that shears did not exist in the Bronze Age most likely because they required the springiness of iron. In the Bronze Age wool was plucked and combed, which results in lower yields of wool than sheared wool, and provides a different quality of wool (Forbes 1957, 7; Barber 1991, 20–30; Melena 1987, 403–4). More than likely, *145 is an ideogram for wool, referring to a unit of MA-RE, related to Greek μαλλός, a somewhat rare word without an accepted etymology which meant 'wool'. Barber (1991, 260) cites Hesychius' reference to a variant of the word, μάλλυκες, meaning, 'hairs'. The more common word for wool in Mycenaean is the adjective *we-we-e-a*, related to Homeric Greek εἶρος 'wool' (Bernabé and Luján 2008, 217)

Having settled the question of the wool ideograms, what can we say about the measurement of wool in the Mycenaean economy? The Mycenaean metrological system is based on the number 60, as is the case in some other Near Eastern economies, such as that at the Hurrian city of Nuzi (Petruso 1986, 28–9). For most goods, Mycenaean scribes mainly used four denominations of measurements, arbitrarily assigned by Linear B scholars alphabetic abbreviations (L, M, N, P): the talent = L (28,900 gr), double mina = M (964 gr.), half mina = N (241 gr) and the 1/24 mina = P (20 gr). Ideogram *145, however, shows that a different unit of measure for wool is equivalent to three double-minas, or one-tenth of a talent, weighing approximately 2,892 grams. In comparison to the Near East once again, it is remarkable that a unique measurement unit specifically for wool is also found at Nuzi, indicated by a fairly uncommon word, the *nariu*, which weighed just over three kilograms (Melena 1987, 397–9). In the Mycenaean Dg tablets, the ratio of sheep to wool was four sheep to one wool unit. Dividing 2,892 grams by four sheep gives an average yield of 723 grams per animal, which fits well within weight ranges calculated from sheep flocks in Medieval Britain and from modern Crete. As Petruso concludes, 'It is evident that, in LBA Crete, the bureaucracy had occasioned a shift away from the natural unit of reckoning wool (the yield of the individual animal) to the yield of four animals' (Petruso 1986, 31). This shift is presumably based on a large and thriving wool industry, and was practiced throughout the Aegean and the Near East.

The *Tarasija* System and the Organization of Labor

By cross checking sheep-shearing documents, target accounts, and workers' rations with various place-names and ethnic descriptions, analyses of Linear B texts allow us to reconstruct a highly structured and well-organized textile industry during the Late Bronze Age. Linear B tablets from Knossos describe flock management (tablet series Da–Dg, Dn), sheep shearing, or more likely 'plucking' (Dk/Dl), and wool allocations (Od) recorded by the palace scribes for outlying areas of the kingdom (Bennet 1988a, 27; Halstead 1991). Raw wool was distributed to textile workers with the expectation that set production targets would be met with finished textiles delivered back to the palace. The distribution and requisition of raw materials to dependent workers is known as the *ta-ra-si-ja* system (Nosch 2000a, 2000b; Killen 2001). The word occurs in later Greek as ταλασία where it is solely associated with textile work, especially with wool spinning (Barber 1991, 265). In Mycenaean times the word is attested in several areas of craft production, including bronze smiths' obligations at Pylos, wheel-making for chariots at Knossos, and in textile industries at Pylos, Knossos, and Mycenae (Shelmerdine 2008, 143).

Collectors and Non-Collectors

Some Mycenaean tablets have masculine personal names, most often written in the genitive, which imply that some raw materials, laborers, and finished textiles, 'belonged' to certain individuals other than the palace. These named figures are known in Linear B scholarship as collectors (or owners) and they occur in tablets from Pylos and Knossos, on sealings from Thebes, and on inscribed stirrup-jars (*Docs¹* 200; Palmer 1957; 1963; Olivier 1967a, 84; 1988; Bennet 1985; Killen 1994; Rougemont 2001). The interpretation of these individuals as collectors is based on the Mycenaean word *a-ko-ra*, related to later Greek ἀγορά, in the sense of collection or *a-ke-re*, Greek αγείρει, the third person singular verb, 'he collects'. This vocabulary item occurs most frequently at Pylos on livestock records. For example:

PY Cc 660
  .1   a-ke-o , a-ke-re
         me-ta-pa , pa-ro   ka-ra-su-no   CAP^m 30

On this tablet, one Alkeos *collects* at Metapa from Karasuno 30 male goats. The collectors operate within various contexts of the Mycenaean economy, not just shepherding, but also in textile production, bronze-working, and perfume manufacture (Killen 1995). While the terms *a-ke-re* and *a-ko-ra* are not fully attested at Knossos, the system of named individuals associated with large flocks of sheep on Crete has been compared with the collector tablets known from Pylos (Bennet 1992, 68). At Thebes the terms *a-ko-ra* and *a-ko-ra-jo* occur among the Wu-series sealings, demonstrating that the 'collector' system was present in several different Mycenaean centers (Aravantinos 1990; Piteros, Olivier, and Melena 1990).

When trying to understand the role of collectors, Killen (1994) stresses that the tablets recording the activities of collectors are found in palace archives, indicating that they were under the supervision of and probably controlled by the Mycenaean palace. The flocks and work groups that they 'own' or 'collect' are administered in the same way that all the other flocks and work groups are recorded in the tablets. The only exception is that they have separate totals for collectors and non-collectors. Finally, references to 'ownership' by named collectors are sometimes found in parallel with references to 'ownership' by divinities. For example, at Knossos the goddess Potnia is recorded as an 'owner' [of sheep] (*po-ti-ni-ja-we-jo*).

The occurrence of similar names in different palaces, such as the collectors named *a-ka-i-jo* and *ko-ma-we*(-*ta*) in texts from both Thebes and Knossos, was once taken to suggest that they were divinities but this idea has been abandoned by most scholars. A more likely explanation, suggested by Killen (1994), is that these names were common to an aristocratic class, comparable to William, Edward, and Elizabeth among British royalty. Killen defines collectors as prominent members of the royal family, high palace officials and the like who have been assigned responsibility for the productive capacity of their kingdoms, for their own benefit. That share, however, was still managed on their behalf by the central authorities (Killen 1994, 213). Comparative evidence from Ur III shows that the queen and officials of both the state and the temple are listed after the king as owners of sheep and wool (Waetzoldt 1972, 107–11). Similarly high-ranking individuals in the Greek world might sometimes be listed in Linear B tablets by their names in the genitive as collectors and at other times are referred to by their rank, title, or position in the Mycenaean hierarchy (*e.g. da-mo-ko-ro*, *e-qe-ta*, and even possibly, the *ra-wa-ke-ta*). The *ra-wa-ke-ta* or *lawagetas,* 'leader of the people,' has been identified as the second highest ranking Mycenaean official after the *wanax* (Deger-Jalkotzy 1978; Nikoloudis 2008a, 2008b). The two titles, *wanax* and *lawagetas*, also appear in Phrygian over the Midas City monument, discussed briefly in Chapter four. The bibliography on these two Mycenaean offices is vast but the identification of the *lawagetas* as a 'collector' is made by Lindgren (1973, 134).

We can see from the *ta-ra-si-ja* tablets that certain types of textiles are made primarily by certain work groups. There are the collector workgroups and there are the non-collectors. The non-collectors include two types of individuals: professionals and work groups that are referred to only by their toponym, known as ethnics. Of the major types of cloth, Nosch

(2000b) has noted that *pa-we-a* is mostly made by collectors or professionals. The cloth called *pe-ko-to* is made by both collectors and ethnics. And *tu-na-no* is made by all groups, collectors and the non-collector professionals and ethnics. One type of cloth *pa-we-a ko-u-ra *161* is made only by professionals.

Mycenaean References to Cloth

Types of cloth are listed in the tablets in three ways: 1) by ligatured cloth ideogram, *i.e.,* an abbreviated Mycenaean word superimposed within the cloth sign, indicating a commodity; 2) by non-ligatured ideograms that resemble various types of cloth; and 3) by specific terms from the abbreviation in the above mentioned ligatures or as a non-ligatured type of cloth. These three types of cloth references are described below.

Ligatures

In addition to the references in Linear B, the ideogram for cloth is found in the two earlier scripts of Crete, in Hieroglyphic, at Malia (see *CHIC* #103, sign *163) and in Linear A (at Hagia Triada, HT 38.4, signs A535 and A536, *GORILA* I). The Linear B ideogram for CLOTH (Latin TELA = *159) occurs frequently in the tablets, and resembles a simple square textile. Arthur Evans unfortunately saw a connection between this sign for textile in Linear A and B with a sign in Egyptian hieroglyphics that meant 'palace'(Fig. 44). He took the sign he found on Crete to also refer to the palace, and the diagonal across to indicate stairs leading to battlements.

The square sign often has a varying number of lines hanging down from the bottom line. In Linear B scholarship a supra-script number after the TELA sign would refer to the number of lines on the cloth ideogram, *e.g.* TELA^2 would refer to two central tassels hanging down (Duhoux 1974, Melena 1975, Tzachili 1997, 46–9). This sign most likely represents a textile from a warp-weighted, vertical loom. TELA occurs in Linear B on its own and with six different ligatures. Each of these variations indicates a different type of textile by an acrophonic abbreviation within the cloth ideogram (Fig. 45):

TELA + the ligature *PU* is the most common of the ligatured ideograms, and the abbreviation probably refers to Mycenaean *pu-ka-ta-ri-ja*, related to the Greek adjective πυκταλιαί or πτυκτός and πυκινός, 'thick, folded', perhaps meaning cloth that is of double-thickness or tightly woven (Palmer 1963, 295–6; Melena 1975, 105–9; Duhoux 1976, n. 232; Killen 1979, 169; Σαλη 1996, 268; Nosch 1999; 2000b, 73–89). This cloth only required one LANA (wool) unit so it was perhaps some sort of loincloth or kilt, as suggested by Melena (1987, 445). Along with *pa-we-a* cloth discussed below, it is often described with color terms, especially red and purple, for example as *po-pu-re-ja* (for example, KN L(7) 474 records 21 pieces, KN L 758 refers to 2 with angular, *o-re-ne-o,* patterns), presumably dyed purple by the murex snail, later Greek πορφύρα. Consequently, it seems unlikely TELA + *PU* would be worn as an undergarment. Rich purple cloth similar to this description is also attested to in Homer (*e.g., Od.* 19.225–6, and *Od.* 4.114–115). Large quantities of this type of cloth are recorded in the tablets: Knossos tablet L 5561 + X 5656, for example, lists 980 units, requiring wool from approximately 4,000 sheep. Nosch estimates 2,500 pieces of this cloth at Knossos (2000b, 74). If this cloth is doubly thick it may be a kind of felt, a fabric from matted wool (Barber 1991, 215–22). The type may also compare to the Homeric cloth, χλαῖνα, (*cf. Il.* 10.133–134) which is used to describe Nestor's great vermilion mantel in a double fold.

On Mycenae tablet X 508 from the House of the Shields, *pu-ka-ta-ri-ja* cloth is being transported *te-qa-de*, 'to Thebes'. This reference is the best evidence for any extra-regional trade or gift-exchange between Mycenaean palaces, if this is indeed the Boeotian city of Thebes (Palaima 1991, 276–7; Nosch 2001b; Shelmerdine and Bennet 2008, 307, n. 58). The cloth seems to have been of high quality, associated with palatial elites, and was often quite colorful.

The ideogram TELA + the ligature *PA* stands most probably for the plural, *pa-we-a/a₂*, *pharwea* or φάρϝεα probably identified with Homeric φᾶρος, often translated as a mantle, cloak, or shroud. The adjective *ko-u-ra* often accompanies *pa-we-a* on the Lc tablets at Knossos, the La tablets at Pylos and L 710.s at Mycenae, although its meaning is obscure. There are some references to this cloth (*e.g.,* KN L 594) made of linen, but normally it is

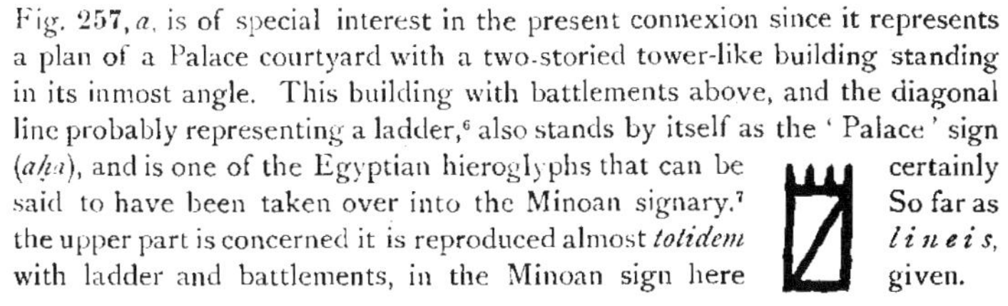

Fig. 257, *a,* is of special interest in the present connexion since it represents a plan of a Palace courtyard with a two-storied tower-like building standing in its inmost angle. This building with battlements above, and the diagonal line probably representing a ladder,⁶ also stands by itself as the ' Palace ' sign (*aḥa*), and is one of the Egyptian hieroglyphs that can be certainly said to have been taken over into the Minoan signary.⁷ So far as the upper part is concerned it is reproduced almost *totidem lineis,* with ladder and battlements, in the Minoan sign here given.

Figure 44. Linear A (or B?) sign for textile from Knossos, upside down, mistakenly read as 'palace' (Evans 1921, p. 358, with permission, Ashmolean Museum, Oxford University).

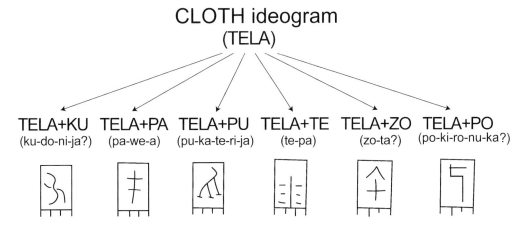

Figure 45. Diagram of Linear B textile ideograms.

a fairly heavy woolen garment, made in the ratio of five wool units for every three units of finished cloth (or conversely, 1.66 units of wool for one PA cloth). So, for example, KN Ld(1) 587 lists 453 pieces of *pa-we-a* cloth, quite a lot for a thick, valuable textile. Barber suspects that this was a thick cloth with three closed edges that could be used as a cloak, a blanket, or a woman's peplos (1991, 358, n. 1). Like *pu-ka-ta-ri-ja,* it is frequently described with color terms, often red/purple.

The ideogram TELA + the ligature *TE* is often paired with TELA + *PA* and is probably an abbreviation of *te-pa* cloth (*e.g.,* KN Ws 8153, MY Oe 107) (Melena 1975, 108, fig. 11; *Docs*^{2} 1973, 585; Killen 1966, 8; Σαλη 1996, 346). The sign TE also appears in Linear A (as sign AB 04) and occurs on the Tel Haror graffito with two other Minoan signs, suggesting that the cloth *te-pa* is not of Greek origin, but most likely Minoan (Finkelberg 1998, 266–7; Olivier 1996, 104). The ratio of wool delivered for the production of TELA + *TE* is one unit of cloth to seven units of wool, making it nearly four times as heavy as the *pa-we-a* cloth described above. Nosch estimates that each unit of cloth weighed approximately 21 kg and would have required wool from 28 sheep (2000b, 16). This cloth was probably a heavy-duty textile, like a cloak or rug, so it was probably fairly simple but made by specialists called *te-pe-ja* (Nosch 2000b, 200). It is possible that this heavy cloth was also made of felt, like the πυκνός variety. Possibly related is Homeric τάπης that occurs most often as thick purple bedding and is often used in epic as a covering for furniture (*Il.* 9.200, 10.156, 16.224, 24.230, 645 and *Od.* 4.124, 298, 7.337, 10.12, 20.150, 24.276) or it may be related to a kind of tapestry.

The ideogram TELA + the ligature *KU* is a difficult textile to identify. No term beginning with KU has been found on the cloth tablets and this is one of the least common ligatures. The KU sign might refer to *ku-do-ni-ja* cloth (*i.e.* cloth from or for 'Chania') or possibly *ku-pi-ri-jo* ('Cyprus', or even 'Byblos') (Melena 1975, 108; Palaima 1991, 280–1) although no other cloth is described by a specific geographic adjective.

The ideogram TELA + the ligature *ZO* occurs rarely in Linear B (KN L 433) but it is probably related to a type of cloth *zo-ta,* restored in KN L 5924 + 6000.a. This reading of L 5924 is based on a parallel tablet, L 5998, by the same scribe at Knossos [103], recording *pa-we-a* cloth. One suggested meaning connects the Mycenaean ligature with the Homeric ζωστήρ (*Il.* 4.132) or ζῶστρον, a type of belt used to secure a θώρηξ. Also related might be the verb ζώννυμι, 'to gird oneself' (*Od.* 6.38 and *Il.* 14.181. See Barber 1994, 42–70). Melena, however, believes that since the sign ZO also appears in Linear A 'it clearly indicates that both the cloth and the ideogram are of Minoan heritage (Melena 1975, 111–2).' Melena discards any possible relationship of *zo-ta* with the Homeric ζωστήρ or ζῶστρον. A Minoan (non-Greek) ancestry for this word, especially one used in elite contexts (Linear B tablets and Homeric poetry), does not necessarily argue against a relationship between the Linear A or B sign and a later Greek word. This could be an example of the so-called 'Versailles effect,' discussed with specific reference to older Minoan textile terms in Mycenaean Greek by Renfrew (1998, 1999).

Finally TELA^2 + ligature *PO* occurs on Lf 139, a tablet from the Arsenal at Thebes, describing 13 units of this type of cloth and a person named *to-po-ne.* This abbreviation *po* may stand for *po-ki-ro-nu-ka* (with multi-colored *onux* discussed below) or two possible red/purple-color terms, *po-ni-ki-ja* or even *po-pu-re-ja* (Aravantinos 1999, 53; Aravantinos, *et al* 2001, 303; Nosch 2001b, 180–2; Dakouri-Hild 2005, 215, n. 46).

Non-Ligatured Ideograms

In addition to the ligatures described above, there are other Linear B signs that indicate various types of cloth or clothing (Fig. 46):

*146 is a rectangle with a triangular or v-shaped indentation on the upper side and has been identified as a simple textile (Duhoux 1974; Robkin 1981; Shelmerdine 2008, 146; Killen 2008a, 190–4; 2008b). It often has the sign *we* superimposed on it

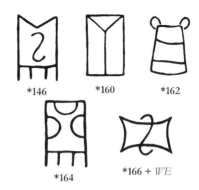

Figure 46. Other Linear B textile signs.

and can be fringed (Robkin 1981; Jones 2005). Prevalent in the Pylos Ma taxation records, *146 is most likely a type of cloth produced in outlying areas of the kingdom and was received along with other taxation commodities by the palace (Douhoux 1976; Killen 2008b; *pace* Palmer 1963, 300–1). The ideogram at Pylos looks like the syllable *pte* with an inserted *we*. The tablets were found in the Southwestern Building along with tablets recording textile *166 + *WE* so they were perhaps related (Robkin 1981; Shelmerdine 1999a). Discrepancies exist, however, in the handwriting of Knossos scribes for ideogram *146 and *166 + *WE*. It has been suggested (Jones 2005, 444–5) that *146 is a religious garment which resembled the dress worn by the veiled dancer shown in fresco from Akrotiri (house Xeste 3), the Linear B evidence suggests that it is an unfinished, linen cloth manufactured throughout the Pylian kingdom and sent to the palace for finishing by specialists. H. Morris (1986, 99) speculates that this was a simple, home-made fabric, possibly required for religious or military purposes. Nosch and Perna (2001) have noted that not all examples of *146 cloth was of linen since it is explicitly stated only on some tablets that it was linen (*ri-no*). It is likely that some examples were of wool. Tablets of the M series at Knossos associate *146 with the religious sphere, and the cloth may have been given to sanctuary officials and to Mycenaean divinities (Nosch 2000b, 97–9). Perhaps people within the orbit of the Mycenaean palaces were instructed to offer this textile to the administrative center in honor of some deity. Or, if *146 was a plain textile of bast fibers, most likely linen based on modern analogues, large amounts of plain linen cloth might have been used as sails for palace-sponsored overseas trade. Waetzoldt (2007) suggests that at around 2000 BC in Mesopotamia there were already specialized sail manufacturers and Tiboni (2005) has suggested that changes in sail technology had a profound impact on Late Bronze Age trade. The Linear B tablets do not provide much information on ship construction but the possibility that the Mycenaeans relied on the subordinate population to manufacture sails seems likely (Palaima 1991). The best way to ensure an adequate supply would have been to require cloth as a tax and have these staple goods converted into specialized cloths by specialists employed by the palace.

*160 occurs only at Pylos in the La tablets and, as Duhoux (1974, 116–8) has shown, is a variant of *146. Similarly, it is often associated with *166 (Nosch 2000b, 95). Tablets of the La series, which recorded this textile, were found in Room 6, the throne room at Pylos.

*162 (at Pylos), or a variant *163 (at Knossos), is shaped like a tunic with shoulder holes, similar to the bronze corselet found in Chamber Tomb 12 at Dendra and may in fact represent a suit of body armor, or a linen cuirass to which bronze plates were attached (KN L 693).

*164 is a rectangle, sometimes fringed, with half-circles on three or four sides (*e.g.* KN L 520). This is a fairly heavy cloth made up of about six kilograms of wool per garment.

*165 and *166 are shaped like an ox-hide ingot and may be related to a Mycenaean kilt (Duhoux 1974, 117). Most of these ideograms include the sign *we,* although *166 can occur on its own (*e.g.,* KN Sc 225 and Sc 5141). These tablets number 140 and were found together in the Room of the Chariot Tablets in the West Wing at Knossos recording the distribution of war equipment and date at least two generations earlier than the bulk of Knossos tablets (Driessen 1990). The occurrence of textile *166 among military equipment is comparable to the Homeric λινοθώρηξ which refers to a linen chiton with attached bronze plates (Sacconi 1971). The term *to-ra-ke* is found at Pylos (Sh 736), and *ta-ra-ka* at Tiryns and *to-ra* at Knossos, all presumably referring to θώρηξ, in the nominative singular (Renfrew 1998, 244–5). *166 + WE is probably an abbreviation for *we-a₂-no* referring to a type of linen cloth, and is perhaps connected with Homeric ἑανός, meaning a fine robe (Shelmerdine 1995, 100–3). The occurrence of the acrophonic abbreviation *ri* in front of *166 + WE on Oa 745[+] 7345 strongly suggests *ri-no,* for Greek λίνον, meaning a textile of linen. Tablets with *166 + *WE* were found above the throne room at Knossos (Oa 878, Oa 745, and Oa 1808) and at Pylos (in the La series, in Ua 1413, and Un 6.6) (Melena 1975, 53). Nosch and Perna (2001, 471) also stress that *166+*WE* and *146 occur on tablets dealing with religion, and Jones (2005, 710) sees ideogram *166 resembling a double-axe rather than an oxhide ingot. Her suggestion that textile *166 was a kilt which "symbolically wrapped the wearer in the double axe, the quintessential religious symbol of the Minoans," is intriguing although based heavily on visual speculation.

Specific Textile Terms

The final method Mycenaean scribes use to list textiles is simply to write out the whole word. Three types of cloth are most common in the target assessment records from Knossos, *pa-we-a, tu-na-no,* and *pe-ko-to* cloth. The abbreviation TELA + *PA* discussed above refers to this same *pa-we-a ko-u-ra* (Killen 1964, 9, 1966, 105–9, 1974, 1979; Chadwick 1988, 82).

In addition to the various references to cloth described above, certain color and status terms are specifically associated with Mycenaean textiles. The stem **po-pu*, related to Greek πορφύρα, 'purple', occurs on four tablets from Knossos and Palaima suggests that, since there are no convincing Greek or Near Eastern etymologies for πορφύρα, it is possible that the word itself derives from Minoan (Palaima 1991, 289–91; 1997). Units of cloth are described on three of the four tablets attesting the stem **po-pu*. One unit of TELA¹ + *TE,* two units of TELA² + *PU*, and 21 units of TELA³ + *PU* are recorded. The fourth tablet refers to professional 'purple' women of *da-*83–ja*, making so much of something '*wa-na-ka-te-ro*', 'royal' (Killen 1987). No ideogram is on this last tablet to indicate that cloth is being made or dyed but this seems likely (Palaima 1991, 291).

Whether the word *po-pu-ra* in the tablets actually refers to purple obtained from the murex snails so famous in antiquity is open to debate, but there is no doubt that imitations of this color made from cheaper plant dyes were exploited by the Mycenaean dyers (Astour 1965; Burke 1999; Nosch 2004). We assume that dyer's madder and alkanet were used for making red, blue, and purple shades imitating the purple color and making textiles more valuable regardless of the source of the dye. Linear B *po-ni-ki-jo* is another word that suggests some purple color (Aura Jorro 1993, 138). This item was understood to describe a spice (*Docs²* 222) but was interpreted as dyer's madder by Astour (1965, 348–9). Dyer's madder (*Rubia tinctorum*) is a plant for red or purple-dye, local to the Levant and Egypt. To Foster (1977), *po-ni-ki-jo* refers to alkanet (*Alkanna tinctoria*), another kind of root used for red-purple dye.

The use of plant roots, alkanet and madder, as dyes calls to mind the Linear B word *wi-ri-za*, Greek ῥίζα, 'root'. The word occurs at Knossos on Od 2026, Od 8202, in both cases it is connected with wool, and not the perfume industry. Based on modern sheep terminology, the term *wi-ri-za* has been interpreted by Linear B scholars as the thicker, base-part of the wool fiber, the 'root' rich in lanolin (Beck and Beck 1978; Killen 1962, 42; *Docs²* 224; Shelmerdine 1985, 18–20; Melena 1987, 406; Aura Jorro 1993, 435). Shelmerdine (1985; 1995) and others have suggested that wool, listed among raw materials used in the perfume industry, was used for straining perfumed oil as indicated by the word *wi-ri-za* (*e.g.,* PY Un 267, 249).

Rather than interpreting the 'root' in Linear B to refer to the oily base of the wool fiber, I believe *wi-ri-za* refers somewhat generically to dyes made from plant roots, such as dyer's madder (*Rubia tinctorum*)(Fig. 47) or alkanet. Still used in Modern Greek for 'root', the diminutive, ῥιζάρι, refers to dyers' madder that grows wild in Greece today, especially on Crete (see also Barber 1991, 232). This word in the Mycenaean texts is often associated with wool and on one tablet it is associated with both wool and perfume (PY Un 249). For example, *wi-ri-za* also appears on Un 249, translated by Shelmerdine (1985, 20) as follows:

PY Un 249
.1a   po-ti-ni-ja-we-jo
    pi-ra-jo ,   a-re-pa-zo[-o] ku-pa-ro₂ AROM 2 T 5
.2   wi-ri-za   LANA 2 [ ] *157 10
.3   *vacat* [ ] KAPO T 6

'Philaios the perfume-boiler of Potnia (the main deity of the Mycenaeans):
cyperus 240 l.
root   wool 6 kg *157 10 units
fruits   58 l.'

The association between *wi-ri-za* and an unguent boiler would be appropriate for dyes

Figure 47. Rubia tinctorum, Dyer's madder (Thomé 1885).

and we assume that the Mycenaeans colored some of their perfume red because they are described as *po-ni-ki-jo*. The wool modified by *wi-ri-za* may have been red and given color to the perfume, or the other way around, the dyed perfume added a red color to the wool.

The Linear B term *tu-ru-pte-ri-ja* may also refer to dyeing textiles if we accept its identification with Greek στρυπτηρία, στυπτηρία, 'alum' or alum stone, ultimately used as a mordant to fix dyes (Baumback 1987; Aura Jorro 1993, 379–80; Firth 2007; Shelmerdine 1985, 136–7; Barber 1991, 276). The word occurs on PY An 35, Un 443, and associate with less information at Tiryns (X 6) and at Knossos (X 986). An 35 and Un 443 record the commodity, *tu-ru-pte-ri-ja,* given 'in exchange for' (o-no) wool, goats, garments of *146, grains, wine, and figs. Most likely the Mycenaean word *o-no* is connected with the Classical Greek verb ὀνίνυμι, 'to derive advantage', and indicates exchange.

Firth demonstrates that *tu-ru-pte-ri-ja* was roasted alum-stone, acquired by traders, named at Pylos, *ku-pi-ri-jo* and *a-ta-ro* (Firth 2007). Alum is a generic term for a naturally occurring material composed of sulphates of aluminum and potassium, with iron, manganese or magnesium sulphate (Baumbach 1987; Forbes 1964, 134–5). Found only in certain parts of the Mediterranean, such as Cyprus, Phrygia, Melos, and Syria, alum was used in antiquity as a fire-retardant, a medicine, and was one of the best mordants for fixing certain dyes to textiles. The occurrence of alum in Linear B with the word *ku-pi-ri-jo* might indicate that the material was imported from Cyprus (Shelmerdine 1985, 137; Barber 1991, 238), although it is also possible that this may just be a personal name.

Various Phases of Cloth Production in the Tablets from Knossos
Da–Dg Series: Tribute or Census?
Ideograms of sheep in the Da–Dg series record large numbers of wool-producing animals pasturing in central Crete, nearly 100,000. Even before Linear B was deciphered, different interpretations of these large numbers of sheep were put forward. For example, Sundwall (1936) suggested that the sheep were part of sacrificial hecatombs for a divinity. Other scholars read the lists of sheep as tokens of exchange, *i.e.* a form of currency similar to the use of cattle in Homeric society. The many sheep were also thought to be tribute (*Docs¹* 198) by local Minoans subject to the Mycenaean Cretan overlord: sheep owners were simply assessed a contribution of so many sheep to send to the palace, regardless of the animals' sex. To a shepherd, rams would be the least valuable member of a flock and his first choice for tribute, thus explaining the high number of rams in the tablets (Finley 1957, 130).

Killen (1964, 1–4) sensibly argues against the Da–Dg tablets as tribute lists. Using modern sheep populations of approximately 530,000 on Crete, he has shown that extracting 100,000 sheep as tribute each year would be neither possible nor practical. That the palace would welcome so many rams as tribute is equally unlikely: rams do not contribute milk and their flesh is inferior to that of ewes or wethers, as is their wool. Uncastrated rams would not have been run together with ewes, which are listed but in the minority. In sheep rearing, the normal ratio of ewes to mature rams is not that reflected in the Mycenaean tablets: usually one ram can service up to fifty or sixty ewes for breeding purposes (Killen 1964, 9; Allison 1958, 104). We find a correspondence on the Da–Dg tablets and other D-series texts, such as the Dk–Dl records, which suggest that the majority of sheep were not tribute but were part of an organized textile industry under the administration of the palace. Although they are not noted as *we-ka-te,* these sheep are likely not true rams, *i.e.,* uncastrated males, which would have been too aggressive and caused problems within the herd; instead they are probably wethers, more suited to running in large numbers and indicative of a thriving textile industry. Compared to ewes, wethers are much more resistant to disease and they yield substantially greater amounts of wool (Bottéro 1957, 248; and Landsberger 1935, 155).

Figure 48. Linear B tablet from Knossos (tablet Dd 1171 ©Trustees of the British Museum).

The tablets in the Da–Dg series only list sheep and a majority of them are written by a single scribe, h. 117 (h. = hand) (Olivier 1988; Halstead 1991). The Da series records rams while the Db tablets list rams and ewes from specific places on Crete. Only rams are listed in the Dc tablets by either the male sheep ideogram alone or with an adjunct syllable that qualifies the sheep in some way (Melena 1975). Finally, the Dd, De, and Df series record rams and ewes either plainly or with adjuncts to the animal sign (Fig. 48). The tablets are all very similar and each one records a separate entry beginning with what is presumed to be a shepherd's name in tall (majuscule) characters. The tablet then usually divides horizontally into two lines. For example,

```
KN Da 1221 + 8200                                    (h. 117)
.A                RAMS 200[
.B        ai-ta-ro-we,/      *56–ko-we
KN Dd 1171
.A                RAMS 20 EWES 72
.B        po-ro    /      pa-i-to pa RAMS 8
```

On 31% of the tablets the top line names a 'collector' in the nominative or genitive (Bennet 1992). The figure known as a 'collector' is described more fully below. These Da-Dg tablets continue usually with a number rounded up to some multiple of one hundred or a series adding up to a round total which records the number of rams and/or ewes, listed by ideograms, with the great majority (*c.* 87%) as rams (Halstead 1991, 344). The lower line gives a place name and information regarding missing, old, or young sheep, most often rams again.

The description of some rams being 'missing' or 'owed' is not uncommon in the Linear B corpus. Absence is indicated by *o,* most likely an abbreviation for *o-pe-ro,* related to Greek, ὄφελον, 'deficit, that which is needed', before the commodity and the total number missing (Chadwick 1988, 46). Killen states that while this term may have already had its later meaning of 'something owed' on some of the tablets, it may, in the context of the sheep records, have two different meanings:

1) It could refer to something that is not there but should be, as in an inventory.
2) It may refer to something lacking which needs to be replaced, such as the total number of sheep under the palace administration (Killen 1964, 8). This could mean that for the flock to be at full strength, the number of '*o*'-sheep had to be supplied by the palace.

Halstead (1991; 1992; 1999) has investigated the evidence for restocking the flocks under palatial control at Pylos and Knossos. While the evidence may be a result of poor preservation of certain tablets, there is some suggestion for the role of the non-palatial sector in supplying the palace with sheep. Using analogies with medieval England, Killen has argued that, at five to six years of age, sheep under palace control at Knossos would have been replaced, at a rate of 17–20% of the yearly total, amounting to 10–12,000 new sheep each year (Killen 1963, 87). As Killen notes, of the tablets that refer to the age of sheep, a remarkable 19% indicate 'yearling' – a number perfectly in line with the replacement estimates. If 10–12,000 new sheep were added each year, this would mean that the same number died or were removed by some means from the palace flocks. The tablets at Knossos that list missing (*o*) and old (*pa*) sheep, however, do not record numbers anywhere near 10,000. At Pylos, however, the tablets record old sheep replaced by young ones suggesting that the absence of missing/old sheep at Knossos is attributable to the time of year that the palaces were destroyed, preserving the tablets in early autumn for Knossos and late spring for Pylos (Godart 1977, 39–40).

Dk–Dl Series: Targets and Yields

Each Da–Dg tablet recorded large numbers of wool producing sheep: the target and the actual wool yield from the Da–Dg sheep were recorded in the Dk and Dl tablets, which are thought to be shearing records (Killen 1984, 50). The Dk records have been divided into two sets based on the two scribes who wrote them, h. 120 writing Dk(1) and h. 119 writing Dk(2). Approximately 30 to 50 tons of wool was produced by these sheep annually for the palace workshops.

In the Dl series the female flocks are assessed a reduced wool target: one unit of wool per five ewes plus five lambs, as opposed to sheep on other tablets. This indicates that these sheep were used for breeding purposes. At least 1939 ewes are listed, with the majority in the Dl(1) set, by h. 118. Dl(1) totals a minimum of 1503 ewes with reduced wool production targets and lambs at a rate of one lamb per ewe. Both the Dk and Dl series record sheep and wool in fixed ratios: the Dl texts have ten sheep (five ewes plus five lambs) per one unit of wool; the Dk texts have four sheep (presumably adult) per unit of wool. The absolute value of weight symbols in Linear B is fairly secure: Late Bronze Age Cretan sheep, it is estimated, yielded on average 0.75 kg of wool and one unit of wool weighed roughly 3 kg, roughly the same as the standard wool unit in medieval England and from second millennium BC Alalakh (Petruso 1986). From this detailed information we can deduce that the D-series tablets are a census or inventory of the palace's holdings and not a record of tribute owed to the palace.

L-Series Tablets

The L-tablets refer to the receipt and delivery of textile targets assessed from outlying villages. The raw material listed in the Dk and Dl wool records finds corresponding targets of cloth production in the Lc records (Killen 1966; 105–9; 1974, 85–6; 1988; Nosch 2000b). Just as we find on the livestock accounts, terms such as *a-pu-do-si*, from Greek ἀπόδοσι, meaning 'restitution, delivery', and *o-pe-ro*, ὄφελον, 'deficit', occur in this series in association with terms for cloth. The tablets refer to various types of cloth expected from different work groups and provide the most detailed information about the amounts of wool used in Mycenaean textiles and their decoration.

Lc Tablets – Receipt and Delivery

Most of the Lc texts generally begin with a feminine ethnic or occupational term written majuscule, (*e.g. se-to-i-ja*, see Lc(1) 525), probably meaning 'the women workers at Siteia', or *da-wi-ja* (*see* Lc(1) 526) 'the women workers at *da-wo*' (Killen 1966). Variations of this pattern exist: for example, some tablets might have a place name written large followed by a small occupational description, such as *ko-no-so te-pe-ja*, 'the (female) *te-pa* makers at Knossos' (*see* L 641). This pattern recurs on tablets by the same scribe in the personnel records of the Ak tablets. Some of the Lc tablets listing individuals in the genitive such as Lc(1) 551 *e-me-si-jo-jo* refer to the owners or collectors of the textile personnel, and follow the patterns found in the Ak series (Killen 1965, 105).

The Lc tablets often divide into two lines, with the upper line reading 'plain' TELA, TELA + *TE*, or both. 'Plain' TELA is always preceded by the phrase *pa-we-a ko-u-ra*, describing a generic kind of textile. The TELA ideogram is then followed by a wool entry. TELA + *TE* is listed once or twice and is also followed by a wool entry. The second TELA + *TE* entry, when it occurs, always has an extra stroke in the characteristic 'fringe' at the bottom of the sign and the first ideogram is always preceded by the qualifications *pe-ko-to* (abbreviated to *pe.* on 551), which is most probably made by professionals called *pe-ki-ti-ra₂*, women who combed wool off of sheep for spinning (Killen 1965, 106; Barber 1991, 262, 283; Chadwick 1988, 82). This was probably a luxury cloth of soft, fine, kempless wool, which required a great deal of sheep and wool (up to 40 sheep per unit of cloth). The lower line of the Lc tablets, when inscribed, begins with 'plain' TELA qualified as *tu-na-no* (see 526) followed by a wool entry.

Two types of cloth, TELA + *TE*, and the 'plain' TELA ideogram, without fringes, described as *pa-we-a ko-u-ra* are recorded in the Lc tablets. The Lc tablets fall into two groups: Lc(1) by h. 103, and Lc(2) with rectos by h. 113 and versos by h. 115 (Killen 1966, 105–9). These two sets cover different geographic areas of Crete: the Lc(1) tablets refer to central Crete, including laborers at Knossos, Phaistos, and Tylissos; the Lc(2) tablets record groups in the far west, at Kydonia (Chania) and *si-ra-ro* (Killen 1976, 121; 1988, 167). Both groups record the targets, or production quotas, established for various work groups of women and children textile workers also listed in the personnel tablets, the Ak and Ap series. Often these two different series, the Lc targets and the A personnel tablets, refer to different aspects of the economy (craft production and personnel maintenance) but are written by the same scribe for the each work group and relate to the same target of production (Shelmerdine 1992). For example, h. 103 writes a target record on Lc(1) 540 + 8075 probably for nine units of '*pa-we-a ko-u-ra*' cloth for the workers of *da-te-we-ja*:

KN Lc(1) 540 + 8075   (h. 103)
.1   'pa-we-a' ko-u-ra TELA¹ 3[
.2   da-te-we-ja /   [
                .1 3[: arrangement suggests 9.

The same scribe also writes tablet Ak(1) 612 recording nine adult women and three children workers, described as *da-te-we-ja* (Killen 1982; Chadwick 1988).

KN Ak (1) 612   (h. 103)
.1   *TA* 1 '*DA* 1' MUL 9
.2   ko-wa ,/ me-zo 1 ko-wa / me-u-jo 1
.3   da-te-we-ja   ko-wo / me-zo 1 [[ko-wo me-   ]]

(*nb.* double brackets [[ ]] indicate an erasure by the scribe but the missing text is still legible)

Killen suggests that these workers were expected to produce the same nine units of cloth referred to in Lc(1) 540 + 8075. The corresponding numbers of nine units of cloth in the Lc(1) tablet and the nine female workers in the Ak(1) tablet, both at *da-te-we-ja*, indicate that these tablets refer to the same workers. This implies the ratio of one unit of cloth per Ak worker, most probably a dependent female weaver. Further, the Lc(1) tablets record approximately 1000 cloths, suggesting that the total Ak work force was about the same, 1000 workers (Killen 1984, 52).

The Lc(2) records by h. 115 refer to assigned tasks and take a standard form (Killen 1979, 163). The recto sides are always by h. 113 and record *pa-we-a* TELA and wool units from western Crete. The term *to-u-ka* occurs on some of these tablets and Björck suggests it corresponds to the Homeric verb τεύξειν, 'to make, render' (Björck 1954, 275). The participal, *te-tu-ko-wo-a*, is also found on a chariot wheel record at Pylos, Sa 682, and, as with the textile records, probably refers to objects that were 'decorated' or 'finished'. Since all the cloth on the rectos of the Lc tablets by h. 113 are identified as 'plain' TELA and the wool listed there is presumably for the manufacture of those cloths, the wool on the verso that is described as *te-u-ka*, by h. 115, is most likely that wool used to decorate or finish the cloth (Killen 1979, 164). Killen also suggests that there is a fairly constant ratio in the wool used for decorating (on the verso, by h. 115) and the number of units of cloth (on the recto, by h. 113), *i.e.* a ratio of 1:4.

At Knossos, the Lc(1) and Lc(2) tablets record a wool entry after certain types of cloth. Either these tablets show the receipt of cloth and wool separately from outlying areas, or, as Killen (1966, 106) suggests, they 'record the weight of wool used in the cloths themselves'. Ratios of various types of cloth to wool units are adhered to fairly strictly on the tablets of the Lc series, indicating that the latter interpretation is correct and that these ratios refer to the wool that was used for these cloths. One case, Od 562, from the series closely related to the Lc series, shows that the three separate wool allotments to certain individuals are 91, 42, and 69 units:

KN Od 562

.1	]o-pi , no-nu-we , 'a-ti-pa-mo' pe-re	LANA	91
.2	]si-da-jo , pe-re 'po-ro-to'	LANA	42
.3	a-po-te , pe-re	LANA	69

In the first two instances, these are multiples of seven. The last entry is one short of 70. The preposition *o-pi* probably means 'at the workshop of' followed by the personal name *no-nu-we* in the dative (Morpurgo Davies 1983, 293; Killen 1968). *A-ti-pa-mo* is probably the subject of the verb *pe-re* (Greek φέρει, 'he brings') in line 1. This suggests a pattern for the other two lines: individuals 'bringing' certain amounts of wool, most likely in units of seven. It seems highly likely that the Od tablets and the Lc records refer to the same wool in different phases of production; in Od the wool is raw and unwoven (Nosch 2007). In the Lc tablets it is a completed cloth of the TELA + *TE* variety or the *pawea* type, discussed in more detail below.

A group of tablets from Knossos, also by h. 103, records units of wool allocated to workers in the textile industry yet the category of tablets is fairly non-distinct and rather miscellaneous. Amounts of wool are recorded in very small quantities, suggesting that this wool was not only sent to weaving workshops but also to finishers and decorators (Killen 1988, 172. See also Killen 1985). New joins of tablet KN Od 765, for example, provide interesting information on craft specialists:

KN Od 765 + 7320 + FRR.

.1	pa-i-to	[
.2	]-ka-ra / a-me-a LANA M	[

The named individual, *a-me-a*, is a man who receives a small amount of wool (M is a fractional accounting unit) for textile finishing. *A-me-a* recurs on Da 1189 as a shepherd and we know that male workers are often associated with finishing (Killen 1979, 167). Other Od tablets (7312, 7326, 7779 + FRR., and 8628 + FR.) list similar quantities of wool and we can presume that at least some of the wool was also going to male workers.

Two totaling tablets of the Lc(1) series, Lc(1) 535 and Lc(1) 536 contain the best source of information about common types of Mycenaean cloth. One tablet totals the amounts of cloth for collectors (535), the other for 'non-collectors' (536):

KN Lc(1) 535 + 538   F10   (h. 103)

.1		ta-ra-si-ja	pa-we-a [
.2		ke-ri-mi-ja	tu-na-no [
.3	to-sa /	pe-ko-to	[

    .3 trace at right consistent with TELA[.

KN Lc(1) 536 [+] 7383 + 7731   F10   (h. 103)

.1	]	'ta-ra-si[-ja'	]pa-we-a[ ]TELA^{x} 200
.2	]	'vest. [']	tu-na-no[ ]TELA^{1} 48 a-ro-zo 'ki-to' TELA1 1
.3	to-]sa /		pe[-ko-to TELA^{1}+ṬẸ]18 TELA$^{?}$+ ṬẸ 267

Since Lc(1) 536 has a cloth total with one less than the single collector targets (Lc(1) 7392), this is probably a total of non-collector cloth (Bennet 1992, 71; Olivier 1967a, 91; Killen

1974, 85–6). Nosch (2000b) has also noted that the amounts of the first four types of cloth listed (200 + 48 + 1 + 18) add up to the total of the final TELA$^?$ + *TE* cloth, 267. It is possible that it is just a coincidence but it is noteworthy. Lc(1) 535 should therefore be the fragmentary remains of the collector totals. How much wool was necessary for each type of cloth cloth, *pa-we-a, tu-na-no,* and *pe-ko-to,* plus TELA + *TE* can be determined (Killen 1964, 9; 1966, 105–9; 1974, 82–90; 1979, 157, n. 13).

pa-we-a: LANA	=	3:5
tu-na-no: LANA	=	1:3
pe-ko-to: LANA	=	1:10
TELA + *TE*	=	1:7

Assuming that one unit of wool weighed three kilograms, one unit of TELA + *TE* would require 21 kilograms of wool – a very heavy garment. One *pe-ko-to* at 10 to 1 would require about 30 kilograms. The total sum is calculated by adding the following: *pa-we-a* if 5/3 = x/200 then x = 333; *tu-na-no* 48 × 3 = 144; *pe-ko-to* 18 × 10 = 180; *te-pa* 267 × 7 = 1869, plus one chiton of 3 units of wool, equaling 2,529 total wool units. From Lc(1) 536 we see that the non-collector target was for 2,529 units of wool, which means approximately 7,587 kilograms (nearly 8.4 tons) of cloth!

Restoring the total targets for the collector tablets of the Lc series is more difficult. Referring to a related target record of *pa-we-a ko-u-ra* cloth, Killen suggests that Ld(1) 587 records a total of 453 cloth units. Building on this theory, Nosch used the individual quotas of collectors for the other types of cloth (*tu-na-no, pe-ko-to,* and TELA + *TE*) to propose a total collector target in Lc(1) 535 as 915 units of wool, based on totals from Lc(1) 551, Lc(1) 7398, and Lc(1) 532.

Adding the collector target total to the wool units from the non-collector targets (Lc(1) 536) [*i.e.* 2,529 units] we get a total of 3,444 units of wool calculated in the *ta-ra-si-ja* tablets. The percentage of wool for collectors and non-collectors corresponds to the estimated percentages in the sheep tablets of collectors *vs.* non-collectors in the Da–Dg series. This works out to a ratio of approximately 30% collectors and 70% non-collectors. The total of wool units (3,444) follows this ratio, with 915 wool units (26.6%) for collectors and 2,529 wool units (73.4%) for non-collectors. This shows that the restored targets for the collectors are not too far off in comparison to the sheep totals.

Ld Tablets – Delivery and Storage
The Ld(1) tablets are all by h. 116 and refer to either the delivery of cloth with its source indicated or to the storage of cloth, without a source given. Most probably these two types, the delivery tablets and storage records, refer to the same cloth but in different phases of administration. They are grouped into two sub-sets: a major group recording cloth in fairly large numbers, including Ld(1) 587 which most probably records the totals from all Ld tablets; and a minor set with smaller numbers and terms not included in the major set for cloth, such as *e-ta-wo-ne(-we)* and *o-nu-ka*. Fourteen tablets refer to storage, with only seven of them preserving the cloth ideograms. From these the average is 27 cloth units on each tablet, giving a projected total of 378 units for the set of 14 tablets (Killen 1979, 151–3).

From personnel records and other tablets we know that there was a wide variety of specialists involved in the textile industry, discussed further below in the A series. Various occupations include the *pe-ki-ti-ra$_2$* ('wool pluckers'), preparers of wool, perhaps carders and combers, related to Greek πέκειν, 'to comb' (Lindgren 1973, 114–115; Barber 1991, 262, 283). The *ri-ne-ja* are certainly flax workers since Linear B *ri-no* corresponds to Greek λίνον, 'flax' (Chadwick 1988, 83; Lindgren 1973, 138). The *a-ra-ka-te-ja* (related to the Greek word, ἠλακάτη, 'distaff', or more likely, 'spindle') may refer 'spinning' women, who receive allotments of wool and flax and presumably spin it into usable thread. We also have male and female weaving specialists at the Mycenaean palaces, as indicated by *i-te-ja-(o)* and one *i-te-we*, both related to Greek ἱστός, 'a standing loom' (Bernabé and Luján 2008, 219). There are also references to *a-ze-ti-ri-ja*, (cf. KN Ap 694, Ln 1568 and M(1) 683), and its alternative forms *a-ke-ti-ri-ja* / *a-ke-ti-ra$_2$*. It was first suggested that this term referred to ἀκέστρια, 'seamstress' (Docs). Lejeune (1971, 105), however, followed an alternative suggestion of Ventris and Chadwick and interpreted the term in relation to later Greek ἀσκεῖν, 'to work with skill'. Based on this interpretation, Lejeune suggests that the women listed as such were apprentices of the wool industry. Killen (1979, 165–7) favors the verb ἀσκεῖν, but interprets it as 'to decorate or dress' particularly since the *a-ke-ti-ri-ja* are closely associated with *o-nu-ke*.

The Ld delivery tablets refer to cloth of the same varieties and in the same relative quantities as the Lc(1) work group records, with the most common type of cloth being that described as *re-u-ko-nu-ka* (Killen and Olivier 1968, 119). Other descriptions include *po-ki-ro-nu-ka* and *ko-ro-ta$_2$*. These epithets, however, are not found in the Lc(1) work group records. Many of the delivery tablets probably did not come directly from the weaver work groups. It is more likely that they came from decorators and finishers who in turn sent on the completed textiles to the palace.

On the Linear B tablets from Knossos, *o-nu-ka* terms are written by two scribes, h. 103 and h. 115. On tablets by h. 115 we find *o-nu-ka* followed by LANA, in parallel with the term *ko-ro-to* (Killen 1979, 162–3). If we accept that Linear B *o-nu-ka* corresponds to Greek ὄνυξ 'nail, claw', it may refer to either an item of decoration or to a type of wool, since it is followed by LANA (For all citations of *o-nu-* see Aura Jorro 1993, 28–30). Whatever '*o-nu-*' is, it clearly is something that can be measured, like wool. This explanation also follows for *ko-ro-to*, probably in the nominative as well. If these decorative terms are compared to *po-ki-ro-nu-ka, re-u-ko-nu-ka*, and to *ko-ro-ta$_2$*, which are followed by the TELA ideogram, it seems likely that they all refer to cloth decorated with woolen *o-nu-ka* or *ko-ro-to*. It has also been suggested that *ko-ro-ta$_2$* is connected with the Greek κροσσοί 'tassels' or 'fringes' (Docs^2 556). The term *po-ki-ro-nu-ka* is related to Greek ποικίλος + ὄνυξ, 'multicolored nails, edges,' while *re-u-ko-nu-ka* must indicate white colored decoration (Barber 1991, 324). Killen suggests that the wool was used to make ὄνυξ-decorations, wool not as yet woven into bands but likely to be used by the finishers, as an elaboration of the cloth. Jones (2005, 712–13) suggests that the term(s) refer to decorative fringes and may even have a connection to the practice of sealing documents in the Near East with impressed finger nails or garment fringes.

Barber (1991, 272–3, n. 10) has suggested that these references are to decorative edgings but not necessarily additions to finished textiles, but rather from woven heading bands.

The weft threads of heading bands would be used as the warp threads on a warp-weighted loom. Barber's interpretation is based on the close connection between the *a-ke-ti-ri-ja*, the makers of the heading bands, and the ὄνυξ-words, (*re-u-ko-nu-ka* and *po-ki-ro-nu-ka*). She suggests that header bands for a warp-weighted loom are either white (*re-u-ko-nu-ka*) or multicolored (*po-ki-ro-nu-ka*), perhaps in a claw-pattern. This suggestion, however, is not entirely satisfactory since the ὄνυξ mentioned in the tablets is always an added element, decorating an already finished textile, not something at the beginning stage of production as we would expect for a 'heading band'.

The Greek term ὄνυξ is found in later authors referring to the claw, or talon of an animal. In the first century AD medical texts, Dioscorides (Dsc. *Eup.* 2.92) uses ὄνυξ to refer to the operculum of the murex, the lid or membrane which retracts to seal the soft body of the snail inside the shell, and other later writers use it similarly (Galen 13.320, Dsc. 2.8). Bronze Age *opercula* have been found with the 14th century BC Ulu Burun shipwreck, proving that these snail-derived items were transported over great distances with other items of trade (Pulak 1988, 5). I wonder if it is possible that the ὄνυξ-based descriptions in Linear B (white, multicolored, etc.) might also refer to opercula from sea creatures, and that they were added beads attached to tassles and fringes on textiles. We can see some examples of attached decorative items and tassels on the skirts of the Aegean ambassadors in the tomb of Rekhmire (Fig. 49)(see detail in Barber 1991, fig. 15.18), in procession frescos from Knossos, and also on the kilts worn by the warriors on the famous 'Warrior Vase' from Mycenae (Fig. 50).

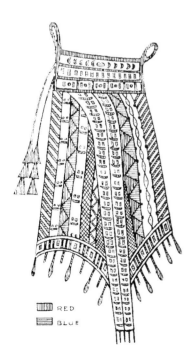

Figure 49 (left). Detail of kilt of tribute bearers, Tomb of Rekhmire (TT 100), c. 1479–1425 BC (A. Evans 1928, p. 744, fig. 479).

Figure 50 (above). Detail of Warrior Vase from Mycenae, National Museum at Athens (B. Burke).

One might wonder why some cloths would be described as simply *o-nu-ka,* and the others with a more specific *po-ki-ro-nu-ka* (multicolored *onukes*) and *re-u-ko-nu-ka* (white *onukes*). The pattern in all the Ld(1) delivery tablets is that first a cloth entry is described by an ethnic or trade-name and then the specific *po-ki-ro-nu-ka* or *re-u-ko-nu-ka* is added. Following that entry is the formula *pa-ro e-ta-wo-ne(-we)* and then the *o-nu-ka* description (Melena 1975, 84). An individual named *e-ta-wo-ne-u* was a finisher of cloth and the cloth described as *pa-ro e-ta-wo-ne(-we)* means 'at the workshop of Etawoneus'. Most likely textiles sent here were finished with any some decoration, either the multicolored or white embellishments, some form of ὄνυξ. Shelmerdine (1995, 103) notes that this decorator, Etawoneus, on tablet KN Xe 7711, receives textiles back from a perfumer who has treated the cloth with scented oil and then returned it to the decorator.

Other modifiers of cloth in the Ld records include *e-qe-si-ja* and *ke-se-nu-wi-ja pa-we-a* TELA. That these terms are written parallel to one another on Ld receipt tablets suggests that their meanings are related. *E-qe-si-ja* derives from *e-qe-ta,* probably related to Greek ἕπομαι, 'to follow'. These individuals are often referred to as 'the followers' (of the king?) and seem to be noblemen who acted as liaison officers between the military contingent and the Mycenaean palace (Driessen 1984). They have fairly high status in the Mycenaean hierarchy, below the *wanax* and *lawagetas,* but were probably leaders on military expeditions, as indicated by the so-called 'oka' tablets, *e.g.* PY An 654. This tablet lists groups of 50 and 60 un-named men under a certain *e-qe-ta* (Fig. 51). Cloth described as *e-qe-si-ja* often varies in color and decoration but is sometimes described as *a-ro$_2$-a,* 'of better quality', further suggesting a high status for the *e-qe-ta.*

The parallel term, *ke-se-nu-wi-ja,* is used to modify 35 units of *re-u-ko-nu-ka pa-we-a* cloth on KN Ld (1) 573 and a variant, *ke-se-ne-wi-ja,* describes cloth on Ld (1) 649. This *ke-se-ne/u* term is thought to relate to Greek ξένος, 'guest-friend', or ξένια, 'hospitality', perhaps meaning cloth that is meant for 'foreigners', 'guest-gifts', or 'for export' (*Docs²* 318, 477ff; Aura Jorro 1999, 353–4; Killen 2008a, 184; Shelmerdine and Bennet 2008, 298). Driessen, however, has suggested that the parallel construction of *e-qe-si-ja* and *ke-se-nu-wi-ja* suggests a military connection for both. The later Greek usage of ξένοι in military contexts, suggesting hired soldiers (*Il.* 24.202; *Od.* 14.102; 17.382; Hdt. 1.77; Thuc. 4.78.30; 6.31.1; 13.5; Ar. *Plut.* 173; Xen. *Anab.* 1.10; 1.2.1), suggests that *ke-se-nu-wi-ja* cloth in Linear B refers to textiles meant for mercenary soldiers. Cloth described as *ke-se-nu-wi-ja* is always the same type, *pa-we-a* cloth with red patterns and white fringes, unlike the varied *e-qe-si-ja* cloth. A possible correspondence in art is found in a papyrus fragment from Amarna discussed at the conclusion of this chapter. This quite possibly indicates payment in cloth or a standardized mercenary uniform for the hired soldiers. The word is also found on oil tablets (PY Fr 1231, 1255) and could imply that hired foreign warriors were supplied with garments and oil by the Mycenaean palaces during the very troubled times at the end of the Late Bronze Age. The association of cloth with mercenary soldiers further supports the wealth finance model, where certain types of cloth have such a standardized value that they can be used as payment for service.

Figure 51. Fresco fragments from Tiryns showing Mycenaean warriors, c. 13th century BC (Rodenwaldt 1912, pl. I.6).

Le Tablets – Receipt

The Le tablets also correspond to the Lc(1) records and are also by h. 103. These tablets record the receipt of cloth most probably from the same work groups listed in the Lc(1) tablets (Killen 1966, 105; 1974, 82). An example of a corresponding Le tablet is:

KN Le 641 + frr.   F14   (h. 103)
.1   o-a-po-te , de-ka-sa-ṭọ , a-re-i-jo , o-u-qe-po[
.2   pa-i-ti-ja , 'pe' TELA + TE 2 mi TELA¹ + TE 1̣4̣ da-wi-ja , pe TELAˣ + TE 1[
.3   do-ti-ja   mi TELA + TE 6 qa-mi-ja TELA¹ + TE 1[
.4   ko-no-so , / te-pe-ja 'mi' TELA + TE 3 tu-ni-ja TELA¹ + TE 1 [
.5 .6   *vacat* [   ]   *vacat*   [

This tablet is classified in the receipt series based on *de-ka-sa-to*, related to the Greek verb δέχομαι 'to receive' (Killen 1966, 107). Who the subject of the verb is remains unclear, either *a-po-te*, if this is a personal name as seems likely from tablet Od(1) 562, or *a-re-i-jo*, perhaps the 'son of Ares'. The varieties of qualified and unqualified cloth (TELA + *TE*) from *pa-i-ti-ja*, *da-wi-ja*, *qa-mi-ja*, and *tu-ni-ja* (women workers of these places), plus the female *te-pe* makers at Knossos, are paralleled on other Lc(1) tablets. KN Lc(1) 546, 526, 543, 547, and 549 refer to similar place names as those on Le 641 and, when the variety of TELA + *TE* is noted, the types also correspond on the tablet. For example, Lc(1) 543 refers to plain TELA + *TE* from *qa-mi-ja*, just as we see plain TELA + *TE* from *qa-mi-ja* on Le 641. Similarly, the *da-wi-ja* on Lc(1) 526 send TELA + *TE* of the *pe-ko-to* type, just as the 'pe' indicates cloth from the same workers at *da-wo* listed on Le 641 (Killen 1979, 152–3). The Le records are interesting because they only record one type of cloth, TELA + *TE*, and they do not mention *pa-we-a ko-u-ra* which occurs so frequently on the other cloth tablets. This is in contrast to the Ld(1) tablets, the storage and delivery records, which show no TELA + *TE* and only the 'plain' TELA, most certainly the same basic type as the *pa-we-a ko-u-ra* on the Lc(1) records.

Since the Le delivery records only list TELA + *TE*, it may be that these textiles went directly to the palace without requiring a separate finishing. On Le 641 we see the receipt of TELA + *TE* from six different sources. Five of them are feminine ethnics, presumably made by the women of these places, e.g. *pa-i-ti-ja*, *da-wi-ja*, and *tu-ni-ja*. The sixth entry on Le 641 has TELA + *TE* described as *ko-no-so* / *te-pe-ja*, that is, cloth from the Knossos *tepe*-making women (Chadwick 1988, 83). If we take TELA + *TE* as an abbreviation for tepe cloth, we recall that this was also a type of cloth recorded by Linear A scribes on Crete. The word itself suggests, possibly, Greek τάπης, 'tapestry', 'thick bedding' or a 'rug'.

In contrast to the TELA + *TE* cloth which went directly from weaver to the palace, the *pa-we-a ko-u-ra* cloth of the Lc(1) target records was sent to finishers where it received decorations. The finishers, in turn, delivered the decorated *pa-we-a ko-u-ra* to the palace, as recorded in the Ld(1) tablets. This type of cloth, *pa-we-a ko-u-ra*, is not found in the Le tablets. What is the connection between these types of records, the work group targets of Lc(1), and the receipt records Ld(1) and Le? The Ld(1) records were found in Magazine XV at Knossos along with Le tablets, by the same scribe, h. 103, suggesting a connection between the two types of storage tablets. In addition, the figures listed as targets of production in the Lc(1) records should correspond to the records of the received cloth. We will examine the totals presently.

From individual collectors, the total number of *pa-we-a ko-u-ra* is at least 356 units of cloth listed in the Lc(1) tablets. In the non-collector work-group tablets there are 200 units of *pa-we-a ko-u-ra* cloth. This gives a total of at least 556 units for both collector and non-collector work groups. From tablet Ld(1) 587 we see that the total number of received *pa-we-a ko-u-ra* cloth is 453. This is 103 short of the corresponding Lc(1) total. What to make of this discrepancy? Killen (1979, 155) suggests that the non-collector work group totals were not considered in the major records of the Ld(1) series. The most likely correspondence, then, would be between the 356 + units of *pa-we-a ko-u-ra* cloth listed on the major Lc(1) tablets from individual collectors with the total in Ld(1) 587 of 453 cloth units. From this we can conclude that the Ld(1) tablets only deal with 'collector' work groups.

Two of the ten minor Ld(1) records refer to what are thought to be non-collector work group, Ld(1) 5955.1 beginning with the ethnic term, *da-*22–ti*[, and Ld(1) 656 *pe-ki-ti*[, probably restored as the occupation of *pe-ki-ti-ra₂* (or *-ri-ja*), combers of wool (Killen 1979, 151 n. 3; Barber 1991, 262). Of the ten tablets, only five have totals preserved, and some only in part. These totals suggest an average of about 15 units of cloth per delivery tablet, for a total of 150, very close to the 200 *pa-we-a ko-u-ra* listed in the Lc(1) totals for the non-collectors.

In summary, the situation seems to be that two varieties of cloth are targeted for production by the Lc(1) work groups (TELA + *TE* and *pa-we-a ko-u-ra*) but they are treated differently at the receipt stage. The Le tablets record the delivery of TELA + *TE*. Ld(1) tablets record *pa-we-a ko-u-ra* cloth, but with epithets such as *re-u-ko-nu-ka, po-ki-ro-nu-ka,* and *ko-ro-ta₂*. As was mentioned above, these terms do not appear in the Lc(1) records. It is probable that the Lc targets merely enumerated the *pa-we-a ko-u-ra* expected by the palace, without further description. But upon delivery to the palace storeroom, this cloth had gone through further processing, such as decorating, which gave it these various qualities. The fullers and decorators may have worked on this cloth prior to final delivery. This system is paralleled in the Neosumerian textile industry, as described by Waetzoldt (1972), where fullers were also responsible for adding decorations of wool to woven garments, such as borders and embroidered designs, since the Neo-Sumerians are known to have received small allotments of wool.

Ak and Ap Series

Mycenaean labor, with reference to the textile industry, is understood from the Ak and Ap series. Work groups made up of women and children are recorded, showing the productive potential of the separate work groups for calculated targets. The tablets also provided the basic information for allocating monthly rations (Killen 1972, 1988).

Once the targets of production were met, the laborers would receive food rations listed in another series of tablets, the Ak series (Gregersen 1997). Concluding the manufacturing stages were the delivery, receipt, and decoration of finished textiles listed in the Ld, Le, and Od series. Small allotments of wool were made to various specialists who edged and finished cloth. Other smaller groups of the D series (*e.g.* Dv, Dw, and Dx) are too fragmentary to be assigned to more specific classes of workers but they refer in some way to the wool industry.

The workers listed in the Ak tablets were probably fully dependent on the palace and fed year round (Killen 1984, 52). They probably lived some distance from Knossos, in central and western Crete, based on what we know from a related group of tablets, the Lc series discussed below. The Lc(1) work groups and the Ak personnel records correspond well in the tablets for laborers in the central part of Crete. No personnel records, however, have been found that correspond to the Lc(1) work groups in the far west. Following an analogy with Pylos ration tablets, Palmer (1963, 113) ingeniously suggested that the missing personnel tablets might be located in the region where the laborers worked, *i.e.* in an archive somewhere in western Crete, and the finds of linear B documents at Chania make this possibility more likely.

Fragments of Knossos tablets stored long ago in the Herakleion museum were joined in 1984 with known Knossos tablets, resulting in a new understanding of western Crete personnel management (Killen 1988). One tablet, Ak 7827 has been joined and records 50 women, probably belonging to some individual whose name is in the genitive (*i.e.*]*jo-jo*). This tablet not only includes features such as the owners, who figure so prominently in the Lc(1) tablets, but it is also possible that it was written by the same scribe, h. 113, although this attestation is based on one sign only -*jo*. Two other newly joined tablets may suggest records of work groups in the far west whose production is recorded in the Lc(2) group, according to Killen (1988).

Women listed in the Ap tablets at Knossos are grouped by profession, although these references are fewer than comparable terms in tablets found at Pylos. Occupational terms provide information on the successive manufacturing stages of Mycenaean textile production and the associated work force. One tablet will serve as an example.

KN Ap 694
.1]-ja ko-u-re-ja   MUL [
.2] ka-ra-we   MUL [
.3] a-ze-ti-ri-ja   MUL [

In tablet Ap 694, the first line probably refers to a certain number (now lost) of women who made *pawea koura* cloth. The second line may refer to 'old' women. The third group of women, *a-ze-ti-ri-ja*, are probably a type of decorator, and would have worked in the later phases of cloth production.

Continuing with the various specialists from the tablets, we have *ka-na-pe-u*, corresponding to Greek κναφεύς, 'fuller or cloth-cleaner', three of whom are named, while one is described as *wa-na-ka-te-ro*, 'royal' (Palaima 1997, 407–9; Lindgren 1973, 71–2; Barber 1991, 283). The *ra-pi-ti-ra₂/ra-pte(-re)*, are probably related to Greek ῥάπτειν, 'to sew', referring to workers who would stitch the textiles. One interesting occupational term that recurs in two Ak tablets, and on other tablets associated with textile workers, is *ne-ki-ri-de*, related to Greek νεκρός, 'corpse' (Killen 1986). The parallel position of this word to other professional textile names suggests that this was a specialized worker, perhaps makers and decorators of funerary shrouds.

Pp Tablets

While no explicit reference to wool and textiles is made in the Pp tablets, Melena (1975) has noted a connection to the wool industry. These seven tablets were found in the West Wing at Knossos, in Magazine VIII, and probably originated in the textile and wool archives on the floor above. Six are one line long with the ligature *168 + *SE* preceded by a toponym and sometimes a personal name. One of the men's names here is *mu-ka-ra* who may be the same person who delivers a quantity of wool recorded in tablet Od 666. The seventh, Pp 498, has a central line division for two lines and does not include the *SE* adjunct with *168 but does include two place-names. Melena suggests that this compression of two place-names on one tablet indicates that this was the last tablet of the series and that the scribe made two entries on one tablet because he was running out of raw clay. Melena (1975, 127) also gives a revised order of the place-names based on the location of the tablets as they were found. The significance of the order of place-names is problematic, and Palmer (1972, 33) has suggested 'scribal routes', or itineraries, reflected in the order that place-names occur in the tablets. Melena (1975, 132) identifies the place-names listed in the Pp tablets as being in the northern and Messara plains of Crete where important flocks of sheep were known to graze.

The ideogram *168 and the ligature *168 + *SE* should also be explained since Melena connects these tablets with the textile industry. The sign *168 was first identified as possibly reflecting adzes based on its resemblance to the wood cutting tool. The sign itself is a four-sided rectangle of fairly wide width in contrast to its height. Often one end seems to taper toward the left giving an unequal appearance to the quadrilateral. At either ends, or rarely just the left end, there is an internal vertical stroke possibly resembling blades. The interpretation by Melena suggests that the sign indicates a basket used for the delivery or storage of wool about to be spun. This object occurs in later Greek as κάλαθος, 'wool-basket', which may occur in Linear B as *ka-ra-to* (MY Ge 603.1a, 605.1). The etymology of κάλαθος is probably related to Greek κλωθεῖν, 'to spin'. This revised view of the sign and ideogram better fits with our understanding of the extensive wool industry on Bronze Age Crete. Melena (1988, 406) further suggests that the 'Pp tablets record deliveries of baskets to be used as part of the equipment for wool plucking.'

Linen at Knossos

Evidence for linen at Knossos is found on the Nc and L(1) tablets (Killen 1968a; 1988). The flax or linen ideogram is generally assumed to be SA, often found on tablets at Pylos and discussed below. At Knossos the ideogram SA is measured by the textile unit M and is found on three fragmentary tablets classified as the Nc series. At Knossos flax is recorded by weight, in one, three and eight kilograms, unlike Pylos where references to flax are followed only by a number (Michailidou 1999, 93). Does SA at Knossos have the same meaning as at Pylos, where it is not measured, counted, or weighed? Does it mean linen or flax as we assume? The sign is not a syllabic abbreviation for flax and appears to have nothing to do with the actual Greek word for the item, similar to the use of sign NI meaning 'figs', which in no way resembles the fruit nor is it an abbreviation. The contexts of the ideogram at Knossos and Pylos are comparable and may indicate similar meanings. On tablets where it occurs, there seem to be references to military matters. SA as linen or flax could have been used as a trophy or payment for soldiers, just as we saw with the *ke-se-nu-wi-ja* cloth, or perhaps it was made into woven linen for tents and ropes used by the squadrons. This calls to mind Homer reference to a λινοθώρηξ in *Il.* 2.529, 830, where linen has a military function and was used as part of lesser Ajax's armor.

The Mycenaean word, *ri-ta,* corresponds to the adjectival, Homeric, accusative plural λῖτα, 'linen cloth' (*e.g., Od.* 1.130), which is probably a light garment worn underneath a heavier tunic or corselet. The six L(1) tablets by h. 103 all refer to *ri-ta pa-we-a* (Killen 1988). One tablet reads:

KN L(1) 594   (h. 103)
.1   ]   ri-ta , pa-we-a
.2   ]da-te-we-ja   TELA¹ 1 TUN + KI 1

This presumably records a suit of clothes: a linen tunic and a cloak worn over it. The mention of the work group *da-te-we-ja* in line 2 is familiar from the Lc(1) target records, also by h. 103. On Lc(1) 540 (discussed above) nine units of *pa-we-a ko-u-ra* cloth are made by the *da-te-we-ja.* In addition, the rations for these workers are listed in the Ak tablets (*infra*). Killen speculates that *pa-we-a* cloth might be made by the same work group but out of different materials, wool (*ko-u-ra*) on the Lc tablets and linen (*ri-ta*) on these L(1) records. The L(1) tablets are probably not targets of production since no raw materials, such as flax or SA , are allotted to workers. But rather tablets like this in the series seem to refer to the receipt of finished cloth (in this case, linen), just as we saw on the Le tablets, also by h. 103.

One well-known tablet from Knossos (*Docs²* 320–1, tablet 222) deals with linen and bronze together.

KN L 693   (h. 103)
.1   ri-no / re-po-to 'qe-te-o' ki-to AES M1 [
.2   sa-pa P 2 Q 1 e-pi-ki-to-ni-ja AES M1[

The phrase, *ri-no re-po-to,* almost certainly refers to 'fine linen' made from flax, rather than wild silk contrary to the conclusion of Panagiotakopulu (Panagiotakopulu, *et al.* 1997, 428; Panagiotakopulu 2000, 78). We can compare *Il.* 9.661, λίνοιο λεπτὸν ἄωτον, 'a fine linen bedspread'. Most interpretations agree that tablet KN L 693 is a list of fine linen with the verbal adjective *qe-te-o*, meaning 'to be paid'. This is followed by the Semitic loan word, *ki-to* for chiton, often associated with armour, and related to Akkadian *kittintu,* Ugaritic *ktn,* and Hebrew *kᵗtonet.* Oppenheim (1967) has also suggested that the word 'chiton' could imply garments made of wild silk, but there does not seem to be much evidence to support this view in Mycenaean. And while the cast of a cocoon and chrysalis from Akrotiri, which may be from a silk producing animal, is extremely interesting, there is little other evidence to suggest wide-spread silk cultivation in Greece during the Bronze Age (*contra* Panagiotakopulu, *et al.* 1997; Panagiotakopulu 2000).

Returning to the tablet, L 693, written in small signs and elevated above the main line, the word *qe-te-o* is clearly and unusually set-off by h. 103. This scribe often tends to elevate certain words to modify specifically the following word, just as modern writers might use a parenthesis mark. Some have suggested that this means *qe-te-o* refers to everything on the tablet. Plenty of room remained on the line and so it does not seem to have been an afterthought by the scribe, and is believed only to modify the chiton. The term, *qe-te-o,* has generally been taken to mean 'to be paid', although this idea is thoroughly critiqued by Hutton (1990–1991) among others. Hamp (1985, 53) closely associates the word with the modifier *lepton*, restoring it to read *qe-te-(j)o, kweiteion,* an adjective meaning 'costly' fine linen. The term is often paired with *o-no* and *o-pe-ro,* and is fairly important for understanding the economic organization of Mycenaean kingdoms, for it suggests equivalencies of value. Killen has suggested that *qe-te-o* refers to something owed by the palace to some individual, in contrast to *o-pe-ro* where something is owed back from an individual *to* the palace. There are 18 attestations of some form of *qe-te-o* in Linear B, including 7 on sealings found at Thebes: six of the total (33%) deal with textiles: L(5) 513, L(5) 5092, L(5) 7380+ 7500, L(5) 7834, L(5) 8441 and L 693 and Killen has restored *qe-te-o* on tablet M 683. All of the L(5) tablets follow the same formula: the first line contains *qe-te-o* and an amount of cloth. The second line begins most probably with a personal name and then more quantities of cloth. For example:

KN L(5) 7380 + 7500

.1]   qe-te-o   TELA¹ 2[

.2]   -ra/   TELAˣ 4 po TELAˣ[

The modifier *po* before the last cloth sign suggests possibly that this was an abbreviation for *po-ki-ro-nu-ka* cloth, decorated with multi-color edges. The consistent, formulaic nature of these tablets, to my mind, suggests an equivalency of values rather than a mere description of quality. The item that is constant in such transactions is textiles, giving the impression that cloth functioned nearly as a kind of currency in the wealth finance of the Mycenaean Bronze Age.

Returning to L 693, the meaning of *e-pi-ki-to-ni-ja* is fairly clear, an over-coat of some kind. Fragmented at the end of this line is also an amount of bronze. The bronze may refer to attachments on garments, *i.e.* a kind of armor (*cf.* λινοθώρηξ in *Il.* 2.529, 830 or χιτών χάλκεος in *Il.* 13.439); it may indicate the weight of the garment in bronze units; or it may be the value of the garments in terms of bronze (Προμπονᾶς 1983, 125). All of these are possible interpretations. The weight values are 1 kg of bronze for the tunic, 45 gr for the *sa-pa* (in line 2, possibly a light cloth), and 1 kg for the *epichiton* (*Docs²* 320–1). As a comparison to this tablet listing fine linen, Ventris and Chadwick cite *Il.* 18.595, where young men on the shield of Achilles are described wearing finely woven tunics 'touched with olive oil'.

An exchange of fine linen is also found at Pylos, on PY Un 1322.5 for example, where the price of this cloth is fixed not in terms of bronze, as at Knossos, but in terms of wheat.

PY Un 1322.5

5.   we-a₂-no[ri]-no , re-po-to *146 GRA 5

The weight of 5 units of wheat equates to about 480 litres. The bronze amount in L 693 is at least one double mina (M), approximately 964 grams. The association of one amount of a certain commodity for another amount of textiles suggests strongly that there is an equivalence of value for certain goods, particularly when textiles are involved in an exchange.

Mycenaean Textile Production at Pylos

As we have seen, wool and linen textiles played a major role in the Mycenaean economy of Knossos. Looking at the texts found at the palace at Pylos, we also see references to textiles and their manufacture administered by the palace authorities. Two major points distinguish textile production at Pylos from Knossos: first, in comparison to Mycenaean Knossos, the palatial economy at Pylos shows a greater degree of regional specialization among its various provinces and towns. The Linear B records found at the Palace of Nestor reflect centralized control of craft activities at two major centers, Pylos and Leuktron, monitoring activities dispersed throughout the kingdom (Shelmerdine 1987a). As Killen (1984) summarizes, Pylos had 28 separate work groups with nearly half containing over 20 women in each group. Leuktron has six or seven work groups, one with 37 women. The other place names in the tablets usually only have one work group with less than a dozen adult workers.

Secondly, linen production had a much larger role in the palace textile industry at Pylos than at Knossos (Robkin 1979; Perna 2005; Rougemont 2007). The various phases of linen cloth production in centers of differing size are fairly well-attested in the Pylian records although much less numerous than the wool records at Knossos. The textual and archaeological evidence for Pylian cloth, both wool and linen, is summarized and discussed below.

Pylian Wool

Wool is not as common in the tablets from Pylos compared to Knossos possibly because, at the time the palace was destroyed, sheep shearing had not yet taken place that year. Sheep records, however, do exist at Pylos: corresponding to the D-series at Knossos, the Cn group at Pylos record primarily male sheep, in the same order of magnitude as the sheep at Knossos and also in round numbers (Killen 1984, 51; Godart 1970; 1973). The Cn tablets often begin with a place name in the dative, a personal name and then livestock information (Bennet 1992, 67–8). There is, however, no explicit connection at Pylos between sheep and amounts of wool, unlike Knossos.

At Pylos there are no *ta-ra-si-ja* target attestations for wool as there are at Knossos but there is evidence for the administration receiving cloth produced according to the *ta-ra-si-ja* system (Nosch 2000b). As in KN Le 642, which also records TELA+TE and *ta-ra-si-ja*, Duhoux (1976, 70), and Killen (1984, 51) have restored the Pylos text La 1393 as:

PY La 1393   SW area 13   S622–H13 (?)
  .1 (o-)de-ka-]sa-to , a-ri-wo , ta-ra-[si-ja
  .2]TELA+ṬẸ 40 [

One individual, Aleios, receives something (raw wool?) according to the *ta-ra-si-ja* system and is assessed forty units of TELA + *TE* cloth. As was mentioned before, TELA + *TE* is most likely a woolen garment using seven units of wool for each unit of cloth, giving a total of 280 wool units for Aleios.

Pylian Linen

Like Knossos, the Mycenaean tablets from Pylos show that textiles were a major industry for the palatial economy. The Pylian kingdom in the southwest Peloponnese during the Bronze Age covered an area roughly equivalent to the region of modern Messenia, an area well suited to the cultivation of flax, the raw material for linen. In the 1950s this region produced over half of the flax in Greece (McDonald and Rapp, Jr. 1972, 240). From the collection records of 100 different towns and villages under the administration of Mycenaean Pylos, we see that textiles and related crops comprise 78% of the records, while goods such as food and livestock are only 16%. We find *ri-no* in the tablets, almost certainly related to λίνον, 'linen'. On the Na, Ng and Nn records, the commodity SA has been identified as some form of flax product (Robkin 1979, 473). From the collection target tablet Ng 319, the Hither province alone yielded nearly 50,000 kg of this fiber in one year. At Knossos,

SA is weighed according to KN Nc 4479. It unlikely refers to linseed since other types of seeds are designated *pe-mo*, σπέρμα, 'seed'. Chadwick, based on modern and ancient land-use productivity, suggests that one unit of SA indicates one Mycenaean talent of un-spun flax fiber, after initial processing, equal to 29 kg.

Often, permission to use land controlled by the palace was given to certain individuals in exchange for payments of flax. For example, we read,

PY Na 396
  1. e-ko-si
  2. wo-no-qe-wa, ko-ro-ku-ra-i-jo SA 30

  1. They have
  2. At Wonoqewa, Korokuraijo 30 units of flax.

These officials, such as (the?) Korokuraijo, administered palace land throughout the kingdom and were assessed certain amounts of flax as payment. Eight of the Na tablets also refer to payment for use of land under the administration of the palace.

The Ma series from Pylos is also relevant to discussion of linen/flax. These tablets are unique in that they demonstrate a regulated taxation system of six set commodities, including textile *146 that was probably linen (Shelmerdine 1973; Nosch and Perna 2001; Killen 2008b). The identification of the other commodities, besides *152 which is an oxhide, is speculative, but suggestions include flax or linen cord (*RI* Killen 2008b, 431), beeswax (*KE*), and honey (Morris 1986, 91–9, discounted by Killen 2008b). Presumably these goods were agricultural commodities that each subdivision of the kingdom's two provinces was capable of producing as payment, like a tax to the center. The use of these goods is disputed by Mycenaean scholars, as summarized by Killen (2008b, 432–3), and range from prestige goods for high level palace personnel, to offerings for gods, or that they are all aromatics needed for religious offerings (Palmer 1963, 300–02). Sign *146 is probably unfinished linen cloth, most likely manufactured throughout the Pylian kingdom and sent to the palace for finishing by specialists. This was probably a simple, homemade fabric, and together with the other goods listed on the Ma tablets may have been used for preparing a military force (Killen 2008b, 440).

As we found at Knossos, some Pylian documents refer to laborers receiving rations from the palace. The Aa, Ab and Ad tablets are of particular interest because of the connections between women workers described in terms of ethnic names and cloth production (*Docs²* 410, 417). The ethnics indicate an origin for the women workers along the Anatolian coast. Women of Knidos (*ki-ni-di-ja*), Lemnos (*ra-mi-ni-ja*), Miletos (*mi-ra-ti-ja*), and possibly somewhere near Halikarnassos (*ze-pu₂-ra₃*, 'Zephyra') are recorded as textile workers at Pylos. Also possible is a reference to women of Chios (*ki-si-wi-ja*) (see Chadwick 1988; Nosch 2003; Nikoloudis 2008a). Any one of these topographical references might be only interesting, but the coincidence of all these names from the same general region of western Ionia is highly suggestive of contact and exchange with Asia Minor in the Bronze Age. A few tablets refer to the occupations of these women with foreign names. Certain ethnics are associated exclusively with particular craft activities suggesting that these women specialized in different aspects of textile production. It may be that their original homeland gave a designation to a kind of trade or craft-guild. For example, the Milesians are spinners and Tinwasians weavers (Ad 684), the Aswian and Zephyrian women are listed as flax-workers (Ad 326, Ad 664), and the Chians are makers of *o-nu-ka* (Ab 194, Ad 675).

The word *ra-wi-ja-ja*, occurring in three Pylian tablets, Aa 807, Ab 586, and as *ra-wi-ja-ja-o* on Ad 686, is probably related to the Homeric adjective ληΐας, 'captured' (*Docs²* 162). Although the women with Anatolian/Ionian names are never explicitly described as *ra-wi-ja-ja*, it is possible that they were prisoners of war won from raids conducted by Mycenaean warriors along the Ionian coast (*pace* Billigmeier and Turner 1981, 4). Alternatively, these women may have been rescued Mycenaean women, previously abducted in the past by Anatolian pirates, and taken back by Greeks. They also could have been refugees from Anatolia, skilled in weaving and attracted to Pylos because of its extensive linen industry. One final interpretation of these foreign names is that they were the names of ancestors of Pylian Mycenaeans who came originally from Anatolia. As an interesting parallel from later Greek history we recall Xenophon (*Mem.* 117.2–8) who refers to female refugees being put to work in Athens, making clothes and baking bread during the Peloponnesian war.

Archaeological evidence for spinning thread and weaving cloth in the kingdom of Pylos is slight, as is the case with other Mycenaean centers. No significant finds of organized cloth production were found at the Palace of Nestor itself. Four loom weights similar in form to those at Nichoria, described below, were found in the aqueduct in the southeast corner of the palace (Blegen, *et al.* (vol. 1) 1966, 301, fig. 305.1, pl. lv; (vol. 3) 1973, 7–16, 336, fig. 105.1–3).

The best evidence for Mycenaean cloth production comes from the site of Nichoria, identified as the Pylian town of *ti-mi-to-a-ke*. This lower-order settlement was assigned one of the largest amounts of flax in the Pylos tablets, suggesting a specialization in linen production (Carrington Smith 1992, 674–711; Shelmerdine 1981). Archaeological data for cloth production included 153 spindle whorls from houses containing mixed ceramic deposits dating to the Middle and Late Bronze Age. The whorls were generally bi-conical in shape and Carrington Smith (1992) compares the Messenia whorls to those found at Troy. She sees a similarity in the new forms appearing in Greece in the Middle Bronze Age to those of Troy VI (Goldman 1931, 198). No new type of loom weight is attested in Greece for the Middle Helladic period, however, and Carrington Smith suggests that different weaving technologies (*i.e.* non-warp weighted looms) were used. Twelve Mycenaean loom weights were found at Nichoria, the majority of LH II–LH IIIA1 date in Area VI. One loom weight and a possible spinning bowl were of Minoan type. These data provide a unique view of a non-palatial, subordinate center from the Mycenaean period.

Thebes and Mycenae

Pylos and Knossos are not the only Mycenaean centers that preserve evidence for centralized textile production. While the Linear B records for cloth are fewer at Mycenae and Thebes, documents from these sites suggest that the centers also relied on a well-organized textile industry.

Thebes

At Thebes, on the corner of Epaminondas and Metaxas Streets, the remains of a two-room structure have been associated with textile production and distribution. Spyropoulos, the excavator, states that the remains of dye vats can be discerned in the form of pits cut into the floor level (Spyropoulos and Chadwick 1975). The area in front of these pits shows a small channel with three post-holes along the sides. Spyropoulos suggested that this was a drying rack for newly washed or dyed textiles although Shelmerdine (1997) has shown that this is unlikely. She suggests instead that this building was a clearing house for wool collected and sent on to workers in outlying areas. In what was identified as a bathroom, there were two holes cut in the floor, in the center of the room, which might indicate post-holes of a warp-weighted or two-beam frame loom. The raised platform in front could have functioned as a bench for the weavers working at the loom. The bath feature may have held spun wool or linen ready for weaving. Shelmerdine, however, reconstructs these post holes as the supports for shelves containing the 16 inscribed Mycenaean tablets found in this room listing quantities and distributions of wool and discounts the identification of a textile workshop (1997, 389).

The 16 tablets in Room 1 are classified in the Of series, dealing with distributions of wool and connect the area to wool working under the administration of the palace (Spyropoulos and Chadwick 1975, 35–7; Shelmerdine 1997, 387; Nosch 2001b). The disbursements of wool (LANA) range between 1 to 30 kg for a total of 69 kg, not a very substantial amount. Wool was probably stored in this room, some for perhaps a long time since the qualifiers meaning 'new' and 'last year' are included on Of 34. The wool would also be sent to outlying areas away from Thebes, such as *a-ma-ru-to-de*, to Euboean (?) Amarynthos, mentioned on Of 25. The sealings found at Thebes, which refer to collectors, also show a strong interest by the central administration in livestock, especially sheep and goats, and provide some indication of a wool industry. On Of 36, one *a-ke-ti-ra$_2$- wa-na-ka* is most likely a 'royal spinner'; on Of 34, there is an 'experienced' distaff-woman/spinner (*a-ra-ka-te-ja pa-ra-ja*).

On the recently discovered tablets from Pelopidou Street, certain specialized craftsmen receive small units of wool from the palace: the Oh tablets record one *o-nu-ke-u* (Oh 206), a 'fringe' or 'bead' maker, and *pe-re-ke-u* (Oh 208), a maker of 'plaits/finisher', according to Killen (1979, 167 n. 30; Dakouri-Hild 2005, 215). In addition, tablet Av 106 sees a cult connection with cloth production at Thebes, since six *ka-na-pe-we* ('fullers') were needed to do their work with a religious feast taking place, presumably meaning that they were going to do the fulling in a religious context.

Mycenae

The West House group at Mycenae provides some Linear B evidence for the administration of a textile industry. Four houses were excavated in the 1950s by the British School at Athens and their contents have been studied by I. Tournavitou (1995). The 29 Oe tablets from the West houses at Mycenae record disbursements of wool to different outlying areas, comparable to tablets found at Thebes. According to Shelmerdine's interpretation amounts of wool disbursed are much higher than originally thought (1997, 390). One tablet (Oe 111) presumably a total tablet, records at least 300 wool units, amounting to over 900 kilograms. In addition, tablet Fo 101 records disbursements of oil sent to textile workers (Killen 1981).

Finally, one tablet from Mycenae provides slight evidence for the extra-regional exchange of textiles between palaces.

MY X 508
.1   ]   te-qa-de , ta-[
         ] ze-ta , / pu-ka-ta-ri-ja ma-ri-ne[

This tablet appears to describe a transaction of *pu-ka-ta-ri-ja* textiles from Mycenae to Boeotian (?) Thebes. Palaima (1997, 276–7) questions why such a relatively common type of cloth would be shipped from Mycenae to an area like Thebes, which, as we have seen, was capable of producing its own woolen textiles. Possible explanations are technical advantages of Argolid wool and weavers, that this was some sort of gift-exchange between elites, or a dedication to a divinity.

The archaeological evidence, besides the Linear B documents, for textile production at Mycenae is slight. Some of our best preserved examples of actual Mycenaean cloth is the oldest, and is found in the early Mycenaean burials of Grave Circles A and B at Mycenae (Schliemann 1880a, 155, 283; Karo 1930, 71, 142, 145, 251; Snodgrass 1967, 16; Åkerström 1978, 52; Papdemetrios 1951, 203; Mylonas 1973, 22).

In addition, nineteen loom weights dating to the LH IIIA period were reported by Wace from the Guard's House at Mycenae but none of these can be located in storage either in Athens, Nauflion, or at Mycenae (pers. comm., E. French 1997).

We also have small objects of clay and stone, sometimes steatite, usually three to five centimeters in diameter, found at Mycenae and at other sites, which were first interpreted as spindle whorls (Schliemann 1880a, 21). These objects come from a full range of contexts within the Late Bronze Age Aegean, being found in cemeteries and settlements, dating to the early through late Mycenaean phases, on the mainland and on Crete (Iakovides 1977; Evely 2006; Rahmstorf 2008). The spindle whorl interpretation of these objects was quickly rejected by Tsountas in 1893 on the weak explanation that one chamber tomb at Mycenae had 160 of these small weights, which would be far too many spindle whorls for one tomb in Tsountas' opinion. Instead they were thought to be buttons (Tsountas and Manatt 1897, 174), or dress weights, based on representations of tassels in Mycenaean figural art (Iakovides 1977, 113–5; Barber 1991, 51–2). Iakovides' typology of this class of object is useful but now supplanted by Rahmstorf's much more detailed presentation (Rahmstorf 2008, plates 47–51, 91.10–11). The belief that the small weights were too light and not of substantial enough size for spindle whorls is not convincing since recent experiments in Scandinavia and in the Aegean have conclusively shown that it is possible to spin fine thread with whorls that weigh less than 10 grams (Anderson and Nosch 2003). Evely's publication of the Late Mycenaean material from Lefkandi is equivocal, primarily following Iakovides and offers no new functional interpretation (Evely 2006, 281). Rahmstorf's publication of the small weights from Tiryns, primarily from the later Mycenaean phases, wisely notes that 'any dogmatic and one-dimensioned functional interpretation is misleading' for this class of item (2008, 296). The ubiquity of the small weights, their relatively light size, and their prevalence through time in the Late Bronze Age suggests to me that their identification as tools related to textile production is not misplaced.

While spindle whorls are rather plentiful in the archaeological record, spindles are rare, primarily since they would most likely have been made of wood. The few extant examples were probably never intended for use since they were made of precious materials, such as gold and ivory, and were deposited as grave goods in burials: a gold spindle comes from Grave Circle A at Mycenae (Karo 1933, 57, pl. xvii, 93, 95, 106); five ivory ones were found at Perati (Iakovides 1970, 350, fig. 155); and a bone one was recovered at Asine (Frödin and Persson 1938, fig. 252). These are comparable to examples found at Hama (Riis 1948, 173 fig. 217) and Enkomi (Schaeffer 1952, 181, pl. xlii). No elite spindles have been reported from Crete.

Late Bronze Age Art

The study of Aegean costume as depicted on wall paintings and figurines is significant for issues related to cultural influence, self-presentation, and modes of production. The Minoan costumes of elite members of society, most especially women, are generally seen as more elaborate and elegant (Jones 2001, 2003; Nosch 2008). The flounced skirt of the snake goddesses and other garments in Minoan art are skillfully crafted garments, showing a great deal of effort by individual seamstresses and weavers (Barber 1994; Jones 2001). These are not mass-produced textiles, as we infer for the cloth listed in the Linear B texts and from Mycenaean representations of plainer cloth. Elite Minoan costumes were probably individually made with a great skill, perhaps the work of ladies of leisure and their servants. Differences in design may be indicative of several things: family/ethnic groups, geographical origins, age, social rank, specialized jobs and ritual activities, such as initation benchmarks. Some work has been done on this topic but the limited nature of the documents and other sources of evidence make further speculation difficult (Trnka 1998; Jones 2001, 2003, 2005, 2009; Marcar 2005; Nosch 2008). In contrast, representations of Mycenaean garments often show plain, white cloth elaborated only with decorative edgings or bands. Elite Mycenaean women continue to use some styles inherited or borrowed from the Minoans, such as the open bodice and full skirt, but the textiles themselves are simpler and less individualistic.

For men, the costumes of both the Minoans and the Mycenaeans remained fairly simple: Minoan men wore a fairly skimpy loin-cloth or breechcloth which is found in bull-jumping frescoes and on male figurines (Barber 1993, 350; Rehak 1996) and Mycenaean men generally wore a kilt in religious and military contexts. The recent analysis of a pictorial papyrus from the royal city of Amarna illustrates Aegean-Egyptian interaction during the Late Bronze Age and provides some illustration of Late Bronze Age Aegean clothing (Schofield and Parkinson 2004). Several warriors are preserved on this unique pictorial papyrus, some wearing what may be a certain type of textile mentioned in Linear B, discussed above perhaps associated with mercenary soldiers. Some wear a fairly typical white Egyptian kilt with finely painted red lines to indicate pleating, but two of the warriors also wear a very unusual tunic around their upper torso of a splotch design and possibly trimmed with metal. This garment finds no parallels in Egyptian art and may have been the *ke-se-nu-wi-ja* type produced by Mycenaean weavers. The soldiers also wear distinctive conical helmets shown in yellow paint with red outlines which are the well-known boar's tusk variety seen in Mycenaean wall painting, ceramics, seal stones, ivory carving, and recorded in later Homeric descriptions (*Il.* 10.260). The actual remains of boar's tusk helmets have also been found in Mycenaean warrior tombs in Greece, Crete and in Egypt at Qantir dating to the LH IIIB period, along with significant amounts of Mycenaean pottery (Warren and Hankey 1989, 158; Cline 1994, 37).

Based on the papyrus the Mycenaeans seem to be fighting as mercenaries alongside the Egyptians. When considering the portrayal of foreigners in the papyrus fragment it is important to acknowledge the processes of iconographical transfer. An Egyptian portrayal of Mycenaeans differed in both intent and detail from images of self-representation in Aegean art, just as the Keftiu in the Theban tombs should be viewed as Egyptian depictions of foreigners. The fragments from Amarna showing a battle scene are rare examples of a pictorial papyrus. From this we should infer that the Amarna fragment is not showing a specific historical event but a general representation of Aegeans and Egyptians engaged together in battle against a common enemy.

Summary

Were textiles a part of a staple-wealth finance system in the Mycenaean economy and did some function as prestige goods? From the discussion in this chapter I hope to have demonstrated that indeed they were. Four criteria have been suggested to determine prestige goods in early state economies and I believe Mycenaean cloth production fits this description (Stein and Blackman 1993, 50). The first criterion requires the presence of craft specialists who are dependent upon the palace center. Personnel records in Linear B list textile specialists of various crafts who receive rations from the palace centers. The Linear B tablets also record disbursements of wool and flax acquired by the state from outlying areas for these same dependent workers to process into cloth. This fulfills the second criterion of workers receiving raw materials from the central administration. The third criterion, a high price/value equivalent for the raw materials or finished products, is evident in Mycenaean tablets that refer to the exchange of one good for another, most often involving textiles. The Mycenaean word, *qe-te-o*, has been discussed and its meaning, 'to be paid' was shown to refer to cloth and other commodities. Exchanges in bronze, alum and aromatic oil are among the goods evaluated and administered by the palaces. The fourth criterion refers to items presented as gifts or payment to individuals of known social rank, and this has also been demonstrated by various types of cloth: *ke-se-nu-wi-ja* cloth listed in the Ld tablets perhaps refers to cloth that was fit for *xenoi*, *i.e.* foreign, mercenary soldiers employed by the palaces just before the great conflagrations that ended the Late Aegean Bronze Age. This cloth may have been payment for services rendered, or part of equipment supplied by the Mycenaeans for their fighting force. Other types of cloth are fit for the '*wanax*' or are meant for the 'followers'. Also fulfilling this last criterion are the Aegean tribute bearers depicted on Egyptian wall-paintings, bringing tribute, including textiles, to foreign elites.

The high value of Bronze Age cloth and its use as a medium of exchange find parallels in the Homeric epics. The wide variety of textiles in Homer can not be discussed fully here but is summarized in the following table (Table 4).

Table 4. Homeric words referring to types of cloth.

Cloth Word	Translations	Iliad	Odyssey
ἡ ἐσθής	Elite clothing, often mentioned with gold and bronze given to highly honored people, *e.g.* to Odysseus from the Phaiakians, to Telemachus from Menelaus, to Eumaios from Odysseus.	24.94 (τὸ ἔσθος – the veil of Thetis)	1.165, 2.339, 5.38, 6.74, 83, 192, 7.6, 8.440, 13.136, 14.510, 15.207, 16.231, 23.290, 341, 24.67
ἡ ὀθόνη	Cloth, usually fine linen, in plural. A sail in singular	3.141, 18.595	7.107
ἡ καλύπτρα	Veil, shroud.	22.406	
ἡ χλαῖνα	A plain, think, fleecy mantle worn over the chiton. A personal garment used as a blanket when sleeping. Simpler than the φᾶρος. Comparable to later Greek ἱμάτιον	2.183, 262, 10.133, 16.224, 22.493, 24.163, 230, 646	3.349, 351, 4.50, 115, 299, 5.229, 7.338, 11.189, 14.460, 520, 17.86, 19.225, 318, 337, 20.4, 95, 143, 21.118, 23.180
ὁ ἑανός	Most often a robe worn by, or fit for, a goddess.	3.385, 419, 14.178, 16.9, 21.507	
ὁ πέπλος	Skillfully woven robe (by Athena, Sidonian women). Purple robe wrapping the body of Hector.	5.194, 315, 338, 734, 6.90, 271, 289, 302, 8.385, 24.229, 796	6.38, 7.96, 15.105, 124, 18.292
ὁ τάπης	Carpter, bedding or coverings for furniture. Sometimes purple.	9.200, 10.156, 16.224, 24.230, 645	4.124, 298, 7.337, 10.12, 20.150, 24.276
ὁ χιτών	An undergarment or tunic.	2.42, 262, 416, 3.57, 5.113, 736, 9.490, 10.21, 13.439	1.437, 439, 3.467, 4.50, 6.214, 8.392, 441, 13.434
τὸ εἷμα	A general term for a man's clothing (usually a cloak and tunic).	2.261, 3.392, 5.905, 16.670, 680, 18.517, 538, 22.154, 510, 23.67, 24.162	2.3, 4.750, 5.167, 6.26, 7.234, 8.249, 10.542, 13.218, 14.132, 154, 214, 320, 341, 396, 501, 516, 15.338, 368, 16.79, 17.550, 21.339, 22.487
τὸ ῥῆγος	A woollen cloth laid down as bedding or thrown over a chair.	24.644	3.349, 351, 4.297, 6.38, 7.336, 10.352, 11.189, 13.73, 118, 19.318, 337, 20.141, 23.180
τὸ σπεῖρον	A cloth, sheet, shroud, or sail.		2.102, 4.245, 5.318 (sail), 6.179, 269 (sail),19.147, 24.137
τὸ φᾶρος	Most often a mantle or cloak worn by a man of distinction. Also, a sail cloth and the web Penelope weaves. Sometimes described as 'sea-purple'.	2.43, 8.221, 18.353, 24.231, 580, 588	2.58, 97, 3.467, 5.230, 258, 6.214, 8.84, 392, 441, 13.108, 15.61, 19.138, 142, 24.132, 147

In the very emotional conclusion to the *Iliad* (24.228–232) Priam puts together a ransom of his most valuable possessions to offer to Achilles for the return of his son Hector's body: Priam takes from 'his clothes-chest …twelve robes surpassingly lovely and twelve mantles to be worn single, as many blankets, as many great white cloaks, and also the same number of tunics.' He also includes ten talents of gold and other objects of metal. A comparable amount of goods was supposedly given as guest-gifts to Odysseus (*Od.* 24.274–279). Along with the metal goods (although only seven talents of gold here) and the dozen mantles, cloaks and tunics, Odysseus includes the four highly skilled female textile workers as part of the gift, perhaps reminiscent of the skilled textile women from Asia Minor listed in the tablets. Telemachos (*Od.* 2.339) takes metals and textiles from Ithaka for his trip and he receives the same from Menelaos and Helen as gifts of honor (*Od.* 15.207). Similarly, Odysseus receives cloth, gold, and bronze from Alkinoös and the Phaiakians (*Od.* 8.440, 13.136, 16.231) before his departure homeward.

From the evidence presented above, textiles played a vital role in the Mycenaean palace economies, as they do centuries later in the Homeric poems and Greek life in general, as illustrated on the Amasis lekythos in New York (Fig. 52). In this chapter I have presented

Figure 52. Attic black-figure lekythos, attributed to the Amasis Painter, c. 550–530 BC (Metropolitan Museum of Art, Fletcher Fund, 1931, 31.11.10, image © The Metropolitan Museum of Art).

most of the textual data relevant to textile production from the Linear B records. I have not included every textual reference related to cloth but have instead isolated key issues and phases of cloth production. Since the archaeological evidence for spinning and weaving is so meager from the Late Bronze Age Aegean we rely on the fragmentary records of the Mycenaean scribes. From this information we see that many different types of wool and linen cloth were manufactured under palace supervision and most probably used as prestige goods and as payment for service within a wealth finance system. These varieties are paralleled in later Homeric Greek. Evidence exists also for common textiles that were assessed as a kind of tax by surrounding communities, especially in the Pylian kingdom (commodity *146).

This investigation of textile production provides a synthesis of views regarding the complex and multifaceted subject of Mycenaean cloth industries and tries to emphasize the archaeological and economic aspects. At the end of the Bronze Age we see a change in social organization in Greece with the collapse of the Mycenaean palaces. Controlling elites no longer administer overseas trade and coordinate craft activities such as cloth production. If we look east, to Iron Age Anatolia, however, we see some holdovers of the Bronze Age Aegean palatial economy. Although the documentary evidence for textile production is not as rich in Anatolia as it is in the Aegean, the archaeological record regarding organized textile production at the palace of King Midas at Gordion in the Phrygian highlands is particularly rich and preserves some of the best evidence for organized textile production anywhere in the eastern Mediterranean.

4 GORDION AND PHRYGIAN CLOTH PRODUCTION

The site of Gordion, located near the modern Turkish village of Yassıhöyük, about 85 kilometers southwest of Ankara (Map 4), provides almost an ideal opportunity to study the organization of a well-developed textile industry in a palatial center of first millennium BC in Anatolia. Evidence from Gordion provides a good comparison to the Bronze Age Aegean, since the Phrygians, with their capital at Gordion, had a palace-centered economy, a fortified citadel, many herds of sheep, access to linen, and skilled craftspeople.

Gordion lies in the Sakarya River plain, about 688 m above sea level, and corresponds

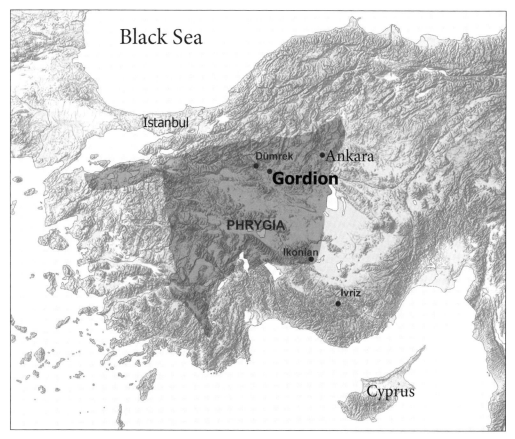

Map 4. Map of Phrygia, based on extent of Phrygian inscriptions. Adopted from K. DeVries.

Figure 53. Gordion, Küçük Höyük and Citadel Mound, 1958 (MJM-004854 © Mellink Archive, Bryn Mawr College).

to a description by the geographer Strabo who says Gordion is on the ancient Sangarios River (surely the Sakarya) and is equidistant from the Pontic and Cilician Seas (Strabo 3.1.11). The main settlement is located on a 'flat mound', giving the Turkish name Yassıhöyük to the nearby village (Fig. 53). The site, conventionally known as the Citadel Mound or City Mound, was first investigated in 1900 by the German Körte brothers. It lay relatively dormant until large-scale excavations were begun by the University Museum of the University of Pennsylvania in 1950, under the direction of Rodney S. Young. The *höyük*, or ancient settlement area, covers approximately 10–12 ha and rises 24 m above the plain. An additional lower town in the flood plain was of comparable size and was enclosed by a mud-brick fortification wall, remnants of which still survive. A 40–60 ha outer town was located on the opposite bank of the Sakarya River, although little is known about this surrounding settlement (Map 5).

This chapter examines the organization and technology of the textile industry at Gordion in order to characterize modes of craft production that might explain the wealth base of a ruler like the Phrygian King Midas and his early Iron Age kingdom. The present investigation of textile production focuses on material from the Early Phrygian destruction level, *c.* 800 BC, in which major structures of the Phrygian capital were burnt (Fig. 54)(DeVries, Kuniholm, Sams, Voigt 2003; DeVries 2005; DeVries, *et al.* forthcoming). The destruction date of 800 BC is a major revision of the long-held view established by Young that the Early Phrygian citadel was sacked by Cimmerian raiders causing King Midas to kill himself (Strabo 1.3.21) in either 696/5 BC (according to Euseb. *Chron* 0.1.21.1 (Latin) 21.2 (Armenian)) or 676 BC (according to Julius Africanus, Cramer, *Anec. Par.* 2.264). Painstaking work by DeVries and Voigt, along with others, has challenged this long-held assumption, which mistakenly connected the suicide of Midas, the Cimmerians, and the Early Phrygian destruction level. This chronological revision has been generally accepted by the scholarly community (see however, Muscarella 2004) and it is the new chronology that is followed in this work.

While the Phrygian material is distant in time and space from the Aegean Bronze Age, we know that Gordion was an active place in the Late Bronze Age since substantial

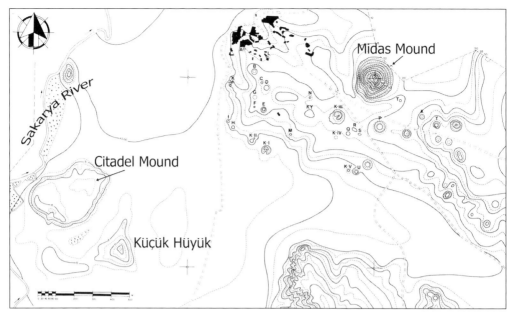

Map 5. Map of Gordion region. (© University Museum, Gordion Archives).

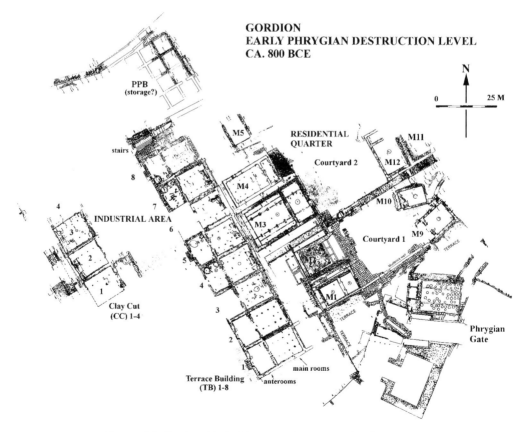

Figure 54. Gordion Early Phrygian Destruction level, 800 BC.

Figure 55. Hittite loom weights from Gordion.

amounts of Hittite material is recorded, although in no way was Bronze Age Gordion a major economic center (Gunter 1991; Güterbock 1980). M. Mellink excavated a large Hittite cemetery near the modern museum at Gordion and published several finds related to cloth production including 16 spindle whorls (Mellink 1956, 42–3, pl. 24). There are also a few examples of the so-called Hittite loom weight from Gordion, shaped somewhat like a curved banana and pierced through either end (Fig. 55).

During the Iron Age, Gordion becomes a major administrative capital with a stratified society and specialized craftspeople, controlling a fairly vast territory. Midas, the most well-known Phrygian, is recorded in various classical sources as an archetypal wealthy king, paranoid of spies as exemplified by having ass' ears (Ovid *Metam.* 11.90–193). He begins the legend of the Gordian knot (Arr. *Anab.* 2.3.1–8; Curt. 3.1.11–18; Just. *Epit.* 11.7.3–5; Plut. *Vit. Alex.* 18.1–2) resolved by Alexander the Great (Burke 2001) and his greed for worldly goods is told in the story of his 'golden touch' (Arist. *Pol.* 1.3.16 (1257b16); Ovid *Metam.* 11.85–145). It is interesting to note that little evidence for gold and gold working has been found at the site, and in fact, the best attested craft activity at Gordion is the production of Phrygian textiles.

Leaving behind the legends of Midas, this chapter looks at the cultural context of Early Phrygian Gordion and the sources of evidence for cloth production. A detailed description of the Iron Age craft-quarters and the tools of textile manufacture found therein is presented. The archaeological evidence provides the most complete picture of organized textile production at a palace center and gives a vivid picture of craft activity on a massive scale during the Early Iron Age. What is lacking from the Phrygian evidence, especially in comparison to the data available from the Aegean, is textual and archival material that would provide a descriptive outline of the palatial economy.

Phrygians of Gordion

The Phrygians most likely migrated into central Anatolia from southeastern Europe sometime after the collapse that marks the end of the Late Bronze Age, according to ancient sources (Hdt. 7.73 and Strabo 7.3.2) and modern research (Drews 1983; Mallory 1989; Henrickson 1993; 1994; Sams 1994). At Gordion, the handmade and burnished ware pottery found in post-Bronze Age levels is probably related to similar wares found in the Aegean and suggests the arrival of newcomers to both regions, although their connection to each other is a point of discussion (Sams 1994; Henrickson 1993). Finds of this ceramic type east of the Halys River in central Turkey may better inform us of this population group (Summers 1990; Genz 2003), but the evidence is in general agreement with ancient sources (Hdt. 7.73 and Strabo 7.3.2) and linguistic data, which indicate that the Phrygians migrated from Europe into modern day Turkey after the Bronze Age calamities that destroyed the political centers of the Mycenaeans and Hittites.

Linguistically, Phrygian is a new branch of the Indo-European family in the east, standing outside the Anatolian language groups (Mallory 1989, Masson 1991). Related to Armenian and Greek, it also shows affinities to Thracian and Illyrian. The Phrygians adapted the Graeco-Phoenician alphabet for public inscriptions and dedications, examples of which can be found on rock-cut monuments at Midas City in the Phrygian highlands (Fig. 56)(approximately 120 kilometers east of Gordion); on wax dedications adhering to bronze vessels found in the Midas Mound tumulus at Gordion; and on other media throughout central Anatolia, even an inscribed spindle whorl from Akhisar, near Manisa (Dinç and Innocente 1999). One of the rock-cut inscriptions at Midas City shows that the Phrygians retained the use of the two highest Mycenaean titles, *wanax* (Phrygian *vanaktei*) and *lawagetas* (*lavagtaei*), in reference to their great king, Midas (Fig. 57)(Mellink 1965; Brixhe and Lejeune 1984, 6–9 (M-01a); De Graaf 1989; Vassileva 2006). These inscribed titles on the façade at Midas City, both in the dative, refer to the time when Midas held both of these positions, 'king or lord' (*vanaktei*), and 'leader of the people' (*lavagtaei*), perhaps implying some military aspect. The chronology for the façade, however, is debated (see DeVries 1988, 53–59, especially note 13): some have proposed that the façades should be dated to the historical Midas of the late 8th century, known from Classical sources (*e.g.*, Hdt. 1.14.35) and from Near Eastern correspondences in the Annals of Sargon II (Huxley 1959); others date the monuments to the 6th century BC and associate it with a successor to the famous Midas (Mellink 1991; Sams 1994). In either case, it should be stressed that the retention of the two titles found in Mycenaean Greek shows a strong continuity and connection between Phrygia and mainland Greece, bridging the Late Bronze Age Aegean and Iron Age Anatolia.

Craft Residues

Literary and historical references to Gordion, the Phrygians, and King Midas help us to understand the cultural context of the great textile industry preserved in the Early Phrygian destruction level. Nothing comparable to the Mycenaean Linear B documents

Figure 56. Phrygian inscription, Arezastis Monument, 7th century BC, Midas City (B. Burke).

Figure 57. Midas façade, 7th century BC, Midas City, 1961 (MJM-01802 © Mellink Archive, Bryn Mawr College).

(or Minoan Linear A) describing the resources and labor organization, however, has been found, and consequently we must rely on the archaeological indicators of craft activity, meaning workshop spaces and craft residues, for a reconstruction of the textile industry. The majority of the finds occurs in the Terrace Buildings (TB) and Clay Cut (CC) area of the Citadel Mound at Gordion and will be described in detail below. The masses of loom weights, spindle whorls, and other tools found in the destruction level of Gordion provide the best archaeological evidence for specialized production of textiles at any site in the Mediterranean region.

Phrygian textiles had a great reputation in antiquity: Strabo (7.6.16; 8.4.14) and Pliny, (*HN* 9.133), among others, refer to the long tradition of skilled weavers and dyers in western Phrygia. Pliny (*HN* 8.74.196) credits the invention of embroidery, decorating textiles with needle and thread designs, to the Phrygians. The assertion that they invented the technology is proven false by finds in Egypt which date to the second millennium BC, earlier than any Phrygian cloth. As Barber (1991, 158–62) has shown, the art of embroidery/tapestry was probably a Syrian technology, appearing suddenly in Egypt after Thutmose III's sack of Megiddo. Although no examples of true embroidery have been found among the Gordion textile assemblages, there are fragments of wool and linen cloth preserved in the

many tumuli surrounding the site and in the destruction level of the citadel itself (Fig. 58). Impressive textile pieces were found in the southeast corner of the largest and most elaborate structure at Gordion, Megaron 3. The fragmentary material is more properly the field of textile conservators and material scientists and can not be adequately discussed in great detail here. In this study of Phrygian economics and craft organization, a preliminary summary of the excavated textile fragments as it relates to cloth production is presented in Appendix 4.1.

Spindle Whorls

Spindle whorls provide us with information about ancient thread, and by extension, qualities of cloth. Lighter whorls

Figure 58. Textile fragments from Gordion (© University Museum, Gordion Archives).

were most probably used for spinning wool, while the heavier outlying whorls could have been used for plying or spinning flax fibers together. Thread can be spun in two directions: with the fiber held vertically in front of the spinner, the whorl and spindle are spun clockwise or counterclockwise. Textile specialists refer to the resulting thread as Z-spun and S-spun, based on the direction of the spun thread following the direction of the central part of the letters, Z or S. According to Ellis, all the fibers from the Gordion tumuli seem to be spun in the Z-direction. Once spun, however, two threads are twisted together but in the S-direction, with a fairly tight angle of twist of about 45 degrees (Ellis 1981, 296).

Spindle whorls recovered from Early Phrygian Gordion number well over one thousand (Fig. 59). These fired clay weights were most likely attached to the end of a wooden spindle and used for drawing out and spinning together wool or linen fibers into usable thread. None of the whorls from the Terrace and Clay Cut buildings showed signs of distinctive decoration. Most examples were asymmetrical, biconical whorls with fairly smooth surfaces. Some had a mica slip. Even though many of the whorls were severely damaged by fire, some revealed traces of vegetable temper in a fairly standardized fabric. In cataloguing these whorls from Gordion I was able to distinguish ten different types, based solely on the shape and profile of the whorls (Fig. 60). Type one was by far the most common, followed by types three and nine. After examining the entire Early Phrygian assemblage of whorls, however, and looking at the distribution of shapes, no discernible pattern was found based on the types of shape. Spindle whorl typologies, such as the 31 types proposed by Blegen for the Early Bronze Age Trojan whorls, seem geared toward distinguishing chronological and cultural affiliation with the whorl-shape types (Blegen 1950, table 128; Balfanz 1995, table 4). The whorls from the destruction level at Gordion are all of the same time period and culture, *i.e.* Early Phrygian. For this reason, and because of the large numbers of whorls, the main classification system used here is based on the weight of the whorls, in ten-gram weight intervals. This, in the end, seems the most meaningful method for reconstructing the types of threads and textiles being produced at Gordion.

The whorls range in weight from very small, almost bead-like, to so large that some may actually have functioned as light loom weights. The average weight of a spindle whorl from Gordion was twenty-four grams but the typical one weighed less than twenty grams – fairly light, and

Figure 59. Early Phrygian spindle whorls from Destruction Level, 800 BC (B. Burke).

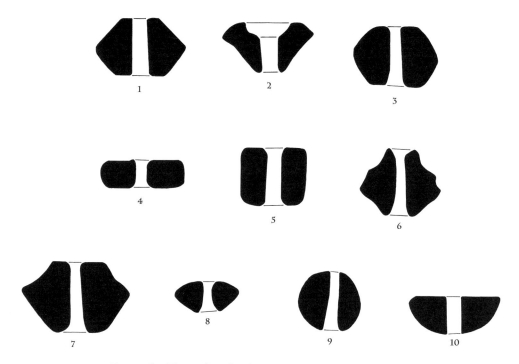

Figure 60. Types of Early Phrygian spindle whorls, 800 BC.

probably used for spinning finer thread. While ethnographic studies of spinners suggest that experienced spinners can spin with a broad range of whorl weights, a lighter weight whorl is preferred for finer thread (Parsons 1972, 65; 1975; Parsons and Parsons 1990, 314–5; Anderson and Nosch 2003). Heavier whorls were more likely used to ply two or more threads together, suitable for weaving fairly heavy textiles.

Loom Weights

The loom weights from Gordion are often referred to as 'doughnuts' because of their round shape and large central hole (Fig. 61). Other shapes of loom weight occur at Gordion in nearly every occupation level but none in such large numbers as the Early Phrygian doughnuts. Catalogued examples vary in quality of preservation probably because all of the weights were originally sun-dried clay from the banks of the Sakarya River and were only preserved accidentally in the fire that destroyed the Citadel in the late ninth century BC. Straw and small pebbles were mixed in with the clay as a kind of temper (Fig. 62). Only a small percentage of the recorded loom weights from Gordion were available for study, as most had either been discarded or deteriorated in storage. Oddly, the two most substantial deposits that were preserved well enough for detailed study were the first and last sets of Phrygian loom weights discovered at Gordion. One assemblage was found in

Figure 61. Crate of Early Phrygian loom weights, 800 BC (B. Burke).

Clay Cut 1, found in 1952, and the other from the anteroom of Terrace Building 2, excavated in 1989. The weights were handmade and fairly coarse. Selected weights and whorls were studied by Johnston in the late 1960s for their ceramic composition (Johnston 1970, 224–242). The various shapes of Gordion loom weights were ovoid, conical, and cylindrical, and like the spindles whorls the shape was probably not related to different weaving technologies. The average weight was around 500 grams. The majority of weights ranged from 400 to 700 grams. These are fairly heavy weights for weaving and suggest that the cloth being made in the workshop units was fairly thick and heavy cloth, probably not fine or elaborate fabrics.

Figure 62. Early Phrygian loom weight, 800 BC (B. Burke).

The shape of the Gordion loom weights, unlike that of some loom weights from antiquity, suggests that warp-threads were directly attached to the unfired clay weights, through the central hole. At least fifteen warp threads could be attached to each loom weight (Fig. 63). The two examples from the Terrace

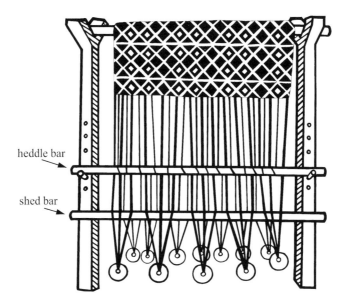

heddle bar

shed bar

Figure 63. Reconstruction of Early Phrygian warp-weighted loom (B. Burke, G. Hill).

Buildings of loom weights found in a row, as if the loom were still standing at the time of destruction, suggest that the looms used about twenty weights each, in two rows for two warp sheds. Various deposits of weights as recorded in the notebooks will be described below.

Ivory and Bone Implements

Flat bone bobbins dating to the Early Phrygian level come from the Terrace and Clay Cut buildings. These flat, pointed implements have long notched heads and may have been used to pass the weft threads back and forth through the warp and for punching small holes in cloth and leather. Pointed implements and awls of bone were also found in the Citadel Mound of Gordion. Descriptions of the bone shuttles and punches from the destruction level at Gordion, based on Sheftel's catalogue (1974), are incorporated into the discussion of each room in which they were found.

Iron and Bronze Tools

Along with the clay finds of spindle whorls and loom weights and the bone and ivory tools, the destruction level at Gordion yielded a significant number of bronze and iron implements which are likely associated with textile production (McClellan 1975). Needles differing in shape and size suggest various uses such as stitching fine cloth, working heavier materials like leather, and carrying out different techniques such as over-casting (Fig. 64). The eyes of the iron needles, though often obscured by rust, seem to have been made by 'drawing the needle to a point and then bending it down against the shank, to form a thin loop', leaving the eye in the shape of an elongated oval (McClellan 1975, 655). The self-soldering character of iron makes this the preferred eye technique. That many of the needles were found with spindle whorls and loom weights, some in the same vessel, suggests that these were kits for textile workers. The rolled hems and other stitches on cloth from the tumuli and Citadel Mound further attest to the use of needles in Phrygian textiles. Although Pliny incorrectly asserted that the Phrygians invented the art of embroidery, we can safely assume that they did know of the technique. In addition, plaques of bronze with holes along the edges, scales of an iron corselet, a cheek piece of a helmet, and fragments of leather shoes all demonstrate that needles were used on a variety of materials at Gordion.

Two iron needles, one very thick and the other slightly curved, were also found at Midas City (Haspels 1972, pl. 42d, 2, 4). All iron needles from Hattusas (Boğazköy) come from Phrygian levels and are comparable in form and manufacture to the Gordion examples (Boehmer 1972, pl 49, 1351–4, 1361–2). From contemporary Iron Age levels at Alishar iron needles are both slit-eyed and looped (Schmidt 1930, 99, fig. 70; Von der

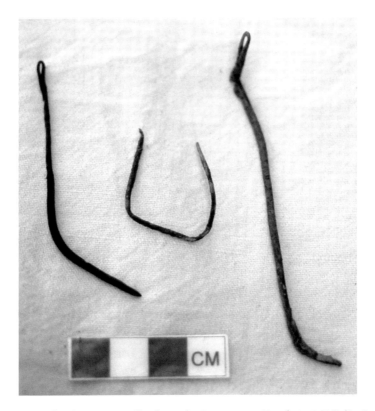

Figure 64. Early Phrygian needles from the Destruction Level, 800 BC (B. Burke).

Osten 1937, 179, figs 200, 203). Interestingly, at these sites, and in the Aegean and the Near East, bronze needles far outnumber the iron examples. As mentioned earlier, bronze needles were also found at Gordion but not cataloged by McClellan. She states that these needles were not associated with other tools for sewing or weaving, but are similar in form to the iron examples (McClellan 1975, 656).

A substantial number of bronze and iron knives were also found in the Terrace and Clay Cut buildings (Fig. 65). They often occur with spindle whorls, needles and ceramic vessels. The knives are either straight or slightly concave in shape with an interior sharp edge. They range in length from about eight to twelve centimeters. The bases of these knives often have pegs for hafting them to wooden, or possibly bone, handles. The majority of them were found in the more northern work room units, TB 7, TB 8, and CC 3.

The large numbers of iron and bronze knives found in the Gordion excavations were possibly used to cut the knotted threads of piled carpet weaves. The shape and size of these blades is appropriate to a hand-held tool used for cutting wool thread. The earliest indications for pile carpet technology come from a special type of bronze knife found in women's graves in the Sumbar Valley, east of the Caspian Sea, dating to the late third millennium BC (Khlopin 1982; Böhmer and Thompson 1991). The earliest known examples of pile carpets come from the astounding burials in Pazyryk, Siberia (Böhmer and Thompson 1991). The origins of these carpets, which date to *c*. 500 BC and bear

Figure 65. Early Phrygian knives from the Destruction Level, 800 BC (B. Burke).

Achaemenid and Greek designs, have been traced to Lydia by Greenewalt and Majewski (1980). That the true origin for this type of textile might be found in Phrygia is another possibility. The knives from Gordion have their inner blades sharpened, in contrast to those found in southern Russia, but their association with warp-woven textiles and their hand-held size may indicate carpet production in the Terrace and Clay Cut units. The decorative patterns found in the mosaic of Megaron 2, discussed below, imitate thrown Anatolian rugs, as is commonly found in mosques today and noted by Young (1965). The small, multi-colored patterns of the great mosaic are certainly suggestive of pile carpets. The hand-tied knots of thread on pile rugs can easily vary in color and design, much more so than on tapestry.

The actual fragments of cloth found at Gordion show that the Phrygians valued high quality textiles. Along with making these fine textiles, we know that Phrygian craftsmen excelled at wooden furniture production, ivory carving and fine metal work. These goods of high quality were most likely used in elite settings, as exemplified by the funerary gifts accompanying the man buried in the great Midas Mound. Gifts of this type could also have functioned as items of exchange with other rulers and officials, bestowing Phrygian authority and approval. This tradition of gift exchange also extended to the sphere of religious dedications, and we are reminded that King Midas is the first foreigner to send dedications to the Greek sanctuary of Delphi (Hdt. 1.14).

Contexts of Production
The Elite Quarter

Within the massive fortification walls of Gordion, excavations have revealed the characteristic Phrygian building form, called the megaron after similarly shaped buildings in the Aegean. The best evidence for organized cloth production anywhere in the Mediterranean is found in these structures which are composed of a single-stepped entrance leading to an anteroom and a main hall behind, often with a hearth located near the center of the room. In this section, I cover in detail the organization of the Gordion citadel because this defines the work area for a massive textile industry of the late ninth century BC in Anatolia.

Defined by courtyard surfaces and internal enclosure walls, the excavated portions of the Phrygian citadel divide into three principal zones: the Palace area, the workshops, and possibly a storage area. The eastern area of the excavations is thought to be the residential quarter of the elite because of the elaborate nature of the freestanding megaron buildings and the luxury goods found within. The monumental Phrygian gateway, located at the southeast, leads the visitor in a direct east-west line through the gate structure, formerly known as the Polychrome House, to a reception area before the first of two courtyards. The entry through the Phrygian gate creates an obtuse angle to the orientation of the main Phrygian buildings, causing the visitor to turn sharply to the right on approach to this first courtyard.

An interior enclosure wall of mud brick was built from the south side-wall of Megaron 1 to the south side-wall of Megaron 9, defining the outer courtyard with its stone-slab paving (Sams 1994, 2). This thin wall was probably a temporary, makeshift enclosure

Figure 66. Megaron 2, Mosaic Building, from the Destruction Level, 800 BC (©University Museum, Gordion Archives).

while renovations to the fortifications were being carried out (DeVries 1990, 387–8). Four freestanding megarons, two on each side, face this area: Megarons 9 and 10 to the east and Megarons 1 and 2 along the west side.

Megaron 1, also known as the Burnt Phrygian Building or the Brick Building, was constructed of mud-brick and wooden timbers and found fairly well-preserved after the conflagration. The building was found relatively empty of goods. The storerooms between the back wall of Megaron 1 and the terrace wall contained some interesting finds, including a jar with 494 astragals (sheep knucklebones), wheat and barley in storage, and the occasional loom weight and spindle whorl (DeVries 1980, 37).

Megaron 2, the Phrygian Mosaic Building or West Phrygian House, was constructed of soft limestone blocks within vertical wooden timber supports. Two small rooms with wooden plank floors flank the threshold to the main room. On the exterior of the walls were rock-cut doodles and graffiti, with both abstract and representational images of birds, humans and building facades (Young 1969, Roller 1987, 1996). These designs may be the casual doodles of people awaiting an official audience, but perhaps the hawk and lion graffiti are evidence for a cultic significance of Megaron 2, dedicated perhaps to an Anatolian mother goddess such as Kybele. The building certainly is special: the main room of Megaron 2 was decorated with one of the earliest known pebble mosaics from

Figure 67. Drawing of mosaic in Megaron 2, by J. Last (Young 1965, p. 11 ©University Museum, Gordion Archives).

antiquity (Figs 66–67). Multi-colored river stones were laid in various patterns, which imitate textile designs. Unfortunately, Megaron buildings 1 and 2 were mostly emptied of their contents at the time of destruction, making further interpretation of the building's function difficult.

Another more substantial dividing wall separates the exterior court from the second one toward the north. Approximately one-third of this dividing wall between Megarons 2 and 3 was demolished when the terrace for the TB and CC rooms was constructed. Through this propylon the visitor entered the most elite area of the citadel, Megaron Buildings 3 and 4, which faced a pebble court and lay in the same orientation as Megarons 1 and 2, facing east. Megaron buildings 11 and 12 ran perpendicular across the courtyard facing north.

Megaron Building 3 is by far the most impressive of all the excavated buildings at Gordion. Its large size required two rows of interior support posts along the side and back walls, presumably supporting a balcony (see Dyson 1980). This building contained very wealthy items, including ivory furniture, fine bronze and clay vessels, a deposit of gold pieces which may be pre-stamped coinage, and finely woven textiles (DeVries 1980, 34–7). Three sides of the exterior walls of Megaron 3 were buried to a depth of nearly 2 m by the piling of terrace fill on the north, south and west.

Megaron 4 was less impressive than Megaron 3 and of fairly simple architecture. Measuring 22 by 12.3 m, the building was entered from the east by a steep ramp covered with cobbled paving. It was constructed entirely of brick, without the vertical and horizontal timber supports of the other megaron units. It may have been one of the last Early Phrygian buildings constructed before the great destruction since it was constructed on an extension of the terrace fill after the TB rooms and at a level higher than Megaron 3. A flight of stairs was also excavated at the northwest corner of the front of the building. These steps led down to the terrace which supported Megaron 5 at a lower level.

The burned deposit was also very thick in Megaron 4, but, unlike the other Megaron units, the debris was highly disturbed, with pieces of joining pottery found in highly disparate places. Luxury finds were also reported from this building, including a large gold figure-eight plate probably once attached to a wooden box or a piece of furniture. An ivory appliqué of two horses running abreast and a mounted rider holding reins gives a good representation of Phrygian horse trappings (Kohler 1962). In addition, there were about twenty-five spindle whorls found in the main room of this building. Behind Megaron 4, a storeroom similar to that behind Megaron 1 contained some interesting items, including hazelnuts and approximately seventy-five doughnut-shaped loom weights.

To the north of Megaron 3 and 4, an earlier phase of the citadel was excavated but the buildings were found mostly emptied of their contents (Sams 1994, 15, DeVries 1987; 1990, 374–7). These remains date to the Early Iron Age, well before the destruction ca. 800 BC. Named Megarons 6, 7 and 8, these buildings are believed to have housed textile and cooking facilities similar to the later Phrygian buildings built perpendicular to them on a large terrace discussed extensively below. Megarons 7 and 8 contained an oven and other food preparation equipment as well as evidence for textile production. As DeVries (1990, 376) points out, already in the early Iron Age, a strong differentiation in function between areas in the Citadel Mound was distinguished. Presumably, a growing economy dictated the demolition of these buildings for an even larger workshop space while still retaining the basic megaron plan and similar functional features. This organized expansion on the built-up terrace behind the Megaron buildings indicates strongly that the activities located in them, cooking and weaving, were of vital importance to the ruling elites.

The Industrial Quarter

Some of the back walls of the elite buildings (Megarons 1–4) served as a retaining wall for the terrace fill upon which the workshop units were built (Sams 1994, 3). Areas between the terrace fill and Megarons 1 and 2 were partitioned into storage areas, as was mentioned.

The entire elevated area seems to have been an industrial center for Phrygian textile and food production, and will be examined in detail below. Farther to the north of these workshops was the so-called Persian-Phrygian Building (PPB). This building was the only Early Phrygian building to be reused in the later Middle Phrygian period. What remains of the PPB is a cluster of rooms without entrances; they are thought to be basement rooms. The PPB was not destroyed by the Early Phrygian destruction level but continued in use after the devastating fire. Further research into these units will help us to better understand the organization of space at Gordion.

In an early report, Young (1958) briefly refers to the 'South Phrygian House' behind the megaron units. The two meter high terrace upon which this 'house' was built is also noted. The pottery found upside-down in stored in stacks rather than in use and revealed fragments of wicker baskets at the bottom. This room marks a transition between two different areas of the citadel: the elite quarters of the Megaron buildings, and the industrial workshop area on the terrace behind.

For the expansion of the citadel that replaced Megarons 6–8, an extensive terrace approximately two meters high was constructed behind the back walls of Megarons 1–4, perpendicular to the demolished megaron buildings. This terrace left limited access to the elite quarter of the megaron buildings in the central court. On it were two very long buildings subdivided into nearly identical megaron units all in a row, with party walls 1.5 m thick. Twelve individual units have been uncovered to varying degrees, and all include a main room and anteroom and measure approximately 11.5 m in width by 21 m in interior length (Fig. 68). The main rooms are about twice the length of the anterooms. The buildings are of different colored sandstone and limestone, with courses of stone, wood, and mud brick. The entire extent of one, called the Terrace Building (TB), has been fully excavated to its length of 105 m. Six workshop units and two storage rooms of nearly identical megaron plan (TB 1–8) subdivide it. All of the main rooms have two rows of four post-holes with a central one between the pair closest to the back of the room. These posts would have supported a second story wooden gallery which surrounded the room on three sides. Twenty meters to the southwest, across a broad street, is the parallel building named the Clay Cut (CC), presumably of the same length as the facing Terrace Building although only portions of four megaron units have been excavated. The two very large buildings were planned and constructed together relatively late in the Early Phrygian period, during one very ambitious program sometime in the late tenth or early ninth century BC

The excavation of each Terrace Building and Clay Cut unit is described below. The Terrace Building and Clay Cut structure were excavated between 1956 and 1989 by many different excavators and in over a dozen different excavation notebooks kept at the Gordion Archives of the University of Pennsylvania. Young at first thought these rooms were the kitchens or pantries of a large palace, comparable perhaps to palaces of the Aegean and the Near East. He did not realize that these were a series of identical rooms of two massive buildings until later. For this reason, the nomenclature for the Terrace Building rooms changed over time, making the various reports even more complicated. Some of the notebooks also refer to trenches in an unsystematic manner rather than by the architectural features within those trenches. One needs to be aware of the many aliases for the Early Phrygian structures at

Figure 68. Terrace Building from South (B. Burke).

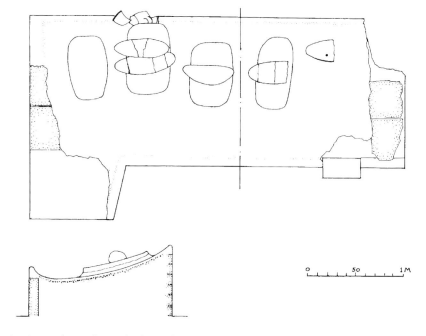

Figure 69. Typical grinding platform from Terrace Building, Destruction Level, 800 BC (© University Museum, Gordion Archive).

Gordion to understand their publication. Compass directions are also problematic in the description of each room since the buildings run askew of true north-south, slightly east of north and west of south. Some of the excavation notebooks for the Terrace Building refer to the back of the rooms as the northern end, with the anterooms to the south. With the Clay Cut rooms, the orientation is a mirror image of the Terrace Building, yet the first two rooms excavated, CC 1 and CC 2, are referred to as the South and North rooms respectively, shifting the conventional orientation once again. While this all seems very confusing, the basic layout of each room is very predictable and the reader can easily follow the excavators' references in consultation with a plan. For the sake of clarity in the discussion below, most references to north in the Terrace Building rooms will be in the direction of the back walls. Each room provides a valuable context for cloth production and by looking at the tools as they were found in each workshop unit we can reconstruct many aspects of the Phrygian cloth industry.

Textile equipment, food processing installations, and large quantities of pottery were the main finds from the Terrace Buildings. Features related to food working included saddle querns and kneading trays (Fig. 69), along with the charred seeds and grains of some of the foods being prepared. The plant remains included wheat, barley, lentils, hazelnuts, and cornelian cherries. The anterooms usually had one or two round dome ovens of brick and clay, a U-shaped construction of crude brick presumably for broiling, and a round, stuccoed hearth. The only exceptions were the anterooms of TB 1 and 2, which also lacked grinding facilities in the main rooms. These rooms did, however, have evidence for textile production, including loom weights and spindle whorls (Fig. 70).

Terrace Building 1 and Anteroom
Excavations along the northern and western sides of TB 1 began in 1961. The entire room was excavated in 1963. The room is referred to as E2, the Phrygian Room. Digging burnt fill in the northwest corner, the excavators comment on the well-preserved, greenish wall-plaster on both the North and West walls. Along the west wall, the excavators discovered a large pile of doughnut-shaped loom weights. A conservative estimate puts the total number at 300 weights in the burnt fill. Found in the SE quarter of the main room, in level 7, described as the top of the burnt fill down to and including the floor, some 95 more loom weights of varying sizes and shapes were found. The floor was cleaned and photographed with pottery and loom weights *in situ*. Five loom weight deposits in the northwest corner of the main room were labeled A through E and sketched. Heap A contained 'hundreds', heaps B and C totaled up to 27, heap D contained 23, and heap E, 45. The excavator notes that the loom weights in these piles are of varying sizes and shapes, as were the other loom weights found in the burnt Phrygian fill of this room. It is difficult to reconstruct what this deposit looked like, since the excavation notebook records shapeless masses of objects in certain parts of the room. The number of loom weights reported, however, 23, 27, and 45, may be the number of weights for single looms, or perhaps two looms for heap E. The total number of loom weights found in the northern half of the main room in TB1, including those in piles on the floor, is recorded at 742, the vast majority of which were discovered near the West wall. This is the largest

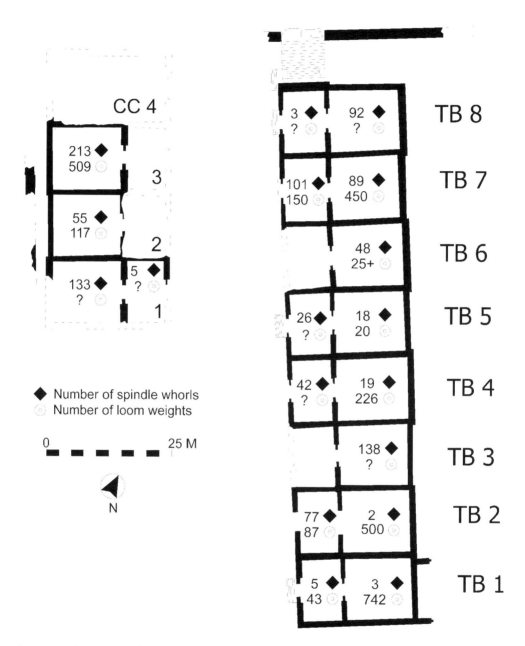

Figure 70. Terrace Building and Clay Cut Building with distribution of loom weights and spindle whorls in Destruction Level, 800 BC (B. Burke, K. Lehmann Insuwa).

number of loom weights from one room. In contrast, only three spindle whorls can be associated with this main room.

The excavation of the Anteroom of Terrace Building 1 (TB 1 A), from the 1963 season, is less well described than that of the main room. Trenches TB-E2 S1 and S2 include the anteroom. In this room spindle whorls were found along with painted sherds and 43 doughnut-shaped loom weights. Again this number of weights may indicate one or two looms. Young states that 'the excavation yielded little more than ordinary interest.' Only five spindle whorls from this anteroom excavation can be located. At the time when excavation of TB 1 began, five of the other Terrace Building rooms were already known. The main aim of the 1962 season was to find an eastern face and corner for this series of rooms on the terrace. As Young states in the season report (1964, 285), 'The Terrace Building was thus shown to have been a single unit consisting of a series of rooms each opening in the same direction to an open area, presumably a street.'

What is most striking about TB 1, however, is what features are missing in comparison to most of the other Terrace Building rooms. While loom weights are abundant in TB 1, there is a curious scarcity of spindle whorls reported from the anteroom of TB 1 and the main rooms of both TB 1 and 2. Neither of these units (1 and 2) had grinding facilities or cooking installations and they clearly had a different function from the other rooms. Young describes the main room of TB 1 as 'an elegant apartment rather than a workroom' (1962, 167). Some finds in this room, however, suggest that it was a storehouse for more valuable items. Among the recorded finds from the main room, for example, is one small rim fragment of a large bronze cauldron. The fragment is bent and the whole cauldron, undoubtedly, was badly crushed in the destruction of the building. Four other bronze cauldrons were found in this room, with bull-protome attachments (Edwards 1963, 45). A bronze goat and furniture tacks were also found in this room. In the anteroom, too, a heavy bronze cauldron with ring handles of iron was found.

Terrace Building 2 and Anteroom

The excavation and detailed record keeping of the finds from this room make it the best example for a detailed analysis of textile equipment. The northern corner of the main room of this building, also known as the TB East Room, was first uncovered in 1957 during the excavation of TB 3, the so-called 'Kitchen'. The trenches for this room were labeled TBT 4-5-6 and are sketched in Notebook (NB) 46. About 100 loom weights were found on the eastern side of the room, and about 25 were found in the south-eastern quarter. Approximately 375 more loom weights were found in other parts of this room, totaling over 500 (Young 1964). The weight measurements of the loom weights, unfortunately, are not recorded and the weights themselves could not be found in the pottery depots at the Gordion dig house. As in the main room of TB 1, very few spindle whorls are reported from this room; only two whorls were found from the Phrygian destruction level in TB 2. A flat bone implement from TB 2 may also be related to textile production if, for example, it was used as a weft-bobbin. Weft thread would be wrapped around the body of the object and then gradually unwind as it was fed through the warp threads.

Other finds from the main room give the impression that TB 1 and 2 were used for storage of valuable items. Find from here include a bronze animal on a plinth, at least two bronze goats, an animal with a bird, tweezers, tacks, and fibulae, some made of precious materials like silver, electrum, and gold. Fragments of an ivory frontlet in the form of a 'mistress of animals' (potnia theron) were found, as were blinkers in the form of a sphinx. Glass beads and other items add to the impression of an artisans store room.

The anteroom of TB 2 was uncovered in 1989 in the renewed excavations directed by Mary Voigt. With careful stratigraphic analysis, Voigt has reconstructed the depositional sequence after the destructive fire (Voigt 1994, 272–3). We can safely extrapolate from this reading a similar pattern of destruction for all of the other Terrace Building rooms, because of the total and simultaneous nature of the structure's collapse. Stone and brick rested upon fire-damaged artifacts on the floor immediately adjacent to the walls of TB 2 A. This primary collapse layer decreased in thickness toward the center of the room. Above this layer and resting on the plaster floor were the remains of the charred roof debris. The roof seems to have been made of wooden beams covered by reed matting and then mud plaster. These remains were fairly well preserved, which suggests to Voigt that the roof debris was not exposed for very long after the initial fire-destruction, meaning a fairly quick rebuilding in the Middle Phrygian period. Eroded brick material and additional wall slabs lay on top of the roof collapse. In the center of the room was a concentration of stone blocks lying horizontally, while along the southern wall, collapsed wall blocks lay vertically.

In total, 87 typical doughnut-shaped, clay loom weights were excavated in 1989. The average weight for the loom weights from TB 2 A was 557 grams, with sixty percent falling in the range of 400–700 grams. The distribution of their weights shows that standardization or uniformity was not strictly adhered to although there was a general range.

One interesting aspect of the loom weights was the change in the recorded weight of each one over a short period of time after excavation. These unintentionally fired weights absorbed moisture once buried in the destruction level and sealed by the later clay rebuilding level. Upon excavation they began to dry out and consequently lose weight. Many of the thousands of reported loom weights from the destruction level were discarded during Rodney Young's excavations because it was thought that they would not survive in storage. Studying the relatively recently excavated doughnuts from the 1989 season, we can see that this was an accurate assumption. Since excavation, many of the poorly fired weights have simply dried out and disintegrated into small mounds of clay and dust. The absorption and evaporation of moisture affected the measured weights to varying degrees. Many of the weights recorded initially in 1989 decreased dramatically in weight by 1996. For example, one weight decreased by as much as 91 grams between 1989 and 1996.

Along with the loom weights in the Anteroom of TB 2 were found 77 spindle whorls (Table 5). The number of whorls in the anteroom is slightly puzzling because of the scarcity of spindle whorls in the other rooms of TB 1 and 2. Perhaps the absence is attributable to incomplete record keeping by the excavators, and to the fact that the excavations were carried out over a long period of time by a large number of people. Of the whorls that we do have from TB 2 Anteroom the largest percentage weighed between 10 and 20 grams, approximately 37 percent. The majority of the whorls weighed less than twenty grams. This is less than the average weight of the whorls from all of the Terrace Building rooms. Some of the spindle whorls were found in groups or clusters. These groups were probably stored in ceramic vessels often found nearby along with metal needles and knives, presumably used in textile production. These whorls are particularly interesting because they may reflect the spinning kits of individual workers. Most of the measured weights of these groups showed a fairly broad range. The Phrygian spinners seem to have used a variety of weighted whorls, probably for different qualities of thread, as is demonstrated by the variety of textile samples preserved at Gordion. One set of thirteen whorls ranged from three to thirty-eight grams. All were of the same pink-orange clay, and they weighed an average of 13 grams. Whorls of another set were found together in pot YH33668 and were made of the same fabric as the other whorls from this room. The measured weights were fairly uniform, ranging only from ten to fourteen grams.

Among the textile equipment was a carefully made comb found in the anteroom of TB 2 (Fig 71). This heavily charred, long-toothed comb is certainly associated with textile production since it has unwoven warp threads adhering to one side and woven textile on the other (Bier 1995). Its use in weaving suggests that it would have had a fairly smooth surface and was probably made out of fine wood, now charred. The comb is catalogued as YH33701, small find 89–583, from locus 100, lot 211, 8/21/89. It had a plain top

Table 5. Terrace Building 2 Anteroom spindle whorls, Gordion.

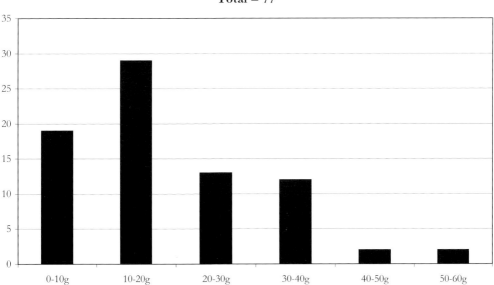

Figure 71. Weaving comb from anteroom of Terrace Building 2, wood, YH33701, SF 89–583, c. 800 BC (B. Burke).

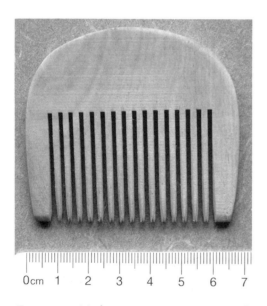

Figure 72. Modern Japanese weaving comb, wood (B. Burke).

and sides with a slightly curved row of teeth perhaps not unlike a modern weavers comb from Japan (Fig. 72). Although it is very fragmentary this find is remarkable because it was clearly in use at the time of destruction. The comb could have been used on a warp-weighted loom or used for band-weaving. The relatively small size of the object from Gordion, approximately 6 cm wide, suggests that it would be used for making small, decorated bands. This comb and the loom weights found within TB 2A are the clearest indicators for cloth production at Gordion at the time of destruction.

As was mentioned above, the first two Terrace Building rooms (TB 1 and 2) were thought to be storage houses, possibly even treasuries. Valuable caches of exotic material were found within, particularly in TB 2. While TB 1 and 2 seem to have been used for storage of wealth items of precious metals and ivory, the cluster of twenty to forty plus loom weights and other tools, including the wooden comb, indicate that weaving occurred even in these rooms.

Terrace Building 3
This workshop was the first of the Terrace Building rooms excavated and portions of the back wall and cross-wall between TB 3 and 4 were uncovered during the 1955 campaign. Based on the utilitarian objects found here, including grinding stones – four pairs were found neatly arranged with boat-shaped upper grinders still in situ along the west end of the north wall, loom weights, spindle whorls, and great quantities of pottery, Young called this room the 'kitchen'. It was known by several other names over the years, including the 'pantry', TB Central Room, TBT 3, and TB W.

In the main room of TB 3, 138 spindle whorls were found with an average weight of 21 grams (Table 6). A few outliers weighed upwards of fifty grams. Fifty-eight percent of these spindle whorls weighed less than twenty grams. One cluster found together had eight whorls and three needles, contained together in a cloth sack which was found inside a Phrygian pinch-pot. These eight whorls were very light compared to other spindle whorls in the room; five were the same weight, five grams each; one was eight grams, the next ten, and the final whorl weighed twelve grams. The range of only seven grams suggests a fairly

Table 6. Terrace Building 3 spindle whorls, Gordion.

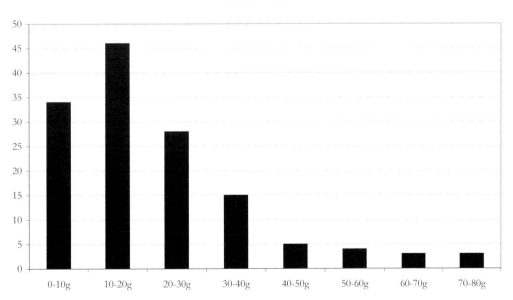

TB 3 Whorls by 10 gram groups
Total = 138

uniform weight and probably indicates that fine thread was spun in this room. Another group of whorls was found with eight needles, which are catalogued by J. McClellan (1975). In addition, two bronze knives with curved blades were found.

Young (1956) mentions a great many loom weights found in the main room of TB 3. Unfortunately there is not a total number given and none of the weights themselves have survived in the storage areas at Gordion for analysis. In comparison to the other main rooms with substantial deposits of loom weights from the Terrace and Clay Cut Buildings, an estimate of approximately 500 loom weights for TB 3 would not be unexpected. The anteroom has not yet been excavated.

Terrace Building 4 and Anteroom
The main room of this Terrace building unit is also known as TB West Room, and TB W1 (Table 7). From Young's notes in NB 67 (1957, 78), we get some understanding of the excavation of this room. He writes, 'We finish digging the burned fill... [finding] more whorls, doughnuts and iron knives. To recount in detail would be tedious.' A total of 226 loom weights and 19 spindle whorls were found in the main room. Seven grinding stands were at the back of the main room, and there was the brick outline of a bin nearby that probably contained whole grain.

The excavation notebooks mention the clearing of the east wall and an assortment of small clay whorls found in a jug. The whorls had evidently been contained in a cloth bag since a few scraps of cloth were found still inside the jug. On average, the whorls in TB 4 and the Anteroom of TB 4 (Table 8) are much heavier than those from other rooms, weighing 35 grams, over ten grams heavier than the average for all the Terrace Building whorls. Eighty-four percent of the whorls from TB 4 weighed more than twenty grams.

Given the central location of this work room along the row, and the heavier whorls found inside, I would propose that the spinning done in this room was the plying together of two finer threads into one larger one, which would be suitable for heavier weaving. This also seems particularly likely given the heaviness of the doughnut-shaped loom weights found here, weighing upwards of 600 grams. We know from the textile finds in the Phrygian buildings and tombs at Gordion that much of the thread was two-ply; that is, fiber spun into one strand of thread was then spun together with another thread to make a stronger, thicker yarn. These heavy spindle whorls from TB 4 may well indicate such plying.

Two further explanations for this kind of spinning in TB 4 are possible. Firstly, the task of plying already spun thread together is a fairly simple one that may be assigned to younger, less experienced spinners as a kind of practice. If this is indeed the case, then the central location of this workroom, TB 4, would seem to be a good place to monitor such junior spinners. The other possibility is that this simpler task was assigned to workers of a slightly higher status, and possibly of an older age, who could in turn monitor the workers on either side of them.

The quality of other goods found in TB 4 is higher than that of what was found in the other workrooms. A cloth and leather piece was found folded up with both faces decorated with rows of bronze studs. This material was found 3.5 m from the south wall and 0.75 m from the west wall, 13 cm above the floor. Its total size is approximately 0.5 m by 0.3 m,

Table 7. Terrace Building 4 spindle whorls, Gordion.

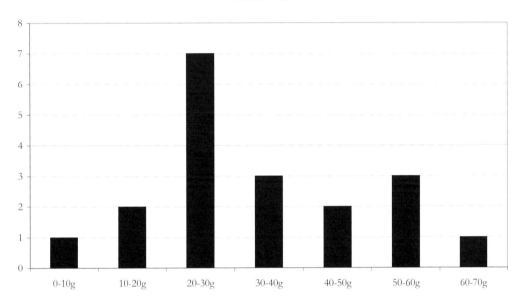

Table 8. Terrace Building 4 Anteroom spindle whorls, Gordion.

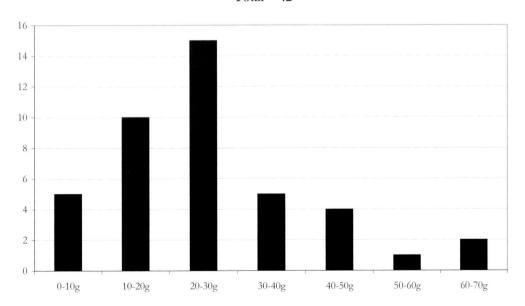

Figure 73. Terrace Building 5, 1961 (MJM-01725 © Mellink Archive, Bryn Mawr College).

and it seems that it had either fallen from the wall or been purposely placed over some pots. A fine necklace was also found in TB 4 as well as six knives, three of them straight-edged, and three curved. Nine other iron objects were found in the main room of TB 4 along the west side.

Terrace Building 5 and Anteroom
Tracing the excavation of this room from the notebooks is difficult because many different trenches were under the supervision of the excavator and recorded in the same notebook, NB 79. Excavation of the main workroom took place in July and August of 1959 (Fig. 73). A well-sketched plan with labeled index can be found in the back notebook flap. The suddenness of the destruction evident in this room by wheat found abandoned on one of the grinding querns in the back of TB 5. A hoard of 20 doughnut-shaped loom weights was found in a half-circle toward the back center of the main room and fairly large pieces of wood were found tumbled together along with these loom weights. The close proximity of the weights suggests that these wooden pieces are the remains of a loom that was standing between the central posts, a convenient location for lighting while still allowing traffic flow through the room.

From this room came 18 spindle whorls. The weight distribution shows that half of these weighed less than thirty grams, while the other half was between thirty and sixty-two

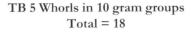

Table 9. Terrace Building 5 spindle whorls, Gordion.

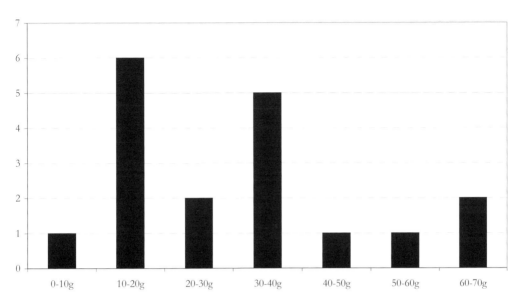

grams (Table 9). Based on the excavation notebooks there were three or four groups of spindle whorls collected in 1959, suggesting that they were 'spinning kits', each possibly used by only one worker before the destructive fire. The lightest of the four groups had four whorls with an average weight of 16 grams, with an interesting distribution wherein two whorls weighed sixteen grams exactly, the smallest one weighed seven, and the largest, twenty-four. This would mean that the whorls were nearly in multiples of 8 gram units. Another cluster of whorls was unusual in that their average weight was around fifty grams. Like the whorls from TB 4, these from TB 5 weighed on average more than the other whorls in the Terrace Building. This discovery suggests that here too was located the plying of thread from two yarns.

The anteroom of TB 5, also known as room W2S2 and TB S2, had been partly opened in 1959. It was excavated simultaneously with the main room, making the notebook references confusing. Work concluded in 1961 along with the excavation of the anteroom of TB 4. Reference is made to a round hearth, two large domed ovens, and a U-shaped construction of crude brick probably used for broiling located in the north-west corner. These cooking features were damaged when the west wall was robbed in later times, and are not as well preserved as the similar constructions in TB 4 A. A typical kneading board of unbaked clay was also found.

For textile equipment we have the usual stray finds but also a few found in clusters.

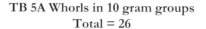

Table 10. Terrace Building 5 Anteroom spindle whorls, Gordion.

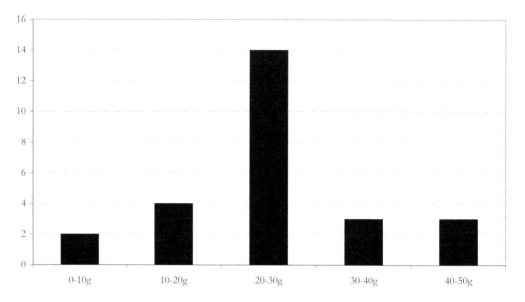

TB 5A Whorls in 10 gram groups
Total = 26

Twenty-six spindle whorls, for instance, were found together. From the notebook references and the label on the spindle whorl bag in the depot, it is assumed that these formed a single group of tools that were originally stored together, perhaps the possession of one Phrygian worker. The weight distribution shows fifty-three percent of these whorls weighing between twenty and thirty grams (Table 10).

The records for loom weights from both the main room and the anteroom are not as specific as one would hope; only a few references are found, such as 'group of three loom weights removed from the floor.' Excavations resumed in 1961, revealing more grinding stones and loom weights, but it is difficult to estimate the numbers because at this point counting the multitude of loom weights seemed pointless to the excavators. In J. McClellan's catalogue of iron implements from Gordion, she records an iron needle found near some loom weights and pottery in the main room. Based on the majority of anterooms with substantial deposits of loom weights, an estimate of between fifty and one-hundred loom weights in TB 5 A would not be extraordinary.

Terrace Building 6
This room was excavated in 1963 along with the anteroom of TB 1, and two of the Clay Cut rooms. It contained 16 grinding querns, the largest number of these found in any of the Terrace Building rooms. There is, however, a striking absence of loom weights in the

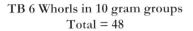

Table 11. Terrace Building 6 spindle whorls, Gordion.

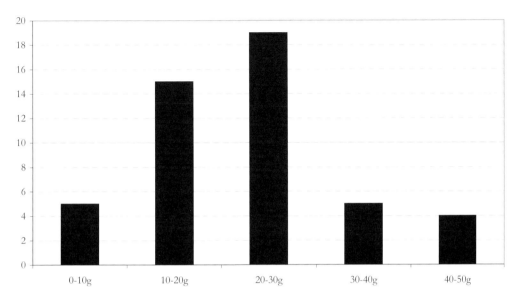

TB 6 Whorls in 10 gram groups
Total = 48

notebooks for this room. It is possible that, after excavating five other large workrooms, counting them in detail would have been tedious for the excavators, as in reference to TB 4 (Young 1957). What can be discerned from the notebook sketches are at least twenty-five loom weights, but it is likely that the actual number was greater.

Forty-eight spindle whorls were studied from this workroom, falling into typical weight distributions for an Early Phrygian workshop (Table 11). Seventy-one percent weighed between ten and thirty grams. The anteroom of TB 6 was left unexcavated.

Terrace Building 7 and Anteroom
This is the best-documented Terrace Building complex, perhaps because of its relatively late excavation in the series, in the 1970s, and certainly because of the careful record-keeping on the part of Keith DeVries. Architectural details, including evidence for reeds and wooden planks in roof construction, are noted but will not be discussed here except where they relate to textile production.

The excavation of TB 7 and 7 A has yielded the clearest description of finds from an entire TB unit at Gordion. In the main room of TB 7, 450 loom weights and 89 spindle whorls were found. Many of these tools seem to be concentrated along the eastern wall. For a main workroom, TB 7 had a fairly heavy concentration of loom weights. The spindle whorls covered a broad range of weights, with a majority weighing less than thirty grams

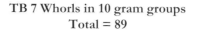

Table 12. Terrace Building 7 spindle whorls, Gordion.

TB 7 Whorls in 10 gram groups
Total = 89

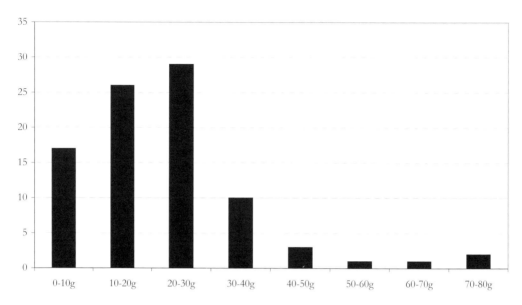

(Table 12). Heavy deposits of pottery were also found along all the walls of the room, while the center was fairly clear.

In addition to the tools of textile production found in TB 7 were indications of another industry; along the back wall were three stations of grinding stands with querns. The main station had six stands, showing evidence for at least six people grinding grain. A mud-plastered bin was located on its western side, perhaps for holding ground grain. Nearby were piles of burned wheat and barley, some of which were contained in baskets. Two more stations for grinding continued along the back wall, facing the same direction as the other six. A large pit in front of these stations was found filled with burned debris, but may have functioned as a storage area for un-ground grain.

The destruction level of the anteroom of TB 7 was excavated in 1971 by K. DeVries (Fig. 74). Work within this room revealed a great deal of equipment related to textile production, including loom weights, spindle whorls, needles, metal tools and stone implements. DeVries records four basic shapes of loom weights: flattened, globular, pyramidal, and cylindrical. These various types were often found in piles together, making it difficult to believe that there was some special function for each shape of weight. The weights and dimensions are similar to loom weights in the other rooms, and they are all grouped together under the generalized nick-name description, 'doughnut'. They are all made from local, coarse river clay and only accidentally fired, although to differing degrees during the great destruction. The spindle whorls from the anteroom are of fired clay for

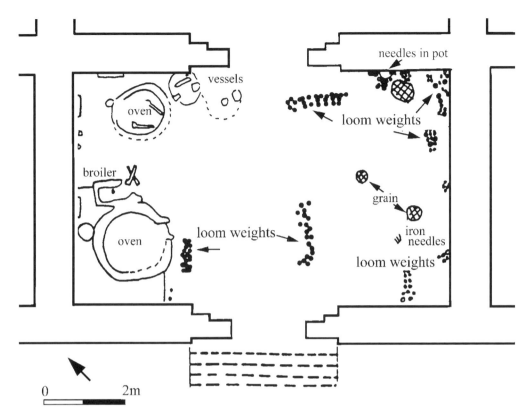

Figure 74. Terrace Building 7 Anteroom plan, 800 BC (adopted from notebook drawing by K. DeVries, 1971).

the most part, and are of the usual range in shape and weight. Clusters of spindle whorls, varying in size, suggest spinning kits for individual spinners. At least 150 loom weights were found in this room. Roughly in the center of the anteroom was a double line, about 1.59 m in length, of 21 doughnut-shaped weights. This length gives us a good idea of the width of the textiles woven on this loom. Again the average cluster of weights numbers around 20. Based on the position of the weights, it is possible that these were two rows of loom weights attached to the warp sheds of a standing loom at the time of destruction. The line of weights, perpendicular to the door leading to the main room, was an excellent location for a loom which would not obstruct traffic yet still get the maximum amount of light for weaving.

While most of the loom weights from this room were concentrated in the eastern half, a cluster of ten loom weights was found along the walls of the large domed oven in the southwest corner. These weights vary in shape and size, from the cylindrical type to the flattened globular kinds. A spindle whorl and two stone tools were also found in the cluster. A low bench measuring 0.37 m high and 0.43 m wide was also found nearby, connecting

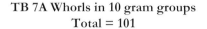

Table 13. Terrace Building 7 Anteroom spindle whorl, Gordion.

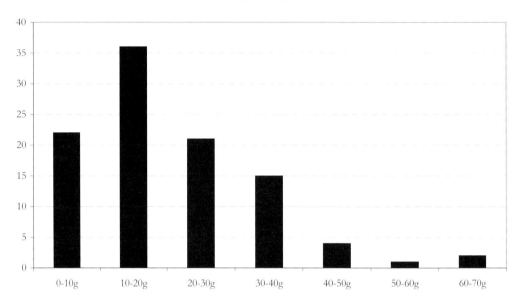

the oven to the interior side of the south (front) wall of the anteroom. The placement of the bench near the loom weights might suggest a seat for weavers, but the location against the wall indicates that this would be fairly cramped. More likely, the bench was used for kneading trays associated with baking. Also found in front of the bench area were an iron rod and an iron hoe. These tools are probably to be associated with tending the fire in the ovens (DeVries 1990, 385). The loom weights in close proximity to the oven might have been intentionally placed there to harden some for use on a loom. More 'doughnuts' were found in this anteroom, particularly along the eastern side in the corners, including a cluster of eleven that was wedged in between two pots and the wall.

At least 101 spindle whorls were found in the anteroom (Table 13). These whorls weighed slightly less than the average for the Terrace Building rooms. Nearly sixty percent of the whorls weighed less than twenty grams, while about thirty-five percent weighed between twenty and forty grams. The whorls were mostly found scattered but a few were clustered together, presumably inside vessels. Iron needles were also found in the clusters, making it seem likely that these were textile tool kits. Eight whorls and six iron needles were also apparently kept in a small vase. In the southeastern corner of the anteroom, just to the right of the entrance thirteen spindle whorls were found next to a heap of loom weights and some needles.

Other unusual tools from the anteroom that might be related to textile production include iron rings, measuring between 3 cm and 5 cm in height, and about 2.5 cm wide. How these rings would have functioned is unclear at this point, but the great quantities of textile equipment found along with them are a good starting point. Examples of similar iron rings are noted in the excavation of other Terrace Building rooms, such as TB 1. There are Egyptian scenes of spinners that show two threads that have been plied together being pulled through small rings attached to the wall: it may be that these rings had a similar function.

At least four dome-shaped stone tools were found in TB 7 A, and they might have functioned as some sort of polisher or beater for finishing heavy textiles. The excavation notebooks describe the half-dome shaped tools having flat undersides. A long, narrow polished stone object with suspension holes on either side was also found which measured 9.2 cm and is described as a pendant. Its shape, however, suggests to me that it could have been a weft-bobbin, with thread being wrapped around it and sent through the warp sheds. At least seven knives were also found in TB 7, two straight edged and five curved. One knife may have been fitted with an ivory handle. Finally, two more bone tools were found that might also have been weft-bobbins.

Terrace Building 8 and Anteroom
The main room and anteroom of this final Terrace Building unit were excavated in 1967. The total length of the entire Terrace Building came to 105 m with the excavation of TB 8. This room was similar to all the others except that it was less well-preserved. The presence of a deep cellar, lined with stones, had resulted in the destruction of much of the northeastern part of the main room. No grind-stones were found on the main grinding stand at the back of the room, but there were some grinders on a smaller subsidiary stand to the southeast. Young (1968) comments on a fortunately well-preserved segment of the wall that fell from TB 8: the remains suggest that the walls were approximately 2.8 m high and made of stone and wood, then capped with a mud-brick superstructure.

A total of 92 spindle whorls were found in the main room, while the anteroom produced only 3 (Table 14). The majority of the spindle whorls in the main room weighed between ten and twenty grams. Some of the whorls were found along with iron needles and knives. Nine bronze knives in total, all curved, were recorded. As for the loom weights, there is the typical problem of no exact count having been recorded in the notebooks. From the excavation sketches and references in the iron catalogue, it seems likely that the anteroom had the usual number of approximately one hundred loom weights. The number in the main room is more difficult to estimate because of the later disturbance. There is, however, no reason to think that this room was appreciably different from the other Terrace Building rooms 3–7.

In the anteroom there was the usual large dome oven, a U-shaped broiler, and a smaller oven or hearth above the floor, but in this room, the cooking features were placed in the southeastern corner rather than the typical northwestern one. Associated with the ovens and broiling stands was a bench with fragments of clay kneading trays, leaning against the wall. These trays were located along the interior wall of the anteroom, toward the door which leads into the main room. The location of the cooking facilities at this opposite side

Table 14. Terrace Building 8 spindle whorls, Gordion.

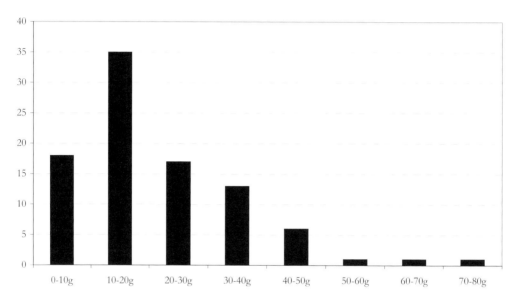

TB 8 Whorls in 10 gram groups
Total = 92

of the room should be attributed to the presence of the entrance and staircase which gave access to the entire Terrace Building complex along the northern side wall of TB 8.

Clay Cut Building (CC)
Traces of four parallel workshop units were located approximately 20 m across a broad street in front of the Terrace Building. That this building was also severely and suddenly destroyed by fire suggests that the destruction of Gordion was a planned, deliberate attack. The burning of Megarons 1–4 and the Terrace Building behind might be explained as an accident if these were the only areas of the Citadel Mound burned. The further destruction of these other units at such a distance from the Terrace Building indicates that it was a separate, contemporaneous, and intentionally set fire.

  This structure is referred to as the Clay Cut Building and is of identical though reversed plan to the Terrace Building, with megaron units each composed of an anteroom and main room behind. The layer of clay placed over the Early Phrygian destruction level by the Middle Phrygian rebuilders gave the conventional name to this excavation area, the Clay Cut. These two parallel workshop buildings, the TB and CC, were presumably built at the same time because they rest on the same terrace fill, and the side-walls of each room are aligned to the mid-point of the workshop unit across the street. For example, the dividing-wall between CC 1 and 2, if continued, would run through the center of TB 6, and interestingly, continue on through the center of Megaron 4 farther behind.

The exact length of the entire CC building is not known, as neither end of the building has yet been excavated. Only traces of the farthest north-west building, CC 4, have been excavated. It is assumed that the CC units continue at least as long as the eight units of the Terrace Building. The conventional names of the rooms excavated to date, CC 1–4, will perhaps someday cause confusion since CC 1 is probably located near the middle of the series of rooms, and if excavations were to continue, they would likely reveal a CC 5 room immediately adjacent to CC 1 toward the south-east!

Clay Cut 1 and Anteroom
After its initial discovery in 1952, excavations in CC 1 continued in 1956 and 1963. This cutting was continued to expose the north end of the building, that is, the front wall facing the TB units. The room is a typical terrace-building type, with cooking facilities in the anteroom and post-holes in two aisles around the walls of the back room. The walls have been preserved highest at the SW corner, where several masonry courses can be counted. Above the sixth course (counting from the bottom) it seems that there ran a horizontal beam course like the one at floor level flush with the inner face of the walls. The main room and anteroom of CC 1 were only partially cleared in excavation, along the north-west side; the side-wall to the southeast was not completely excavated. It is assumed that CC 1 adjoined other identical workshop units running toward the south, parallel to the Terrace Building rooms across the broad dividing street.

In the back room was a grind-stone bench very similar to one in the North room, CC 2. Both were built in exactly the same way, with mud-brick sides and a curved brick edge. The notebook from CC 1 records that a section of the installation in that room with millstones *in situ* can be seen in the south scarp of the trench. The grindstone had slipped into the platform edge but the original arrangement is clear. The outer, western face of the bench was plastered down to floor level with thick mud plaster.

Found in the main room were 133 spindle whorls covering a broad range of weights, from five to 68 grams (Table 15). Some needles were also found in this room, as well as three bronze knives. The distribution of whorl weights from the main room of CC 1 was much more typical of the other Terrace Building workshops than that of the whorls from the anteroom of CC 1, noted below.

The anteroom was relatively free of pottery, but contained one large oven with grains of barley inside, two smaller ovens, and a round hearth. Only one large pot appears to have rested *in situ* against the western wall near the larger of the two ovens. At least 57 spindle whorls are known to have come from this anteroom (Table 16). What is striking about these whorls is the limited range in weights. A large majority, 90%, of the whorls from this room weighed less than 20 grams while the other ten percent were under 30 grams. This suggests that light-weight, relatively fine thread was being spun in this room on these very light-weight spindle whorls.

Table 15. Clay Cut Building 1 spindle whorls, Gordion.

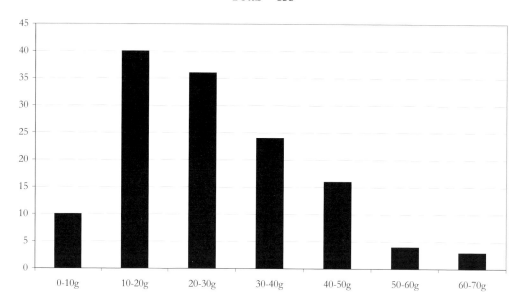

Table 16. Clay Cut Building 1 Anteroom spindle whorls, Gordion.

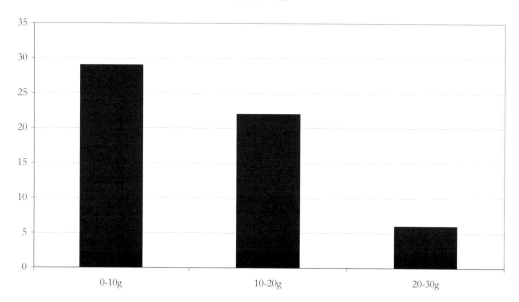

Clay Cut 2

This unit is sometimes referred to as the North Room, while CC 1 was known as the South Room. Only the main room of CC 2 was excavated. It has the usual arrangement of two rows of four post-holes with a central one between the innermost pair, presumably for supporting a balcony. Along the walls runs another set of post-holes echoing the interior ones. A circular hearth is located off-center, roughly in line with the third post-holes down from the North end of the building. The pottery deposit was fairly heavy in this room. Broken jars near the wall contained burnt wheat and barley, samples of which were saved. A fragmentary red-polished jar with rim revealed a piece of fairly thick cloth inside, along with thick thread all bundled up. In the corner, many loom weights were found in fallen rows and piles.

Two large grinding stands were found along the back wall, one of which was excavated by Machteld Mellink in 1956. A total of five querns rested in place on the bench, three of these having hand grinders; just to the east of the westernmost quern was the hollow for a sixth, which was not present. Lying scattered about on the floor of the room were 8 complete querns (four upside down, four right-side up) and one end of a ninth quern: there were also 3 saddle querns, all right-side up (scraping end down), but one resting against the side of a rectangular quern. The plaster surface around the grinding stone platforms was also well-preserved.

North of the grinding bench, approximately in line with the fifth saddle quern from the west end, a cluster of 27 loom weights sat on the floor, including two very large weights. Another pile of 90 loom weights in the eastern corner was removed. Three of the weights from this pile are cone-shaped, pyramidal types and are quite large – 0.14 m high, 0.12 m wide, and pierced horizontally. The excavator suggests that these weights must have belonged to special places on the loom. It is probable that these were used to reinforce the edges of the textile, giving heavier tension to the warp threads on either end to prevent an incurving edge.

Fifty-five spindle whorls in total were found in CC 2. Five of these were found lying as if strung together, two large and three medium-sized, under a burned, brittle jar. The weights of these whorls fall within the usual range (Table 17). The average of all whorls from CC 2 was 24 grams, fitting with the average weight for all of the TB and CC whorls. In addition to the spindle whorls and loom weights, several iron knives and a needle were also found in the northeastern corner of CC 2. McClellan notes that an additional group of iron needles was found here, but not catalogued, along with several pieces of fabric.

Clay Cut 3

This room contained the usual post-holes to support a balcony on three sides and a hearth in the center. The grinding stand seems to have been destroyed in a later disturbance, though grinding stones were still present. North of this stand was perhaps a bin for the flour produced at the grinding stand. In a circular area of the floor, the grain found was 'the sort of tail-corn and wild seeds that is normally separated from the better grain during the final stages of cleaning the grain with sieves.' (G. Hillman, in DeVries 1990, 386).

A pile of sprouted barley may have been set aside for Phrygian beer production. Based on

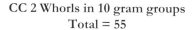

Table 17. Clay Cut Building 2 spindle whorls, Gordion.

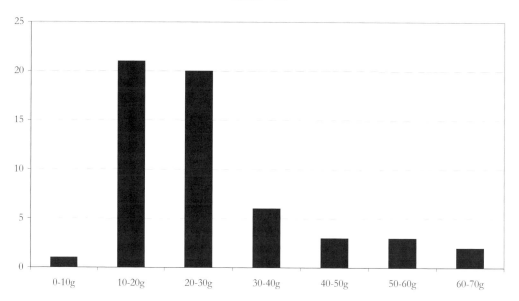

literary references and certain types of sipping vessels found at the site, Sams has suggested that beer was brewed at Gordion (Sams 1977, 1994). Side-spouted sieve jugs, referred to as beer mugs, had built-in tubes which would filter floating husks from the brew (Fig 75). Xenophon (*An* 4.5.26) also remarks on the straw-sipping Phrygians and their beer. These Phrygian beer mugs are found in elite contexts at Gordion, in burials and in the citadel, as well as in Phrygian levels at other Anatolian sites. Other indications of food production include the skeletons of two partially butchered calves and traces of hazelnuts found together with spindle whorls in a jug in this room.

A total of 213 spindle whorls were recorded from CC 3. More than half of these weighed less than twenty grams (Table 18). Five hundred and nine loom weights were discovered in the main room, some with traces of thread still in their holes, although they may have fallen from the balcony above since they were in no discernable row (DeVries 1990, 387). These threads could either be from the warp-threads, or, more likely, they were the remains of cords used to fasten the weights to the warp. The weights were found in large groups, up to 72 per pile. The find spots of the weights do not suggest that they were attached to a loom when the destruction occurred, though it could be that they fell from the balcony above. This deposit of textile tools makes the main room of CC 3 the workshop with the largest concentration of textile equipment excavated at Gordion.

Five spindle whorls were found inside a carved, round, wooden box with the remains of braided thread. Clumps of coarsely twisted fibers were also found, which may be rove. A

Table 18. Clay Cut Building 3 spindle whorls, Gordion. Types of Specialization, from Costin (1991).

CC 3 Whorls in 10 gram groups
Total = 213

Figure 75. Early Phrygian beer mug from Tumulus III (Körte and Körte 1904, pl. 3).

bone tool that may be a weft-bobbin was also found in CC 3. In addition to the spindle whorls and loom weights, pieces of thread, needles, and metal knives were also found. At least eleven bronze knives were catalogued from this room, three straight-edged, the rest curved.

Summary

A great deal about Phrygian political and social organization is unknown, including aspects of military organization, but we can assume from the Near Eastern documents that refer to the Phrygians as 'Mushki', and their King Mita, that military might was a necessity in the belligerent times of Early Iron Age Anatolia. Alliances and loyalties switched quickly among people facing the Assyrian war-machine: power and politics were based on military strength. Historical records seem to indicate that smaller kingdoms of Anatolia appealed to the Phrygians for military aid against the Assyrians, suggesting that a powerful Phrygian army existed. Some militaristic aspects are found in Phrygian plaques and other examples of Phrygian art (Prayon 1987, 161–163, Pl. 32–33).

Three aspects are vital to the strength of any fighting force: social organization, adequate supplies, and troop mobility. The standardized architectural features of the workshop units along the great terrace and the elaborate nature of the Phrygian gateway and Megaron buildings show a high degree of planning and social organization among the Phrygians. The political force that mobilized the labor, technology and resources necessary for building the capital of Gordion would certainly have been able to organize and maintain a standing army.

Supplies for an army would include weapons, food, and textiles. The Phrygians were skilled metal workers, crafting fine objects of precious metal, and also strong tools of bronze and iron. Among these metal goods would have been weapons, such as the long spears and shields shown in Phrygian art (Fig. 76). The furniture fragments from Megaron 3 showing horse and riders depict mounted warriors equipped with such weapons (Fig. 77). The grinding platforms, hearths, ovens and bins in the Terrace and Clay Cut units, could have supplied a fighting force as well as fed supporting craftsmen and women. The famed Phrygian beer may have been brewed in the Citadel Mound and been supplied to the army as both an enjoyable payment and a good source of calories. Finally, evidence for the mass production of textiles by attached, dependent workers has been adequately demonstrated from the loom weights, spindle whorls, needles, and other tools found within the Terrace and Clay Cut buildings. The heavy duty cloth made here could have been used as a reward for service, a protective armor, and it would have provided temporary shelter to an army abroad.

Another possibility for the textiles at Gordion is that they were a form of payment or medium of exchange. This would be in keeping with a long tradition in the Near East and Mesopotamia. Since the mid-third millennium BC, textiles, metal objects, and semi-precious stones were the most widely recognized prestige goods in the Mediterranean region (Stein and Blackman 1993). Comparing the organization of craft activities in Mesopotamia to that of textile production at Early Phrygian Gordion nearly two millennia later may seem a great stretch, especially since Gordion lacks the archival evidence of earlier Near Eastern centers. The workshops in close proximity to the elite quarters, enclosed within the fortifications, the artistic depictions of Phrygian garments worn by royal figures, dedications of cloth-associated goods in Greek sanctuaries, and finds of well-made cloth in elite burial

Figure 76. Phrygian horse and rider plaque, ivory, from Megaron 3 (from DeVries 1980, fig. 7, ©University Museum, Gordion Archive).

Figure 77. Phrygian furniture inlay, ivory, from Megaron 3 (from DeVries, 1980, fig. 8. ©University Museum, Gordion Archive).

chambers at Gordion, all suggest that textiles were both a prestige item and a medium of exchange in Early Iron Age Anatolia. This is paralleled in the evidence from third and second millennia BC, at centers such as Ebla, Mari, and Nuzi.

Archaeological evidence from Gordion demonstrates that cloth production and food preparation were the major activities in the Terrace and Clay Cut Buildings at the time of the Early Phrygian destruction. As in many Aegean palaces, craft residues of industries such as bronze working and pottery production are lacking at Gordion (Henrickson and Blackman 1996, Henrickson 1994). The location of textile production and food preparation (including beer) in standardized workshop units within the massive Phrygian fortification walls suggests that these were the two most important products of the Phrygian political economy: food and cloth.

As Mellink states, "The organization reflected in the citadel plan is one of a privileged society preparing for war and siege... The Phrygians show themselves heirs to a long tradition, to which Trojans of Troy II and VI belonged and to a branch of which, on the other side of the Aegean, the Mycenaeans were also indebted" (Mellink 1991, 629). As with cloth in the Minoan and Mycenaean kingdoms, Phrygian textiles probably functioned as both a kind of currency or medium of exchange, and as a prestige good. The research presented here suggests that different qualities of cloth were woven in the Terrace and Clay Cut Buildings. The large numbers of spindle whorls and loom weights of fairly similar shape and standardized size indicate cloth made on a massive scale, for distribution directed by the ruling elite. The heavy weight of the doughnut-shaped loom weights might imply that the woven textiles were strong and durable. Heavy-duty textiles could have been used to equip a standing army of the Phrygians, or perhaps as some means of payment or compensation to the soldiers. Alternatively, some of the cloth woven just before the great conflagration may have been meant for tribute to assuage an aggressive neighbor.

Rodney Young, director of Gordion from 1950–1974, stated "we can have little admiration for the Phrygians as neat and orderly housekeepers. In a palace, as at Knossos for example, one would expect many storerooms for stowing of goods and equipment of all kinds, one would expect also workrooms in which chores of daily living were performed. But one would expect at least a modicum of neatness and order: one for the storage of bronzes... perhaps one for the archives" (Young 1960, 242–3). While the organization of the Terrace Buildings may not have conformed to Rodney Young's original conception of a palace, his later research and that of others have broadened our understanding of Phrygian economy and culture.

From this investigation of textile production and related craft activities we can see that the Phrygians had a highly developed system of cloth manufacture. The masses of spindle whorls and loom weights contained in the destruction level of the Terrace and Clay Cut buildings suggest that a great deal of importance was placed on textile production in the Phrygian economy and political structure. Cloth can serve many purposes in a state-level economy. It can function as a kind of currency in tribute demands placed upon commoners. Cloth of various qualities and grades bestowed by a ruler can signify certain levels of authority to peers and subordinate officials. Textiles can also function as protection and payment for members of a fighting force.

From surveys and excavations in central Anatolia, the geographical extent of Phrygia is estimated to have covered a large portion of central Turkey. It is possible that some amount of tribute was demanded by the central authority, and some of this may have been in the form of textiles sent to the center, or textiles manufactured at Gordion were distributed as payment to loyal vassals. Artistic representations far from the capital, such as the Ivriz relief, show cloth that appears to be Phrygian in style. King Warpalawas' garment is decorated with traditional Phrygian designs, and fastened with a fibula of a well-known Phrygian type, suggesting that textiles and bronze pins were diplomatic gifts from the capital at Gordion, in keeping with a long tradition of royal gift-exchange. Finally, from diplomatic records we also hear of shifting alliances between the various rulers of Anatolian city-states and the Assyrian kingdoms. The citadel at Gordion was a complex center where people were heavily invested in a textile industry, located along with food production. Who consumed these goods will remain a subject of speculation but by looking at contemporary kingdoms and ones of similar scale and power, we can suggest both a military and peer-to-peer system of elite exchange with a heavy emphasis on cloth.

APPENDIX 4.1: TEXTILE FRAGMENTS

Analyses of textile fragments from Gordion by Bellinger (1962), Brown (1980), Ellis (1981), Barber (1991) and Ballard (2006; 2007) have shown that cloth production was fairly sophisticated and made use of advanced technologies. By looking at the actual pieces of cloth from the tumuli and Citadel Mound we can see the wide variety and different qualities of Phrygian cloth that were almost certainly made within the Terrace and Clay Cut Buildings.

The first account of textiles from Gordion was by Louisa Bellinger in 1962, then at the Textile Museum in Washington DC, who identified various types of fibers: linen, hemp, wool and mohair. Cotton and silk were not present. How these identifications were made is not clear though this range of fibers is not unexpected for Iron Age Anatolia. Bellinger does not give the total number of textile fragments she examined, only 'groups of specimens'. Also, no context for the textile finds is mentioned, so we are uncertain as to whether Bellinger is referring to finds from the tumuli or from the Citadel Mound. The sketches accompanying the dull photographs do indicate that the textiles from Gordion were elaborately decorated and finely made.

The dissertation by K. Brown (1980) was primarily concerned with the influence of textile patterns on Greek vase painting of the Orientalizing period. She thoroughly exams the decorative designs of the preserved fragments, which are still poorly housed in the Gordion archives of the University Museum, University of Pennsylvania as of 2009. That these extremely important fragments of cultural property should be properly conserved and housed goes without question.

The study of Gordion textiles by Richard Ellis is an appendix to the first Gordion Studies volume, *The Three Great Early Tumuli* (1981). Ellis states that this is a preliminary study because it focuses only on textiles from the three great tumuli, MM, P, and W, not from the Citadel Mound itself, and because the examination of the fibers was made only with a binocular microscope rather than a scanning electron microscope or chemical analysis. Consequently, no complete publication of all the textile remains from Gordion has as yet been made. Ellis was unable to confirm the fiber identifications of Bellinger and prefers a more cautious identification of threads as either animal or vegetable. The thread-spin is examined, which provides interesting data in relation to the thousand-plus spindle whorls found at Gordion.

Continuing the textile analysis today is Mary Ballard, Senior Textiles Conservator, Museum Conservation Institute, at the Smithsonian Institution. She reports that the condition of the Gordion textiles varies greatly; some are well preserved, fairly pliable and strong. Others, however, are brittle, nearly dust, which makes identification of their structure difficult if not impossible. Some samples are very brittle but have a fairly easily identifiable structure due to preservation in the proximity of copper alloys, which has turned them into pseudomorphs. Ballard reports that many of the fibers at Gordion appear to be wool or goat-hair and some are very fine, with diameters falling into the range of cashmere, mohair, and merino, at 19–20 microns (pers. comm. 1996). In some examples, the epicuticle is abraded off so none of the characteristic scales of animal fibers are present. Sometimes crystalline material obscures the fiber structure or, in other cases, the fiber has collapsed. Of the bast fibers, Ballard reports that they are probably flax, with diameters in the 10 micron range, comparable to Egyptian linen in fineness. Like Bellinger and Ellis, however, she was unable to distinguish between hemp and linen under the microscope.

In 2003, at the behest of the Gordion furniture project, Ballard and her Smithsonian-based team began studying 11 textile samples from Tumulus MM, the Midas Mound (Ballard 2006, 2007). At first examination the textiles did not seem very impressive, and most were actually pseudomorphs: that is, the organic fiber element had mostly disappeared because of the close proximity of metal artifacts. A hollow shell had formed creating a textile fossil. With spectrographic analysis of the surface of the fibers it was discovered that Goethite was evident, a gold-colored iron oxide (α-FeOOH) which has been used as a pigment since Paleolithic times. Using sophisticated dyeing methods, which the Phrygians seem to have perfected, the fibers would take on the brilliant gold color of the Goethite, perhaps giving some credence to the legend of King Midas and his 'golden touch' (Ovid *Metam.* 11.85–145). These results by Ballard have not been formally published at this point and it is unclear to me which of the samples examined by Ellis, described below, were included in the new study, but the results suggests that textile technologies at Gordion were quite sophisticated. The remains indicate a very discerning and highly developed textile industry at Gordion.

Three different types of fabric structure are reported for textiles from Gordion: plain weave with variations, weft wrapping (Soumak), and felt. The tumuli textiles are only plain weave and felt. No examples of the Soumak were found in the burials, but only in the Citadel Mound at Gordion. Ellis groups the fragments into nine different 'fabric' groups, based on fiber and technical similarities. These are labeled Fabric A through K, numbering eleven different fabrics. Each fabric is thoroughly described by fiber, color, spin, weave, and a description of the starting borders and hems. The find spot and probable function of each fabric are also given.

Figure 78. Phrygian textile fragments from Tumulus MM (B. Burke).

Fabric A

Fabric A was found in the great tumulus MM, at the head and foot of the coffin and in the bronze cauldron, MM 13. The fragments from the bed may have been the sheets underneath heavier blankets. From the cauldron, the fabric was probably a bag containing unidentified food, presumably grains. This Z-spun thread, double plied in the S direction (hereafter referred to as Z2S), is yellow-brown to orange-brown, and was identified by Bellinger as mohair, but to Ellis it is a vegetable fiber. The thread diameter varies between 0.1 and 0.6 mm. The fabric is interesting because the edges show a separately woven band that is only found on two other fabrics from the tumuli (C and F discussed below). A band is woven separately with long looped weft threads which, when placed on the warp-weighted loom, act as the warp threads on the final textile.

Fabric A is a balanced plain weave, *i.e.* with the same number of warp threads as weft per centimeter, over one, under one. On average, there are 16 to 24 threads per centimeter. Some of the warp threads are fairly crowded, resulting in a slightly striped appearance on the fabric. One error in this fabric is the failure of some warp thread to actually weave. This, according to Ellis, is due to a heddle of improper length so that at the change of sheds, one warp thread does not fully return but gets caught in the other shed (see Barber 1991, 198–9). Paired Z-spun thread of the same fiber as fabric A was sewn through rolled hems of two fragments of Fabric A.

Fabric B

This vegetable fabric varies in color from yellowish-white to brown and has strongly plied (Z2S) thread. The thread diameter is about 0.2 to 0.3 mm, with about 18 threads per centimeter. The fabric is generally very similar to Fabric A but comes only from Tumulus P. Young refers to this cloth as 'cheesecloth' and found fragments of it on one of the pegs of the tomb chamber walls, suggesting that it may have covered these walls. The preserved piece was red with a simple white stripe and was probably a wall hanging.

Fabric C

This is a single piece of plain weave fabric, light yellow-tan in color, presumably of linen, in the Z2S ply, and with a thread diameter of 0.15–0.2 mm. This is a fairly fine, thin textile, with 18 warp threads per centimeter and 22 weft threads. It presumably was part of the cloth bag that contained many of the bronze fibulae found in the Midas Mound burial chamber. This identification is not certain because there is no textile sample number in the Gordion record system, but Ellis suggests the identification based on the description of Bellinger and on evidence from the excavation notebooks.

Fabric D

This fabric is similar to fabric C in general description, except that examples are found in narrow strips or tapes. There are on average 40 warp threads set at 24–26 threads per centimeter, and a widely placed weft at 10 to 12. These strips are found in all three major tumuli and may have been used to tie up bundles of cloth and wrap bronze objects.

Fabric E

This is a plain weave fabric, probably of brown wool, though it is very poorly preserved and matted together, making analysis very difficult. Ellis states that most of the examples of this fabric are balanced with about 18–22 threads per centimeter. All of the examples come from Tumulus W, two from inside a bronze bowl, one from the wall of the chamber, and two others found between two pieces of leather. Brown felt and a strip of Fabric D were also found in the same bronze bowl. There may be similarities between Fabric E and Fabric F.

Fabric F

This fabric is unique among the Gordion textiles in that it uses two different yarns, one animal and the other vegetable. The two different fibers are found in various combinations in the same fabric. Some areas are made completely with the animal fibers, others with vegetable ones, and still others with the vegetable fibers as the warp and the animal fibers as the weft. Ellis suggests the possibility that these combinations of fibers were used to make checks and stripes. The vegetable fiber is yellowish-white (some blackened by the conflagration), Z-spun, double S ply, and measures in at 0.1 to 0.5 mm in diameter. The animal fiber is either a natural yellow-brown, or sometimes dyed red to purple. This is a single Z-spun fiber, moderately twisted to 0.15 to 0.25 mm in diameter. All four samples of this fabric were found in Tumulus MM and had been in contact with bronze objects: a cauldron, the lion-head and ram-head situlae, and a fibula. The cloth was probably used to wrap the bronze objects, or, in the case of the fibula, it may have fastened a group of various textiles together.

Fabric G

Just as fabric F was found only in Tumulus MM, fragments of fabric G with decorative bands were all found in Tumulus P. The textile is made of two yarns, A and B. A is similar in color, yellowish-white, to the vegetable yarn of fabric F (Ellis 1981, 305). Likewise, yarn B is similar to F's animal yarn, in that it is dark red to purple in color. Fabric G seems to have been predominantly red or purple with white patterns. The warp threads dominate in this fabric, using both yarns A and B, in warp-faced plain weave and sometimes with complementary warps. Ellis reports that the system is set at 50–60 threads per centimeter. Some of the patterns of Fabric G are meanders in white against red, with white triangles at the edges. These patterned rectangular designs are depicted on the Ivriz and Bor reliefs showing King Warpalawas of Tyana, a contemporary of King Midas (Boehmer 1973, 149–72; Dalley 1991, 126–7). Selvages found on Fabric G suggest that some examples were attached to other fabrics, including a piece of Fabric B.

Fabric H

This fabric was found in various contexts, in Tumuli MM, P, and W. It seems to be an animal fiber, yellow or bluish-gray in color, spun in fairly tight Z-singles. Not many examples are preserved but what can be said is that they were a balanced weave with 9–18 threads per centimeter.

Fabric I

This fiber is identified by Bellinger as 'mohair' (1962, 14). Eleven samples were found in Tumulus MM, all Z2S, moderately twisted, and of very consistent size at 0.1–0.2 mm in diameter. They were all found at shoulder, elbow and hip level beside the body and were in contact with the copper-bronze fibulae which helped in their preservation. This fabric is likely the remains of a funerary cloak or blanket made of layers of cloth fastened together by pins.

Fabric J

Examples of this fabric are fairly small, so little can be said. The fiber is presumably wool. Made of two yarns, both brown in color, it is woven in plain weave: yarn A is Z2S, moderately twisted at 0.3–0.7 mm; yarn B is probably the weft thread, spun Z single and lightly twisted, with a smaller diameter than A, at 0.2–0.3 mm. Two fragments of this fabric are known, one from Tumulus MM, found with leather near a fibula, and the other from Tumulus P.

Fabric K

The final fabric from Gordion is non-woven but instead, is matted together as felt. This fabric was found under the bodies in all three Great tumuli and found as padding for a stool and possibly as wall-hangings and tablecloths. The samples were very difficult to examine due to their fragmentary state. No decorative pattern can be discerned from the many different colored threads found on the surface of the thickly wadded masses.

APPENDIX 4.2: PHRYGIAN FIBULAE
AND TEXTILES

Among the four hundred items that accompanied the man buried in Tumulus MM at Gordion were many fibulae, that is, elaborate bronze 'safety-pins' of distinctive Phrygian design (Muscarella 1967b; Blinkenberg 1926, 204) In total, over 677 examples of Blinkenberg's Asia Minor type xii fibula were found at Gordion, 512 coming from the excavated tumuli. Some were placed on the burial shroud, while others were contained in woven bags (Fabric C), perhaps as burial offerings. Fibulae were also found in the Citadel Mound, including pins of gold and silver from the Terrace Buildings (Muscarella 1967b, 16, Pl. III.12–13). Examples of Phrygian fibulae are also found outside of Gordion, dedicated at a number of Greek sanctuaries along with other Phrygian artifacts. These sites include Lindos, Samos (Jantzen 1972, 48–53), Olympia (Völling 1998), the Argive Heraeum, and perhaps Perachora, Paros and Sparta (Muscarella 1967a). Similarly, eastern Greek-imported 'leech-type' fibulae were found in the destruction level at Gordion and in two of the

Figure 79. Relief from Ivriz showing King Warpalawas of Tyana before a fertility god, wearing a Phrygian textile, fastened with a Phrygian fibula (B. Burke).

eighth century tumuli (G and Y) (Muscarella 1967b, 82). That Phrygian clothing was also dedicated along with the Phrygian pins in Greek sanctuaries is a distinct possibility.

Representations of Phrygian fibulae in sculpture show how the pins were fastened and worn (Muscarella 1967a; Boehmer 1973). Most often one fibula was worn on the torso, attaching two parts of one large outer garment. One Neo-Hittite relief of King Warpalawas of Tyana (fl. 738 BC), suggests that Phrygian fibulae and cloth were also likely gifts between ruling elites. Warpalawas was a competitor of Tiglath-pileser III (745–727) and his image is carved on a rock relief standing before a fertility god at the source of an important spring in south central Anatolia (Boehmer 1973, 151–9). The king's outer garment is secured by a

Figure 80. Detail, relief from Ivriz showing King Warpalawas wearing a Phrygian textile, fastened with a Phrygian fibula (B. Burke).

fibula similar to the Phrygian types found at Gordion and Ankara, identified by Muscarella as type xii 9, with characteristic arcs and a double pin masked by a rectangular transverse plate rather than a single exposed pin. The plate is detachable and serves to shield the pins. Not only is the pin of Warpalawas of likely Phrygian origin, but also the garment worn by the king. The carved designs are typical of Phrygia and the cloth may have been an item of royal gift-exchange.

From historical sources we know that Warpalawas, or Urballa, of Tyana, sent envoys to the Assyrian governor of Que along with messengers sent by King Midas (Saggs 1958, 182–212; Mellink 1991, 622–23; 1979). His diplomatic moves also parallel those of other southeastern Anatolian kings. He is known to have sent tribute to Tiglath-pileser III in the late eighth century BC, as did Pisiri of Carchemesh. The recent explorations at the site of Göllüdag may have located one of Warpalawas' strongholds (Schirmer 1993, 121–131). Warpalawas' dedication of the Stele of Bor (Kemerhisar) again shows him wearing a possible Phrygian garment and probable fibula. According to Mellink (1991, 625), this stele might be best viewed as the Tabal equivalent of the Phrygian dedication by Midas preserved on the Black Stone of Tyana.

Another probable representation of Phrygian cloth is seen on an ivory figurine found in a wealthy tomb at Baynıdır, in the Elmalı plain, along with Phrygian inscriptions and metal objects of Phrygian style. The garment of the young boy standing at his mother's side shows the typical Phrygian lozenge patterns. Inscriptions, tomb goods and the tumuli found in the Elmalı plain strongly suggest Phrygian habitation in this region of Anatolia.

5 COMPARATIVE TEXTILE PRODUCTION AND CONCLUSIONS

In different parts of the world the many stages of fiber processing are often organized along the same general principles. I hope to have highlighted some of these aspects in this book. My other aim was to demonstrate how much can be said about textile production, even when, in most cases, few finished products of the craft itself have survived.

One gap in our knowledge of Minoan, Mycenaean, and Phrygian cloth is its function, or, that is to say, the consumption of the finished textile. Among many uses, some evidence has been cited that connects intensive textile production with military preparations and even payment to soldiers: the *ke-se-nu-wi-ja* cloth recorded in the Linear B tablets is perhaps to be associated with mercenary soldiers, as either a kind of uniform supplied by the palace or a payment for services rendered (Driessen 1984). All of the Linear B tablets recording the phases of cloth production and distribution were preserved in fires that destroyed the Mycenaean citadels. The citadel at Gordion may also have faced a similar fate prior to the great conflagration that destroyed the Phrygian capital and preserved so much of the textile production equipment discussed earlier. Perhaps the textile activity within the palace walls of Knossos, Pylos, and Gordion was intensified during times of crisis to supply a standing army, to pay mercenaries, and to curry favor with allies. Concurrently more slave labor may have been employed to fulfill this increased need for cloth, and in cyclical fashion this fed back on the economic system, increasing demands for provisions and procurement of other goods and services.

An examination of cloth production in other parts of the world, in Egypt, the Near East, and in the New World, provides cross-cultural parallels that supplement our understanding of Mediterranean textiles and their uses. Comparative examples demonstrate the important role of cloth in financing an elite power base. These forays through time and space are not meant to prove a preconceived notion of what I think all textile industries should be like, but rather this comparative evidence better directs my own line of inquiry in the Aegean and Anatolian spheres.

Egypt

The evidence for textiles from Egypt is plentiful because the warm, dry conditions are good for the preservation of thread and other organic matter. Study and publication of linen garments and their construction seems to have been more common in the early years of Egyptology. We also have a good deal of art historical and archaeological data related to textile working. Petrie, for example, studied many of the tools related to cloth production and the workshops associated with the funerary monuments in Pharaonic Egypt (Fig. 81)(Petrie 1917). Evidence

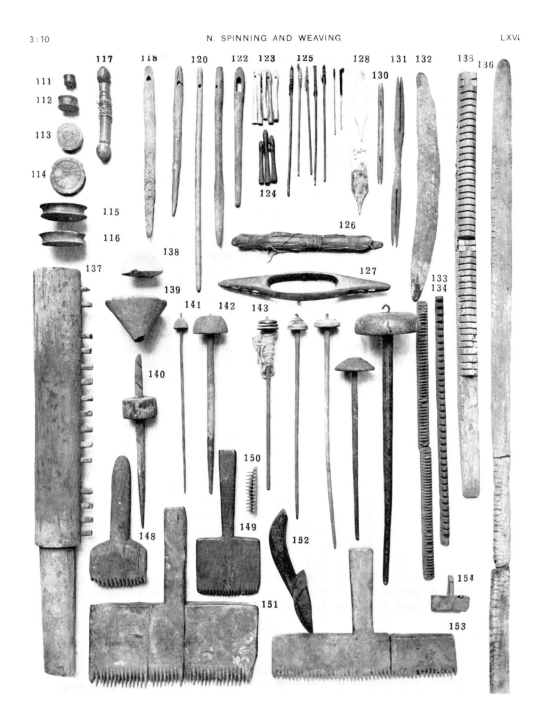

Figure 81. Textile tools found in Amarna (Petrie 1917, pl. 66).

for textile working is found as early as the Neolithic in Egypt, at the site of Kom W in the northern Faiyum, dating to about 6000 BC. This site was excavated by G. Caton-Thompson in 1924–26, who found spindle whorls and evidence of flax, which would indicate long-term settlers rather than seasonal hunters-gatherers. Cloth, needles, whorls, and other related material was also found southeast of Cairo at the Predynastic settlement of Omari by Debono in the mid-20th century although it is not yet published (David 1996, 229). At Abydos, Peet in 1913 discovered evidence for domestic cloth production.

Fortunately, there has been a sort of renaissance in recent years of cloth production studies in Egypt (see Kemp and Vogelsang-Eastwood 2001 especially). The study of textile production at Amarna presents evidence for a complex proto-industrialized textile economy, where production and consumption was done in both domestic and public arenas. Egypt was a society that stored goods heavily and tended to perhaps over-produce goods by outside estimations. According to Kemp and Vogelsang-Eastwood (2001, 427) cloth production was one of the most common industries, performed in nearly every household, perhaps next in importance and frequency to baking and brewing. By the second millennium BC, there is more evidence of industrialized production of cloth in Egypt, from texts, art, and archaeology. One example is the Lady of Teye (Chasinot 1901) from Gurob, who illustrates nicely that women were actually playing an active role in overseeing cloth production, as the title 'Chief of the Weavers' is inscribed on her ebony statuette, dating from the period of Amenophis III (1386–1349)(Fig. 82).

Figure 82. Lady Teye (Chassinat 1901, pl. 2.1).

Near East

We know a great deal about the organization of textile production during the third and second millennia from palace and temple records at centers such as Ebla (Pinnock 1984, Sollberger 1986), Ur (Jacobsen 1970; Waetzoldt 1972; Szarzynska 1988), Lagash (Maekawa 1980, Van de Mieroop 1997) and Ugarit (Elliott 1991) in the Near East. Mortuary data and iconographic evidence indicate that textiles were a marker of status and prestige. Generally, subordinate city-states and professional herders under palatial administration sent enormous amounts of wool, goat hair, and finished textiles to a 'wool office' once each year. Mari often sent wool to Ebla, for example (Pinnock 1984, 27). Raw wool could either be sent to an urban center or spun locally and then disbursed to weaving workshops. The 'wool houses' were a distribution center for weaving, storage, and disbursement and are perhaps comparable to the structure at Thebes discussed in Chapter three. Finished garments were also sent on to wool houses: one inventory at Ebla lists various qualities of 7,000 garments in one wool house. In exchange for the yearly tribute of wool, herders would presumably be granted land of their own to raise palace sheep along with private livestock and/or crops of their choice.

Regarding the organization of labor in Bronze Age Mesopotamia, almost no craft specialists that were attached to administrative centers can be called a slave except for male and female textile workers (Zaccagnini 1983, 24). It took at least five years for an apprentice weaver to learn the necessary weaving skills, and it is estimated that 13,200 weavers were employed around Ur on a full-time basis, entirely dependent on the palace for their food and clothing (Van de Mieroop 1997, 186). Most of these workers were female and lived at home each day since they are known to have had children. The children would be taken to work each day, out of necessity early on in the child's life and then later for additional labor. The keen eyesight and small hands of older children made them especially desirable for fine textile manufacture, just as child labor is still exploited today in some parts of the world. In the Iron Age, Neo-Elamite tablets and art (Fig. 83), particularly from Susa, inform us greatly about textile production in the seventh century BC and show a mixture of Elamite and Iranian populations, fully acculturated, as craftsmen working for the palace (Briant 2006, 21).

After the textiles were woven they were sent on to fullers and finishers also located in the nearby villages around Ur. Less is known about these workers but their tasks were obviously arduous and required a great amount of water. Van der Mieroop (1997, 187) reproduces one text that fully records the phases of a single, three and a half kilogram, garment of second rate quality. The total amount of time spent on this piece is well over one year by laborers twisting, cleaning, trimming, sewing, pressing, beating, and picking the garment. This example gives a good idea of the attention and effort that went into making cloth under the Mesopotamian temple-state.

Access to raw materials was the major way centers controlled the production of certain goods, primarily metals. Since natural deposits of precious metals were lacking in Mesopotamia, raw materials had to be imported from Anatolia, Oman, and Iran (Stein and Blackman 1993, 52). Textual evidence from Assyrian trading colonies in Anatolia,

Figure 83. Woman with a spindle, c. 750 BCE. Neo-Elamite period, from Susa, Iran (Hervé Lewandowski © Réunion des Musées Nationaux / Art Resource, NY, for permission fee).

primarily the cuneiform documents at Kültepe Karum Kanesh, provides information on the two main items of exchange at the trading colonies of Anatolia: metals and textiles (see Barber 1994, chapter 7). Wool and linen cloth woven in communities surrounding Assur were sent by caravan northward. In Anatolia these garments would be exchange for valuable metals lacking in the home cities.

With textiles, however, access to the raw material wool was much more difficult to control. As Stein and Blackman (1993, 52) suggest, 'The centralized institutions might have maintained their control over high-prestige, luxury textiles through a strategy of close control over the knowledge and skills of the specialists themselves.' The absence of metal sources on Crete has already been noted and one wonders if the Minoans organized their metal and textile industries in a way similar to the Mesopotamian palace-temple states, by controlling access to certain textile technologies, such as purple dyeing or whatever kind of weaving was done with the spherical 'melon'-weights.

Tell es-Sa'idiyeh

The University Museum of the University of Pennsylvania excavations at Tell es-Sa'idiyeh, between 1964 and 1967, under the direction of J. Pritchard, provide a striking comparison to textile production at Gordion. Located in modern Jordan, the mound has been reinvestigated by J. Tubb and the British Museum, and has yielded evidence for occupation from the Early Bronze Age through the seventh century AD. The site has been associated with the biblical city of Zarethan. Traces of fortification walls and a dominating presence in the landscape demonstrate that the tel was obviously an important center in the region. From the published findings by Pritchard interesting questions about the organization of this site and its industrial potential are raised in comparison to the remains from Gordion.

A substantial phase at Tell es-Sa'idiyeh roughly contemporaneous with the Early Phrygian period is called Stratum V by the excavators (Fig. 84). This stratum provided the most substantial information from the excavations and shows a group of building units that are very similar to the Terrace and Clay Cut buildings at Gordion. These structures are identified by the excavator as domestic houses. The standardized plan and shared walls show that all of the units were planned and constructed at the same time. Pritchard (1985, 30) states that, 'every indication is that these were private dwellings, with the furniture and artifacts appropriate to residences.' The finds, however, and the architectural units, when viewed in comparison to the Terrace and Clay Cut buildings, would seem to me to imply an industrial quarter of specialized workshops. The major classes of artifacts from these units are ceramic bowls and storage vessels, doughnut-shaped clay loom weights, grinding stones, and clay bake-ovens. The standard architectural unit consists of a main room and a smaller room built in a line with shared side walls. The one feature of comparison found at Gordion and not at Tell es-Sa'idiyeh is a large number of clay spindle whorls. All of the other evidence, however, strongly suggests that the main activities in these buildings were grinding grain, baking, and weaving. These buildings suggest a nucleated workshop aggregated within a single community.

Six identical units are built in a line with their entrances facing a north-south street at Tell es-Sa'idiyeh. A smaller chamber is found behind the main room through an internal doorway, similar to the Gordion megaron plan but inverted with the smaller chamber behind the main room rather than in front. Through the thresholds one enters the main room of the unit, rather than an anteroom as at Gordion. The back wall of these rear chambers is shared by a parallel set of units built directly behind this first set of six. The second set of rooms corresponds to the facing Clay Cut building at Gordion in that the plan is a mirror image of the units across the way. Their organized plan and consistent features of cooking facilities and textile equipment are highly reminiscent of the remains from Gordion.

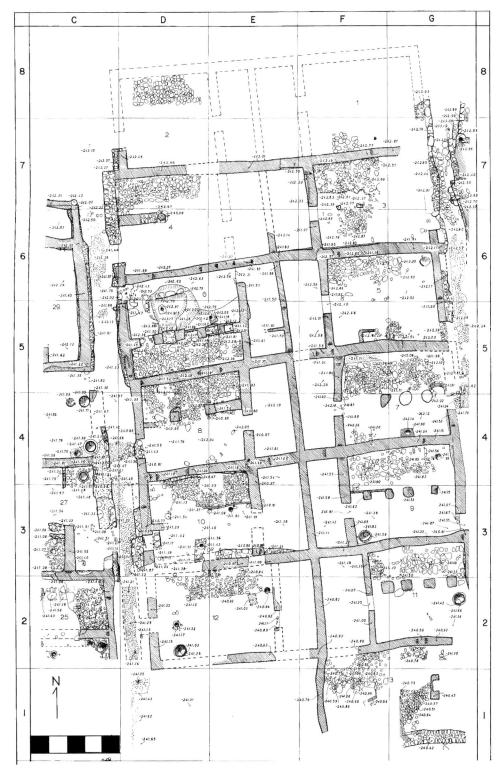

Figure 84. Tel es-Sa'idiyeh plan (Pritchard 1985, fig. 179 © University Museum).

New World Evidence

Comparative evidence for organized textile production is also found in kingdoms of the New World. By examining evidence from the Aztecs in Mexico and from the Inca at the center of Huánuco Pampa in Peru we can understand better the role of cloth in early states. While the complexity and scope of the Aztec and Inca empires are greater than what we might reconstruct for the Aegean and Phrygia, similarities in the organization of craft activities do yield useful comparisons.

Aztec

In the early part of the second millennium AD, the Aztecs expanded throughout large portions of Mesoamerica as leaders of the Triple Alliance. Aztec culture, like Bronze Age Greece, was an amalgamation of many native and subjugated groups. Tribute, trade, and war financed a large empire. Aztec textile production played a large part in all of these spheres (Berdan and Anawalt 1997). Like linen and wool in the Aegean and Anatolia, two fibers dominate Aztec textiles: cotton was the finer fabric used for elites and in ceremonial contexts. Maguey fabrics were coarser and less expensive and could be worn by commoners. This distinction appears in the archaeological record with two different types of spindle whorls, light ones for cotton and heavier ones for maguey (Smith and Hirth 1988; Brumfiel 1991; Parsons 1975; Parsons and Parsons 1990).

Aztec tribute lists from the 38 provinces are preserved in codices recording tallies of various goods required by the ruling elites at Tenochtitlan. Among these are assessments of cloth that might be compared to the Mycenaean records. The Aztec pictographic script depicts images of various types of cloth with identifying markers inside the sign (Fig. 85)(Berdan and Anawalt 1997). The Aztec (Nawat) words used to identify the textile do not describe what the cloth looks like but they inform the reader what technology was used for making the cloth. This representational system compares well with the ligatured ideograms of TELA in Mycenaean Greek. Like the Mycenaean ideograms, the signs are in the shape of cloth with distinguishing features drawn inside the textile unit. The scribes

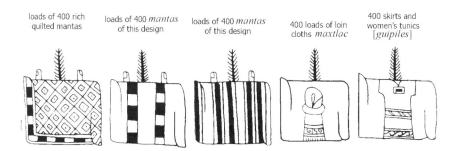

Figure 85. Aztec textile ideograms, Codex Mendoza 1992 Vol.4: folio 43r (Coayxtlahuacan) (Berdan and Anawalt 1992, with permission).

Figure 86. Ceramic Aztec spindle whorl decorated with incised fine ornament, from Calixtlahuaca Matlazinca (Am1946.16.118 © Trustees of the British Museum).

use a generic form for any textile and then within the sign they give it a distinguishing design. Some Aztec ideograms indicate extra thick cloth, fabric from different areas, specially dyed cloths, and finely woven textiles, all noted by the marker inside. This is the same scribal method used by the Mycenaeans and the Minoans as described above. The graphic representation might also suggest that those required to pay tribute in textiles were illiterate but could recognize a cloth representation in an ideogram.

Brumfiel (1991) has looked at weaving and cooking as gendered activities in Mesoamerica and examined the changes over time in tribute demands when the Aztecs rose to power. Because the Aztecs placed increasing demands on subjects for textiles in their tribute payments, it was expected that many spindle whorls would be found in surveys of urban Aztec centers (Fig. 86). There were, however, fewer spindle whorls found than expected. This dearth in evidence compares well with the absence of spindle whorls noted at Minoan palaces. Brumfiel explains that in urban areas, Aztec rulers gave cloth to commoners who served the state. These people could then go to the market to exchange the textiles for food. The farmers would then take the cloth and give it back to the state as tribute. Textiles had become a kind of currency in this finance system, and a similar explanation and use for Aegean textiles is not impossible.

Spindle whorls collected from survey in the valley of Mexico were studied extensively by M. Parsons (1972, 1975, with J. Parsons 1990). Parsons was able to suggest that certain areas predominated in cotton textile production even though the spinners most likely did not wear what they made but sent the goods on as tribute. She also did ethnographic work with local spinners asking them to test various weights of spindle whorls to see which kind of thread they could spin. While the spinners said they could make most thicknesses of thread with any weight, they preferred a certain range, 16 to 74.8 grams. This interesting work has applications to the assemblage of spindle whorls from Gordion which have comparable weight ranges.

Inca

In the Andean highlands the Inca Empire, called Tahuantinsuyu, or Land of the Four Quarters also financed itself with many different industries between 1438 and 1532. While the complexity of the Inca Empire is greater than that of anything known from the Bronze Age Aegean and Anatolia, there are similarities in the administration of labor, craft activities and storage. The distinguishing features of Inca art are standardization of design and technical precision, which can be seen in the mortarless stone masonry at sites like Machu Picchu and in tapestry-woven textiles.

The Inca Empire was divided into four provinces, each with its own provincial capital, but the imperial capital was at Cuzco. Only the most valuable wealth goods were sent to this city. An early 16th century traveler recounts that only two kinds of goods were sent here, 'gold and cloth', because they weighed little, were easily transported, and were highly valuable (Murra and Morris 1976).

In each region of the empire, the Inca built store houses with a full range of goods, supplying the local population and thus eliminating the need for one area to be in contact with any other center but the capital. These secondary centers are comparable to the outlying places known in the Minoan and Mycenaean kingdoms. Another possible similarity with Aegean palaces is that the Inca were known for ceremonial feasts and public hospitality at the state centers. Some of the royal gifts at such ceremonies were elaborately woven textiles (Murra 1989; Costin 1993; 1996; Rowe 1995–1996). These cloths would bestow authority on loyal chiefs and legitimize the dominant Inca system. Drinking vessels, certain architectural features like wide-open, public spaces, and the quantities of goods recorded in the Aegean administrative documents have suggested to some that these centers also functioned as communal feasting areas, as a way of 'redistributing' the kingdoms' wealth, possibly including finely woven textiles (Killen 1994).

Two major types of Incan cloth are recorded in ethnohistoric documents. The first type was a thick, rough cloth called *'awasqa*. Women weavers in nearly every provincial household would receive wool and cotton from local storage facilities, administered by a subordinate Incan lord called the *kuraka* (Costin 1996). They could use this fiber for their own household needs but they were also required by the Incan state to make a specific amount of cloth for the state each year (Murra 1989, 282). Officials would inspect each community to account for the raw materials and finished goods. One source states that one blanket and one shirt was the annual tax required of a household, although other sources disagree (Costin 1993, 4, citing the 16th century chronicler Cieza).

The other type of Incan cloth was a finer textile called *qompi* or *kumpi*. This was a colorful, soft textile often decorated with shell beads and feathers. These garments seem

Figure 87. Inca Textile, featherwork, cotton plain warp-faced weave with overlapping rows of feathers, made in Peru, 1530–1660 AD (Am 2006.Q.12 © Trustees of the British Museum).

to have been made by male weavers, *qompi-kamayoq*, and have particular associations with soldiers and warfare (Murra 1989, 278). One settlement near Lake Titicaca is reported to have housed one-thousand full-time male weavers of this feather-cloth. The *qompi* was tapestry-woven, with a high thread count, much more so than contemporary textiles of Europe. Sixteenth-century chroniclers from Spain note that some Aztec men wore tunics with chessboard patterns, suggesting a military association (Kotz 1997, 176).

One Inca center of particular interest to textile production is Huánuco Pampa (Morris 1974; Murra 1989; Murra and Morris 1976). Excavations within one part of this site revealed a large concentration of textile equipment and food processing. This area, Unit 5, was built in a standardized architectural idiom, with secured and controlled access. From sixteenth-century accounts, it is believed that this unit housed the *aqlla*, 'the chosen' or, more accurately, 'abducted' women who were specialists of cloth manufacture and may have had a role in supplying food for military personnel (Morris 1974, 52; Costin 1996). The high density of liquid storage jars in Unit 5 also suggests that liquids were being prepared here, most probably *chicha*, corn beer (Morris 1974, 53). It is most significant that no other craft activities have been found at Huánuco Pampa, such as pottery kilns or evidence for metal working: only textile production and food processing were the visible crafts in the archaeological record.

All Andean households had both obligations and claims to the stores of community fibers and textiles. As a valued commodity, textiles were required from peasants as payment to the crown. In exchange they would receive the right to work state lands. As with the Aztecs, textiles given by the king were used as gifts to other kings, members of the royal family, and to administrators as a way of ensuring loyalty (Fig. 87). Finally, textiles were used in ceremonies and as funerary gifts (Murra 1989). The role of state textiles supplying the military recalls some of the uses of cloth suggested for the Mycenaeans and Phrygians.

Conclusions: Tying it all Together

Textile production of the type described above and in the preceding chapters is a highly specialized craft with attached laborers participating in staple/wealth finance economies. Most probably these industries were administered by centralized bureaucracies, although little evidence for this has yet been found from Gordion. This kind of organization could only occur at urban centers that had close ties to rural hinterlands. The evidence available from the Minoan, Mycenaean and Phrygian kingdoms shows that there was a close interaction between these two spheres. The development of surplus agriculture may have been the result of increased trade and commerce in Minoan Crete, including the production of valuable textiles. Food rations are recorded in the Linear B records as payment to the textile workers. The evidence from Gordion shows that textile and food production were the two major activities the Phrygians chose to locate within their citadel walls, under the watchful eye of the ruling elites.

Evidence presented above demonstrates that differences in social complexity and productive strategies translate into differential distributions of textile equipment. For this book, the unit of analysis has been, for lack of a better term, the Aegean and Anatolian

Table 19: Types of Specialization, from Costin (1991).

Costin's Specialized Production Types	Archaeological Examples
Specialization by autonomous individuals for unrestricted local consumption	Little evidence in examples studied
Dispersed specialists working for unrestricted local consumption	• Middle Neolithic Knossos, • Early Minoan Knossos (?)
Community specialization by autonomous individual or household-based production units, aggregated within a single community, producing for unrestricted regional consumption	• Later Neolithic Knossos • Early Minoan II A–B Myrtos (Fournou Korifi)
Large, nucleated workshops aggregated within a single community, producing for unrestricted regional consumption.	• Perhaps at Early Minoan II A–B Myrtos (Fournou Korifi) • Vasiliki
Dispersed corveé labor, working part-time for elite and government institutions within households or local community settings.	• Mycenaean Nichoria • production of textile *146
Individual retainers and individual artisans usually working full-time for elite patrons or governments	Little evidence in examples studied
Nucleated corveé laborers working part-time, recruited by government for special purposes.	• Perhaps some evidence at Mycenaean palaces.
Retainer workshops reflecting large-scale operations with full-time artisans working for an elite patron or government institution within a highly segregated, specialized setting or facility.	• Old Palace at Knossos (Loom weight Basement) • Houses around Knossos (MUM, North House, South House) • Gordion

palace. Rather than seeing specialization as a 'presence or absence' at palatial centers, I have tried to look at textile production in terms of degrees. Costin (1991) proposes an eight-part typology of increasing complexity for the organization of specialized production. Applying these criteria to examples presented in this book provides a summary of organized textile production in the Bronze and Iron Ages (Table 19).

Having looked at many examples of centralized textile production, both with textual and archaeological sources, what can we say about palace production? From the Mycenaean period we have documentary records of cloth manufacture in archives at palace centers. Many archaeologists have focused a great deal of attention on the Mycenaean palace while not investigating smaller settlements where activities such as pottery, metallurgy and textile production are more likely to be located. It is highly probable that the production of cloth occurred in smaller Mycenaean villages located in the hinterlands of the palaces, at settlements like Nichoria. It seems that large scale production of textiles was primarily the work of women dependent upon the central authority, possibly against their will. Similar to the Inca *aqlla*, some of the women laborers at the Mycenaean palaces may have been prisoners captured in war, from areas across the Aegean, like Miletus, Lemnos, and Halikarnassos. Palace-made cloth was probably used to appease potentially hostile neighbors, impress valuable trading partners, and to legitimize the elite power base. Textiles produced by commoners in household settings were often assessed and collected as tribute by the center and then redistributed as a form of currency to non-food producers. This circulation of textiles would have continued as long as the system was working.

The Mycenaean system contrasts with the earlier Minoan period on Crete, where both administrative documents and artifactual evidence for textile production are located at the palaces. The Mycenaeans may have adopted some of the administrative aspects of the Minoan system but they do not seem to have employed the same production system. The Minoans might be closer in organization to the Phrygians, who, as we saw, located their textile production within the citadel walls of their capital.

After the Bronze Age the organization of textile production changes dramatically in the archaic and classical periods in Greece. The contribution of women's labor to Classical household economics, as described in Xenophon (*Oec.* 7), and the role of textiles in Greek religion, are subjects for further investigation. This book has examined the many different sources of information for understanding the role of controlled textile production at large palatial centers of the Bronze Age Aegean and the Anatolian Iron Age. This investigation shows that cloth manufacture in the eastern Mediterranean is an industry of wealth-based economies and that changes in textile technology and organization reflect developments in both complexity and craft specialization. The rich archaeological record demonstrates that humbler artifactual evidence can inform us about larger issues of emerging complexity.

BIBLIOGRAPHY

Abbreviations, in addition to those in the preface, follow the conventions of the *American Journal of Archaeology.*

Adovasio, J. 1983. "Notes on the Textile and Basketry Impressions from Jarmo," in *Prehistoric Archaeology along the Zagros Flanks*, ed. L. Braidwood, R. Braidwood, B. Howe, C. Reed, and P. J. Watson, Chicago, 425–426.

Adovasio, M., O. Soffer, and B. Klìma 1996. "Upper Palaeolithic Fibre Technology from Pavlov I, Czech Republic," *Antiquity* 70, 526–534.

Åkerström, Å. 1978. "Mycenaean Problems," *OpAth* 12, 19–86.

Albright, W. 1965. "The Role of the Canaanites in the History of Civilization," in *The Bible and the Ancient Near East*, ed. G. Wright, Garden City, 438–87.

Alexiou, S. 1987. "Minoan Palaces as Centres of Trade and Manufacture," in *Function of the Minoan Palace*, 251–53.

Allison, K. J. 1958. "Flock Management in the Sixteenth and Seventeenth Centuries," *Economic History Review* 11(1), 98–112.

Anderson, E. and M.-L. Nosch 2003. "With a Little Help from my Friends: Investigating Mycenaean Textiles with help from Scandanavian Experimental Archaeology," in *METRON*, 199–203.

Aravantinos, V. 1990. "The Mycenaean Inscribed Sealings from Thebes: Problems of Content and Function," in *Aegean Seals, Sealings and Administration*, (*Aegaeum* 5), ed. T. Palaima, Liège, 149–174.

Aravantinos, V. 1999. "Mycenaean texts and contexts at Thebes: the discovery of new Linear B archives on the Kadmeia," in *Floreant Studia Mycenaea*, 45–102.

Aravantinos, V. 2001. *Thèbes, fouilles de la Cadmée I: Les tablettes en Linéaire B de la Odos Pelopidou (édition et commentaire)*, Pisa and Rome.

Aravantinos, V. 2002. *Thèbes, fouilles de la Cadmée III: Corpus des Documents D'Archives en Linéaire B de Thèbes*, Pisa and Rome.

Aravantinos, V., L. Godart and A. Sacconi 1995. "Sui nuovi testi del palazzo di Cadmo a Tebe: note preliminari," *RendLinc* 6, 809–845.

Astour, M. 1965. "The Origin of the Terms 'Canaan', 'Phoenician', and 'Purple'," *JNES* 24, 346–50.

Aura Jorro, F. 1999. Reprint. *Diccionario Micénico* I, Madrid.

Aura Jorro, F. 1993. *Diccionario Micénico* II, Madrid.

Balfanz, K. 1995. "Bronzezeitliche Spinnwirtel aus Troia," *Studia Troica* V, 117–144.

Ballard, M. 2006. "MCI: 5277: King Midas' Tomb," *Project Summaries 2006 MCI*, http://www.si.edu/ MCI/ downloads/AnnualReports/MCI_Executive_Summaries_2006.pdf, p. 16.

Ballard, M. 2007. "Textile Production at Gordion," paper delieved at University Museum of the University of Pennsylvania Conference: The Archaeology of Phrygian *Gordion*. Philadelphia, April 20–22, 2007.

Banti, L., F. Halbherr and E. Stefani 1980. "Haghia Triada nel periodo tardo-palaziale," *ASAtene* 55, 37–61.

Barber, E. 1991. *Prehistoric Textiles: The Development of Cloth in the Neolithic and Bronze Ages, with Special Reference to the Aegean*, Princeton.

Barber, E. 1992. "The Peplos of Athena," in *Goddess and Polis: The Panathenaic Festival in Ancient Athens*, ed. J. Neils, Hanover, 102–117.

Barber, E. 1993. "Late Bronze Age Kilts and the Reconstruction of Aegean Textile Connections," *AJA* 97, 350.

Barber, E. 1994. *Women's Work: The First 20,000 Years*, New York.

Barber, E. 1997. "Minoan Women and the Challenges of Weaving for Home, Trade, and Shrine," in *TEXNH*, 515–519.

Barber, E. 1998. "Aegean Ornament and Designs in Egypt," in *The Aegean and the Orient in the Second Millennium. Proceedings of the 50th Anniversary Symposium Cincinnati, 18–20 April 1997*, (*Aegaeum* 18), ed. E. Cline and D. Harris-Cline, Liège, 13–17.

Barrett, J. and P. Halstead eds 2004. *The Emergence of Civilisation Revisited*, Sheffield Studies in Aegean Archaeology. Oxford.

Baumbach, L. 1987. "Mycenaean tu-ru-pte-ri-ja and Herodotus II.180," in *Tractata Mycenaea: Proceedings of the VIIIth International Colloquium on Mycenaean Studies, held in Ohrid, 15–20 September 1985*, ed. P. Ilievski and L. Crepajac, Skopje, 49–54.

Beck, L. and C. Beck 1978. "*Wi-ri-za* wool on Linear B Tablets of Perfume Ingredients," *AJA* 82, 213–215.

Bellinger, L. 1962. "Textiles from Gordion," *The Bulletin of the Needle and Bobbin Club* 46(1), 5–34.

Bennet, J. 1985. "The Structure of the Linear B Administration at Knossos," *AJA* 89, 231–249.

Bennet, J. 1987a. "Knossos and LM III Crete: A Post-Palatial Palace?" in *Function of the Minoan Palace*, 307–311.

Bennet, J. 1987b. "The Wild Country East of Dikte: The Problem of East Crete in the LM III Period," in *Studies in Mycenaean and Classical Greek Presented to John Chadwick* (*Minos* 20–22), ed. J. T. Killen, J. L. Melena, and J.-P. Olivier, Salamanca, 77–88.

Bennet, J. 1988a. "Outside in the Distance: Problems in Understanding the Economic Geography of Mycenaean Palatial Territories," in *Texts, Tablets and Scribes* (*Minos* Supplement 10), ed. J.-P. Olivier and T. Palaima, Salamanca, 19–42.

Bennet, J. 1988b. "Approaches to the Problem of Combining Linear B Textual Data and Archaeological Data in the Late Bronze Age," in *Problems in Prehistory: Proceedings of the 1986 Manchester Conference*, ed. E. French and K. Wardle, Bristol, 509–518.

Bennet, J. 1990a. "Knossos in Context: Perspectives on the Linear B Administration of LM II–III Crete," *AJA* 94, 193–211.

Bennet, J. 1992. "'Collectors' or 'Owners'? An Examination of their Possible Functions Within the Palatial Economy of LM III Crete," in *Mykénaïka: Actes du IXe Colloque international sur les textes mycéniens et égéens organisé par le Centre de l'Antiquité Grecque et Romaine de la Fondation Hellénique des Recherches Scientifiques et l'École française d'Athènes, Athènes, 2–6 octobre 1990* (*BCH* Supplement 25), ed. J.-P. Olivier, Athens, 65–101.

Bennet, J. 1999a. "*Re-u-ko-to-ro-za-we-te*: Leuktron as a Secondary Capital in the Pylos Kingdom?" in *A-NA-QO-TA: Studies Presented to J. T. Killen* (*Minos* 33–34), ed. J. Bennet and J. Driessen, Salamanca, 11–30.

Bennet, J. 1999b. "The Mycenaean Conceptualization of Space or Pylian Geography …yet again!" in *Floreant Studia Mycenaea*, 131–57.

Bennett, E. and J.-P. Olivier eds 1973. *The Pylos Tablets Transcribed*, Vol. I, Rome.

Bennett, E. J.-P. and Olivier eds 1976. *The Pylos Tablets Transcribed*, Vol. II, Rome

Benzi, M. 1987. "Evidence for MM Settlement on the Acropolis at Ialysos," in *The Minoan Thalassocracy: Myth and Reality*, ed. R. Hägg and N. Marinatos, Stockholm 93–105.

Berdan, F. and P. Anawalt, trans. and eds 1992. *Codex Mendoza*, 4 Vols, Berkeley.

Bernabé, A. and E. Luján 2008. "Mycenaean Technology," in *A Companion to Linear B: Mycenaean Greek Texts and their World*, ed. Y. Duhoux and A. Morpurgo Davies, Leuven, 201–233.

Betancourt, P. 2000. "Vasiliki", in *Crete 2000: A Centennial Celebration of American Archaeological Work on Crete (1900–2000)*, ed. J. Muhly, Athens, 119–21.

Betancourt, P. 2007. "Textile Production at Pseira: the Knotted Net," in *Ancient Textiles: Production, Craft, Society,* ed. C. Gillis and M. -L. Nosch, Oxford, 185–9.

Bieber, M. 1928. *Griechische Kleidung*, Berlin and Leipzig.

Bier, C. 1995. "Textile Arts in Ancient Western Asia," in *CANE*, New York, 1567–88.

Billigmeier, J. and J. Turner 1981. "The Socio-Economic Roles of Women in Mycenaean Greece: a Brief Survey from the Evidence of the Linear B Tablets," in *Reflections of Women in Antiquity,* ed. H. Foley, New York, 1–15.

Bintliff, J. 1977. *Natural Environment and Human Settlement in Prehistoric Greece* (*BAR* Supplement 28), Oxford.

Björck, G. 1954. "Pour le vocabulaire des tablettes 'à bannieres' de Knossos," *Eranos* 52, 271–275.

Blegen, C. 1928. *Zygouries: A Prehistoric Settlement in the Valley of Cleonae*, Cambridge.

Blegen, C. 1950–58. *Troy: The University of Cincinnati Excavations*, 1932–1938, Princeton.

Blegen, C. and M. Rawson 1966. *The Palace of Nestor at Pylos in Western Messenia* I, Princeton.

Blegen, C., M. Rawson, W. Taylour and W. Donovan 1973. *The Palace of Nestor at Pylos in Western Messenia* III, Princeton.

Blinkenberg, G. C. 1926. *Fibules grecques et orientales,* Copenhagen.

Boehmer, R. 1972. *Die Kleinfunde von Boazköy: Aus den Grabungskampagnen 1931–1939 und 1952–1969*, Berlin.

Boehmer, R. 1973. "Phrygische Prunkgewänder des 8. Jahrhunderts v. Chr. Herkunft und Export," *AA* 11(2), 149–172.

Böhmer, H. and J. Thompson 1991. "The Pazyryk Carpet: A Technical Discussion," *Source: Notes in the History of Art* 10(4), 30–36.

Bosanquet, R. 1904. "Some 'Late Minoan' Vases found in Greece," *JHS* 24, 317–329.

Bosanquet, R. 1939–1940. "Dikte and the Temples of Dictaean Zeus," *BSA* 40, 60–77.

Bosanquet, R. and R. Dawkins 1923. *The Unpublished Objects from the Palaikastro Excavations 1902–1906* (*BSA* Supplement 1), London.

Branigan, K. 1970. *The Foundations of Palatial Crete*, New York.

Branigan, K. 1988. *Pre-Palatial: The Foundations of Palatial Crete*, Amsterdam.

Branigan, K. 1995. "Social Transformation and the Rise of the State in Crete," in *Politeia*, 33–40.

Briant, P. 2006. *From Cyrus to Alexander: a history of the Persian Empire* (trans. P. Daniels), Winona Lake.

Brice, W., ed. 1961. *Inscriptions in the Minoan Linear Script of Class A*, Oxford.

Brixhe, C. and M. Lejeune 1984. *Corpus des inscriptions paléo-phrygiennes*, Paris.

Broodbank, C. 1992. "The Neolithic Labyrinth: Social Change at Knossos before the Bronze Age," *JMA* 5(1), 39–75.

Broodbank, C. and T. Strasser 1991. "Migrant farmers and the Neolithic colonization of Crete," *Antiquity* 65, 233–45.

Brown, D. 1991. *Human Universals*. New York.

Brown, K. 1980. *The Question of Near Eastern Textile Decoration of the early First Millennium B.C. as a Source for Greek Vase Painting of the Orientalizing Style*, Ph.D. diss., University of Pennsylvania.

Browning, D. 1988. *The Textile Industry of Iron Age Timnah and Its Regional and Socioeconomic Contexts: A Literary and Artifactual Analysis*, Ph.D. diss., Southwestern Baptist Seminary.

Browning, D. (personal communication). "Loom weights in Iron Age Israel: Evidence of production for Assyrian Tribute?"

Bruin, F. 1970. "Royal Purple and the Dye Industry of the Mycenaeans and Phoenicians," in *Sociétés et compagnies de commerce en Orient dans l'Ocean Indien,* ed. M. Mollat, Paris, 73–90.

Brumfiel, E. 1989. "Factional Competition in Complex Society," in *Domination and Resistance,* ed. D. Miller, M. Rowlands, and C. Tilley, London and Boston, 126–139.

Brumfiel, E. 1991. "Weaving and Cooking: Women's Production in Aztec Mexico," in *Engendering Archaeology: Women and Prehistory,* ed. J. Gero and M. Conkey, Oxford, 224–251.

Brumfiel, E. and T. Earle eds 1987. *Specialization, Exchange, and Complex Societies,* New York.

Brysbaert A. 2007. "Murex and Marine Shell Use for Lime Production and in Plaster Surfaces in the Aegean and Eastern Mediterranean Bronze Age," *Mediterranean Archaeology and Archaeometry* 7–2, 29–51.

Burke, B. 1997. "The Organization of Textile Production in Bronze Age Crete," in *TEXNH,* 413–424.

Burke, B. 1999. "Purple and the Aegean Textile Trade of the Early Second Millennium BC," in *Meletemata: Studies in Aegean Archaeology Presented to M. H. Wiener as he enters his 65th Year,* (Aegaeum 20), ed. P. Betancourt, V. Karageorghis, R. Laffineur, and W. Niemeier, Liège and Austin, 75–82.

Burke, B. 2001. "Anatolian Origins of the Gordian Knot Legend," *GRBS* 42, 255–261.

Burke, B. 2003. "The Spherical Loom Weights," in *Knossos: The South House* (BSA Supplement 34), P. Mountjoy, London, 195–197.

Burke, B. 2005a. "Textile Production at Gordion and the Phrygian Economy," in *The Archaeology of Midas and the Phrygians: Recent Work at Gordion,* ed. L. Kealhofer, Philadelphia, 69–81.

Burke, B. 2005b. "Materialization of Mycenaean Ideology and the Ayia Triada Sarcophagus," *AJA* 109, 403–422.

Burke, B. 2006. "Textile Production at House II, Petras," Πεπραγμενα Θ' Διεθνους Κρητολογικου Συνεδριου *2001 Τομος Α.2,* 279–95.

Cadogan, G. 1986. "Why Was Crete Different?" in *The End of the Early Bronze Age,* ed. G. Cadogan, Leiden, 153–71.

Carington Smith, J. 1975. *Weaving, Spinning and Textile Production in Greece: The Neolithic to Bronze Age,* Ph.D. diss., University of Tasmania.

Carington Smith, J. 1992. "Textiles at Nichoria," in *Excavations at Nichoria in Southwestern Greece, Vol. II: The Bronze Age Occupation,* ed. W. McDonald and N. Wilkie, Minneapolis, 674–711.

Casson, L. 1971. *Ships and Seamanship in the Ancient World,* Princeton.

Catling, H. 1989. *Some Problems in Aegean Prehistory, c. 1450–1380 BC,* Oxford.

Catling, E., H. Catling and D. Smyth 1979. "Knossos 1975: Middle Minoan III and Late Minoan I Houses by the Acropolis," *BSA* 74, 1–78.

Chadwick, J. 1963. "The Two Provinces of Pylos," *Minos* 7, 125–141.

Chadwick, J. 1964. "Pylos tablet Un 1322," in Mycenaean Studies: Proceedings of the Third International Colloquium for Mycenaean Studies held at 'Wingspread' 4–8 September 1961, ed. E. Bennett, Madison, 19–26.

Chadwick, J. 1973. "The Geography of the Further Province of Pylos," *AJA* 77, 276–278.

Chadwick, J. 1988. "The Women of Pylos", in *Texts, Tablets and Scribes* (Minos Supplement 10), ed. J.-P. Olivier and T. Palaima, Salamanca, 43–96.

Chapin, A. 2008. "The Lady of the Landscape: An Investigation of Aegean Costuming and the Xeste 3 Fescoes," in *Reading a Dynamic Canvas: Adornment in the Ancient Mediterranean World,* ed. C. Colburn and M. Heyn, Cambridge, 48–83.

Chassinat, M. 1901, "Tombe inviolée de la xviii dynastie découverte aux environs de Médinet el-Gorab dans le Fayoùm," *Bulletin de l'institut français d'archéologie Orientale* 1, 225–234.

Cherry, J. 1983. "Evolution, Revolution, and the Origins of Complex Societies," in *Minoan Society: Proceedings of the Cambridge Colloquium 1981,* ed. O. Krzyszkowska and L. Nixon, Cambridge, 33–45.

Cherry, J. 1986. "Polities and Palaces: Some Problems in Minoan State Formation," in *Peer Polity Interaction and Socio-Political Change,* ed. C. Renfrew and J. Cherry, Cambridge, 19–45.

Çilingiroğlu, Ç. 2009. "Of Stamps, Loom Weights and Spindle Whorls: Contextual Evidence on the Function(s) of Neolithic Stamps from Ulucak, İzmir, Turkey," *JMA* 22.1, 3–27.

Cline, E. 1995. "Tinker, Tailor, Soldier, Sailor: Minoans and Mycenaeans Abroad," in *Politeia*, 265–283.

Colburn, C. 2008. "Exotica and the Body in the Minoan and Mycenaean Worlds," in *Reading a Dynamic Canvas: Adornment in the Ancient Mediterranean World*, ed. C. Colburn and M. Heyn, Cambridge, 13–47.

Coldstream, J. and G. Huxley 1987. "The Minoans of Kythera," in *Function of the Minoan Palace*, 106–108.

Costin, C. 1991. "Craft Specialization: Issues in Defining, Documenting and Explaining the Organization of Production," in *Archaeological Method and Theory*, ed. M. Schiffer, Tucson, 1–56.

Costin, C. 1993. "Textiles, Women, and Political Economy in Late Prehispanic Peru," *Research in Economic Anthropology* 14, 3–28.

Costin, C. 1996. "Craft Production and Mobilization Strategies in the Inka Empire," in *Craft Specialization and Social Evolution: In Memory of V. Gordon Childe*, B. Wailes, Philadelphia, 211–228.

Crewe, L. 1998. *Spindle Whorls: A Study of Form, Function and Decoration in Prehistoric Bronze Age Cyprus.* Jonsered.

Crowfoot, G. 1936. "Of the Warp-Weighted Loom," *BSA* 37, 36–47.

Cummer, W. and E. Schofield 1984. *Kea III. Ayia Irini: House A,* Mainz on Rhine.

D'Altroy, T. and T. Earle 1985. "Staple Finance, Wealth Finance, and Storage in the Inka Political Economy," *CurrAnthr* 26(2), 187–197.

Dabney, M. 1996. "Ceramic Loomweights and Spindle Whorls," in *Kommos I: The Kommos Region and Houses of the Minoan Town,* ed. J. Shaw and M. Shaw, Princeton, 244–262.

Dalley, S. 1977. "Old Babylonian Trade in Textiles at Tell al Rimah," *Iraq* 39, 155–59.

Dalley, S 1984. *Mari and Karana*, London.

Dalley, S 1991. "Ancient Assyrian Textiles and the Origins of Carpet Design," *Iran* 29, 117–135.

Davis, J. 1984. "Cultural innovation and the Minoan Thalassocracy at Ayia Irini," in *The Minoan Thalassocracy: Myth and Reality,* ed. R. Hägg and N. Marinatos, Stockholm, 159–166.

David, R. 1996. *The Pyramid Builders of Ancient Egypt: A Modern Investigation of Pharaoh's Workforce,* London.

Dawkins, R. 1903–1904. "Excavations at Palaikastro II," *BSA* 10, pp.192–226.

Day, P., D. Wilson and E. Kiriatzi 1997. "Reassessing Specialization in Prepalatial Cretan Ceramic Production," in *TEXNH: Craftsmen, Craftswomen and Craftsmanship in the Aegean Bronze Age Proceedings of the 6th International Aegean, Philadelphia, Temple University, 18–21 April 1996, (Aegaeum* 16), ed. R. Laffineur and P. Betancourt, Liège and Austin, 276–290.

Deger-Jalkotzy, S. 1978. *E-QE-TA: Zur Rolle des Gefolgschaftswasens in der Sozialstruktur mykenischer Reiche*, Vienna.

De Graaf, F. 1989. "Midas, Wanax, Lawagetas," in *Thracians and Mycenaeans,* ed. J. Best and N. Devries, Leiden, 153–155.

Deshayes, J. and A. Dessens 1959. *Mallia: Exploration des maisons et quartiers d'habitation II 1948–1954 (Études Crétoises* XI), Paris.

DeVries, K. 1980. "Greeks and Phrygians in the Early Iron Age," in *From Athens to Gordion: The Papers of a Memorial Symposium for Rodney S. Young,* ed. K. DeVries, Philadelphia, 33–50.

DeVries, K. 1987. "Phrygian Gordion Before Midas," in *Anatolian Iron Ages,* ed. A. Çilingiroğlu and D. French, Izmir, 6–12.

DeVries, K. 1988. "Gordion and Phrygia in the Sixth Century BC," in *Phrygian Art and Archaeology* (*Source: Notes in the History of Art* 7), ed. O. Muscarella, New York, 51–59.

DeVries, K. 1990. "The Gordion Excavation Seasons of 1969–1971 and Subsequent Research," *AJA* 94, 371–406.

DeVries, K. 1998. "The Assyrian Destruction of Gordion?" *AJA* 102, 397

DeVries, K. 2005. "Greek Pottery and Gordion Chronology," in *The Archaeology of Midas and the Phrygians. Recent Work at Gordion*, ed. L. Kealhofer, Philadelphia, 36–55.

DeVries, K., P. Kuniholm, K. Sams and M. Voigt 2003. "New Dates for Iron Age Gordion," *Antquity* 77.296, http://antiquity.ac.uk/projGall/devries/devries.html.

Dimopoulou, N. 1997. "Workshops and Craftsmen in the Harbour-Town of Knossos at Poros-Katsambas," in *TEXNH: Craftsmen, Craftswomen and Craftsmanship in the Aegean Bronze Age,* (*Aegaeum* 16), Liège and Austin, 433–438.

Dinç, R. and L. Innocente 1999. "Ein spinnwirtel mit phrygischer inschrift," *Kadmos* 38, 65–72.

Dothan, M. 1988. "The Significance of Some Artisans' Workshops along the Canaanite Coast," in *Society and Economy in the Eastern, c. 1500–1000 BC: Proceedings of the International Symposium held at the University of Haifa from the 28th of April to the 2nd of May, 1985*, ed. M. Heltzer and E. Lipìnski, Leuven, 295–303.

Dothan, T. 1963. "Spinning Bowls," *Israel Exploration Journal* 13, 97–112.

Doumet, J. 1980. *A Study on Ancient Purple*, Beirut.

Drews, R. 1983. "Myths of Midas and Phrygian Migration from Europe," *Klio* 75, 9–26.

Driessen, J. 1984. "Some Military Aspects of the Aegean in the Late Fifteenth and early Fourteenth Centuries BC, Part I: Mercenaries at Mycenaean Knossos," *BSA* 79, 49–56.

Driessen, J. 1990. *An Early Destruction in the Mycenaean Palace at Knossos: A New Interpretation of the Excavation Field-Notes of the South-East Area of the West Wing*, Leuven.

Driessen, J. and J. Sakellarakis. 1997. "The Vathypetro Complex," in The Function of the "Minoan Villa". Proceedings of the eighth international symposium at the Swedish Institute at Athens, 6–8 June 1992, ed. R. Hägg, Stockholm, 63–77.

Duhoux, Y. 1974. "Idéogrammes textiles du Linéaire B *146, *160, *165, et *166," *Minos* 15, 116–132.

Duhoux, Y. 1976. *Aspects du vocabulaire économique mycénien*, Amsterdam.

Durand, J-M. 1983. Textes administratifs des salles 134 et 160 du palais de Mari, transerits, traduits et commentés. *ARMT* XXI, Paris.

Dyson, R. 1980. "The Question of Balconies at Hasanlu," in *From Athens to Gordion: The Papers of a Memorial Symposium for Rodney S. Young*, ed. K. DeVries, Philadelphia, 149–157.

Edwards, G. R. 1963. "Gordion: 1962," *Expedition* 5(3), 42–48.

Efstratiou, N., A. Karetsou, E. Banou and D. Margomenou 2004. "The Neolithic Settlement of Knossos: New Light on an Old Picture," in *Knossos: Palace, City, State*, 39–49.

Elliott, C. 1991. "The Ground Stone Industry," in *Ras Shamra Ougarit* VI: *Arts et Industries de la pierre*, ed. M. Yon and A Caubet, 9–99, Paris.

Ellis, R. 1981. "The Textile Remains," in *Gordion Excavation Reports I: Three Great Early Tumuli (P, MM, W)*, R. Young, Philadelphia, Appendix V.

Evans, A. 1906. *Essai de Classification des Epoques de la Civilisation Minoenne*, London.

Evans, A. 1909. *Scripta Minoa. The Written Documents of Minoan Crete with Special Reference to the Archives of Knossos*: Vol. I, *The Hieroglyphic and Primitive Linear Classes* I, Oxford.

Evans, A. 1921. *The Palace of Minos at Knossos* I.2, London.

Evans, A. 1928. *The Palace of Minos at Knossos* II, parts 1 and 2, London.

Evans, J. D. 1964. "Excavations in the Neolithic Settlement at Knossos, 1957–60, Part I" *BSA* 59, 132–240.

Evans, J. D. 1968. "Knossos Neolithic, Part II," *BSA* 63, 239–276.

Evans, J. D. 1994. "The Early Millennia: Continuity and Change in a Farming Settlement," in *Knossos: A Labyrinth of History,* ed. D. Evely, H. Hughes-Brock, and N. Momigliano, London, 1–20.

Evely, D. 2000. *Minoan Crafts: Tools and Techniques: An Introduction*, Jonsered.

Evely, D. ed. 2006. *Lefkandi IV: The Bronze Age. The Late Helladic IIIC Settlement at Xeropolis* (*BSA* Supplement 39). Athens.

Evely, D., H. Hughes-Brock and N. Momigliano eds 1994. *Knossos: A Labyrinth of History,* London.

Finkelberg, M. 1998. "Bronze Age Writing: Contacts between East and West", in *The Aegean and the Orient in the Second Millennium. Proceedings of the 50th Anniversary Symposium Cincinnati, 18–20 April 1997*, (*Aegaeum* 18), ed. Cline, E. and D. Harris-Cline, Liège, 265–73.

Finley, M. 1957. "The Mycenaean Tablets and Economic History," *Economic History Review* 10, 128–141.

Firth, R. 2007. "Re-considering alum on the Linear B Tablets", in *Ancient Textiles: Production, Craft, Society,* ed. C. Gillis and M. L. Nosch, Oxford, 130–8.

Fletcher, B. 1921. *A History of Architecture on the Comparative Method*. Sixth edition. New York.

Forbes, R. J. 1964. *Studies in Ancient Technology* IV, Leiden.

Forstenpointner, G., U. Quatember, A. Galik, G. Weissengruber and A. Konecny 2007. "Purple-dye production in Lycia – results of an archaeozoological field survey in Andriake (south-west Turkey)," *Oxford Journal of Archaeology* 26.2, 201–14.

Foster, E. 1977. "*Po-ni-ki-jo* in the Knossos Tablets Reconsidered," *Minos* 16, 52–66.

Foster, E. 1981. "The Flax Impost at Pylos and Mycenaean Landholding," *Minos* 17, 67–121.

Fouqet, H. and H. Bielig 1971. "Biological Precursors and Genesis of Tyrian Purple," *Angewänte Chemie* 10, 816–817.

Frödin, O. and A. Persson 1938. *Asine, Results of the Swedish Excavations 1922–1930*, Stockholm.

Furtwängler, A. and K. Reichhold 1904–1932. *Griechische Vasenmalerei*. 1932.

Gamble, C. 1982. "Animal Husbandry, Population and Urbanism," in *An Island Polity: The Archaeology and Exploitation of Melos,* ed. C. Renfrew and M. Wagstaff, Cambridge, 161–171.

Genz, H. 2003. "The Early Iron Age in Central Anatolia," in *Identifying Changes: The Transition from Bronze and Iron Ages in Anatolia and its Neighboring Regions,* ed. B. Fischer, H. Genz, E. Jean, and K. Koroğlu, Istanbul, 179–191.

Gillis, C. and M. -L. Nosch eds 2007. *Ancient Textiles: Production, Craft, Society.* Oxford.

Godart, L. 1970. "The Grouping of Place-Names in the Cn Tablets," *BICS* 17, 159–161.

Godart, L. 1973. "Valeur des idéogrammes OVISm, OVISf, CAPm, SUSm, SUSf, BOSm et BOSf dans les tablettes de Cnossos," *Minos* 13, 113–129.

Goldman, H. 1931. *Excavations at Eutresis in Boeotia,* Cambridge: Harvard University Press.

GORILA I–V: Godart, L. and J.-P. Olivier. 1976–1985. *Recueil des inscriptions en Linéaire A* I–V (*Études Crétoises* XXI), Paris.

Graham, J. 1975. "The Banquet Room of the Little Palace," *AJA* 79, 141–145.

Greenewalt, C., Jr. and L. Majewski 1980. "Lydian Textiles," in *From Athens to Gordion: The Papers of a Memorial Symposium for Rodney S. Young,* ed. K. DeVries, Philadelphia, 133–40.

Gregersen, M. -L. 1997. "Pylian Craftsmen: Payment in Kind/Rations or Land?" in *TEXNH*, 397–405.

Guarducci, M. 1935. Inscriptiones Creticae: Opera et Consilio Friderici Halbherr Collectae I, Rome.

Gunter, A. 1991. *Gordion Final Reports III: The Bronze Age Occupation*, Philadelphia.

Gurney, O. 1948. "Mita of Pahhuwa," *AnnLiv* 28, 32–47.

Güterbock, H. 1980. "Seals and Sealing in Hittite Lands," in *From Athens to Gordion: The Papers of a Memorial Symposium for Rodney S. Young,* ed. K. DeVries, Philadelphia, 50–55.

Hägg, R. ed. 1997. *The Function of the Minoan 'Villa': Proceedings of the Eighth International Symposium at the Swedish Institute at Athens, 6–8 June, 1992,* Stockholm.

Hallager, E. 1977. *The Mycenaean Palace at Knossos: Evidence for Final Destruction in the III B Period*, Stockholm.

Hallager, E. 1996. *The Minoan Roundel and Other Sealed Documents in the Neopalatial Linear A Administration,* (*Aegaeum* 14), Liège.

Hallager, E., M. Vlasaki and B. Hallager 1992. "New Linear B tablets from Khania," *Kadmos* 31, 61–87.

Halstead, P. 1981a. "Counting Sheep in Neolithic and Bronze Age Greece," in *Pattern of the Past: Studies in Honour of David Clarke,* ed. I. Hodder, G. Isaac and N. Hammond, Cambridge, 307–339.

Halstead, P. 1981b. "From Determinism to Uncertainty: Social Storage and the Rise of the Minoan Palaces," in *Economic Archaeology,* ed. A. Sheridan and G. Bailey, Oxford, 187–213.

Halstead, P. 1988. "On Redistribution and the Origin of Minoan-Mycenaean Palatial Economies," in *Problems in Prehistory: Proceedings of the 1986 Manchester Conference*, ed. E. French and K. Wardle, Bristol, 519–530.

Halstead, P. 1991. "Lost Sheep? On the Linear B Evidence for Breeding Flocks at Knossos and Pylos," *Minos* 22, 343–365.

Halstead, P. 1992a. "Agriculture in the Bronze Age: Towards a Model of Palatial Economy," in *Agriculture in Ancient Greece: Proceedings of the Seventh International Symposium at the Swedish Institute at Athens, 16–17 May 1990*, ed. B. Wells, Stockholm, 105–117.

Halstead, P. 1992b. "The Mycenaean Palatial Economy: Making the Most of the Gaps in the Evidence," *Proceedings of the Cambridge Prehistoric Society* 38, 57–86.

Halstead, P. 1995. "From Sharing to Hoarding: the Neolithic foundations of Aegean Bronze Age Society," in *Politeia*, 11–21.

Halstead, P. 1999a. "Texts, Bones and Herders: Approaches to Animal Husbandry in Late Bronze Age Greece," in *A-NA-QO-TA: Studies Presented to J. T. Killen* (*Minos* 33–34), ed. J. Bennet and J. Driessen, Salamanca, 149–190.

Halstead, P. 1999b. "Missing Sheep: On the Meaning and Wider Significance of *O* on the Knossos SHEEP Records," *BSA* 94, 145–166.

Halstead, P. 2001. "Mycenaean Wheat, Flax and Sheep," in *Economy and Politics in the Mycenaean Palace States* (*PCPS* Supplement 27), ed. S. Voutsaki and J. Killen, Cambridge, 38–50.

Halstead, P. and J. O'Shea 1982. "A Friend in Need is a Friend Indeed: Social Storage and the Orgins of Social Ranking," in *Ranking, Resource, and Exchange,* ed. C. Renfrew and S. Shennan, Cambridge, 92–99.

Hamp, E. 1985. "Kn L 693 *qe-te-o* and *mantis,*" *Minos* 19, 51–53.

Hardy, K. 2008. "Prehistoric String Theory. How Twisted fibres helped to shape the world," *Antiquity* 82, 271–280.

Haspels, E. 1971. *The Highlands of Phrygia: Sites and Monuments*, Princeton.

Hauser, F. 1903. "Disiecta membra neuattischer Reliefs," *ÖJh* 6, 79–107.

Hazzidakis, J. 1934. *Les villas minoennes de Tylissos*, Paris.

Hecht, A. 1989. *The Art of the Loom: Weaving, Spinning and Dyeing Across the World*, London.

Helms, M. 1988. *Ulysses' Sail: An Ethnographic Odyssey of Power, Knowledge, and Geographical Distance*, Princeton.

Helms, M. 1993. *Craft and the Kingly Ideal: Art, Trade, and Power*, Austin.

Henrickson, R. 1993. "Politics, Economics and Ceramic Continuity at Gordion in the Late Second and First Millenia BC," in *Social and Cultural Contexts of New Ceramic Technologies,* ed. W. Kingery, Westerville, 111–122.

Henrickson, R. 1994. "Continuity and Discontinuity in the Ceramic Tradition of Gordion during the Iron Age," in *Anatolian Iron Ages 3: The Proceedings of the Third Anatolian Iron Ages Colloquium,* ed. A. Çilingiroğlu and D. French, London, 95–129.

Henrickson, R. and M. Blackman 1996. "Large-scale Production of Pottery at Gordion: Comparison of the Late Bronze and Early Phrygian Industries," *Paléorient* 22(1), 67–87.

Hiendleder, S., B. Kaupe, R. Wassmuth and A. Janke 2002. "Molecular analysis of wild and domestic sheep questions current nomenclature and provides evidence for domestication from two different subspecies," *Proceedings of the Royal Society B: Biological Sciences* 2002, 893–904.

Hiller, S. 1988. "Dependent Personnel in Mycenaean Documents," in *Society and Economy in the Eastern, c. 1500–1000 BC : Proceedings of the International Symposium held at the University of Haifa from the 28th of April to the 2nd of May, 1985*, ed. M. Heltzer and E. Lipìnski, Leuven, 53–68.

Hillman, G. 1975. "The Plant Remains from Abu Hureyra: A Preliminary Report," *PPS* 41, 70–3.

Hitchcock, L. and D. Preziosi 1997. "The Knossos Unexplored Mansion and the 'Villa-Annex Complex," in *The Function of the Minoan 'Villa': Proceedings of the Eighth International Symposium at the Swedish Institute at Athens, 6–8 June, 1992*, ed. R. Hägg, Stockholm, 51–62.

Hoffman, M. 1964. *The Warp-weighted Loom: Studies in the History and Technology of an Ancient Implement* (*Studia Norvegica* 14), Oslo.

Hogarth, D. 1900–1901. "Excavations at Zakro, Crete," *BSA* 7, 121–149.

Hooker, J. 1987. "Minoan and Mycenaean Administration: a Comparison of the Knossos and Pylos Archives," in *Function of the Minoan Palace*, 313–16.

Hutchinson, R. 1939–40. "Unpublished Objects from Palaikastro and Praisos," *BSA* 40, 47–49.

Huxley, G. 1959. "Titles of Midas," *GRBS* 2(2), 85–99.

Iakovides, S. 1970. *Perati B*, Athens.

Iakovides, S. 1977. "On the Use of Mycenaean Buttons," *BSA* 72, 113–119.

Jacobsen, T. 1970. "On the Textile Industry of Ur under Ibbi-Sin," in *Toward the Image of Tammuz and Other Essays on Mesopotamian History and Culture*, ed. W. Moran, Cambridge, 216–230.

Jameson, M., C. Runnels and T. van Andel 1994. *A Greek Countryside: The Southern Argolid from Prehistory to Present Day*, Stanford.

Jantzen, U. 1972. *Ägyptische und orientalische Bronzen aus dem Heraion von Samos*, Bonn.

Jarman, M. and H. Jarman 1968. "The Fauna and Economy of Neolithic Knossos," *BSA* 63, 241–64.

Jensen, L. and F. Jensen 1965. *The Story of Royal Purple*, Champaign.

Johnston, R. 1970. *Pottery Practices during the 6th–8th Centuries BC at Gordion in Central Anatolia: An Analytical and Synthesizing Study*, Ph.D. Dissertation, The Pennsylvania State University.

Jones, B. 2001. "The Minoan 'Snake Goddess': New Interpretations of her Costume and Identity," in *POTNIA: Deities and Religion in the Aegean Bronze Age. Proceedings of the 8th International Aegean Conference, Göteborg University, 12–15 April 2000*, (*Aegaeum* 22) ed. R. Laffineur and R. Hägg, Liège and Austin, 259–65.

Jones, B. 2003. "Veils and Mantles: An Investigation of the Construction and Function of the Costumes of the Veiled Dancer from Thera and the Camp Stool Banqueter from Knossos," in *Metron*, 441–50.

Jones, B. 2005. "The Clothes-line: Imports and Exports of Aegean Cloth(es) and Iconography," *Emporia*, 707–15.

Jones, B. 2009. "The 'Mykenaia' and a Seated Woman from Mycenae," *AJA* 113, 309–37.

Joukowsky, M. 1986. *Prehistoric Aphrodisias: An Account of the Excavations and Artifact Studies*, Providence.

Joyce, R. 2005. "Archaeology of the Body," *Annual Review of Anthropology* 34, 139–58.

Kanta, A. 1980. *The Late Minoan III Period in Crete: A Survey of Sites, Pottery, and their Distribution* (*SIMA* 58), Göteborg.

Karo, G. 1933. *Die Schachtgräber von Mykenai*, Munich.

Kemp, B. and G. Vogelsang-Eastwood 2001. *The Ancient Textile Industry at Amarna*, (*Excavation Memoir* 68, EES), London.

Kenna, V. 1960. *Cretan Seals*, Oxford.

Khlopin, I. 1982. "The Manufacture of Pile Carpets in Bronze Age Central Asia," *Hali* 5(2), 116–118.

Killen, J. 1962. "The Wool Ideogram in Linear B Texts," *Hermathena* 96, 38–72.

Killen, J. 1963. "Some Adjuncts to the Sheep Ideogram on Knossos Tablets," *Eranos* 61, 69–93.

Killen, J. 1964. "The Wool Industry of Crete in the Late Bronze Age," *BSA* 59, 1–15.

Killen, J. 1966. "The Knossos Lc (Cloth) Tablets," *BICS* 13, 105–109.

Killen, J. 1968a. "The Knossos Nc tablets," in *Studia Mycenaea: Proceedings of the Mycenaean Symposium at Brno,* ed. A. Bartonek, Brno, 33–38.

Killen, J. 1968b. "The Knossos o-pi Tablets," in *Atti e memorie del 1.o Congresso Internazionale di Micenologia* (Incunabula Graeca 25), Rome, 106–113.

Killen, J. 1972. "Two Notes on the Knossos Ak Tablets," in *Acta Mycenaea. Proceedings of the Fifth Inernational Colloquium on Mycenaean Studies, Salamanca, 30 March–3 April, 1970,* ed. M. S. Ruipérez, Salamanca, 425–440.

Killen, J. 1977. "The Knossos Texts and the Geography of Mycenaean Crete," in *Mycenaean Geography,* ed. J. Bintliff, Cambridge, 40–47.

Killen, J. 1979. "The Knossos Ld (1) Tablets," in *Colloquium Mycenaeum. Actes du sixième Colloque International sur les textes mycéniens et égéens à Chaumont sur Neuchâtel du 7 au 13 Septembre 1975,* ed. E. Risch and H. Mühlestein, Neuchâtel, 151–181.

Killen, J. 1981. "Some Puzzles in a Mycenae Personnel Record," *ZivaAnt* 31, 37–45.

Killen, J. 1982. "TA and DA," in *Concilium Eirene,* ed. P. Oliva and A. Frolikova, Prague, 121–126.

Killen, J. 1983a. "PY An 1," *Minos* 18, 71–79.

Killen, J. 1983b. "On the Mycenae Ge tablets," in *Res Mycenaeae: Akten des VII. Internationalen Mykenologischen Colloquiums, 1981,* ed. A. Heubeck and G. Neumann, Göttingen, 216–232.

Killen, J. 1984. "The Textile Industry at Pylos and Knossos," in *Pylos Comes Alive,* ed. C. Shelmerdine and T. Palaima, New York, 49–64.

Killen, J. 1985. "The Linear B tablets and the Mycenaean Economy," in *Linear B: A 1984 Survey,* ed. A. Morpurgo Davies and Y. Duhoux, Louvain-la-Neuve, 241–305.

Killen, J. 1986. "Two Mycenaean Words," in *O-o-pe-ro-si: Festschrift für Ernst Risch zum 75. Geburtstag,* ed. E. Risch and A. Etter, Berlin, 279–284.

Killen, J. 1987. "Piety Begins at Home," in *Tractata Mycenaea: Proceedings of the VIIIth International Colloquium on Mycenaean Studies, held in Ohrid, 15–20 September 1985,* ed. P. Ilievski and L. Crepajac, Skopje, 165–170.

Killen, J. 1988. "Epigraphy and Interpretation of Knossos Woman and Cloth Records," in *Texts, Tablets and Scribes* (*Minos* Supplement 10), ed. J.-P. Olivier and T. Palaima, Salamanca, 167–183.

Killen, J. 1994. "Thebes Sealings, Knossos Tablets and Mycenaean State Banquets," *BICS* 39, 67–84.

Killen, J. 1995. "Some further Thoughts on Collectors," in *Politeia,* 213–226.

Killen, J. 2001. "Some thoughts on *TA-RA-SI-JA*," in *Economy and Politics in the Mycenaean Palace States* (*PCPS* Supplement 27), ed. S. Voutsaki and J. Killen, Cambridge, 161–180.

Killen, J. 2007. "Cloth Production in Late Bronze Age Greece: the Documentary Evidence," in *Ancient Textiles: Production, Craft, Society,* ed. C. Gillis and M. -L. Nosch, Oxford, 50–58.

Killen, J. 2008a. "Mycenaean Economy," in *A Companion to Linear B: Mycenaean Greek Texts and their World,* ed. Y. Duhoux and A. Morpurgo Davies, Leuven, 159–200.

Killen, J. 2008b. "The Commodities on the Pylos Ma Tablets," in *Colloquium Romanum: Atti del xii Colloquio Internazionale di Micenologia, 20–25 Febraio 2006,* ed. A. Sacconi, M. Del Freo, L. Godart, M. Negri, Rome, 431–447.

Killen, J. and J.-P. Olivier 1968. "155 raccords de garments dans les tablettes de Cnossos," *BCH* 92, 115–141.

Killen, J. and J.-P. Olivier eds 1989. *The Knossos Tablets,* 5th Edition. *Minos* Supplement 11, Salamanca.

Kitchen, K. 1966. *Ancient Orient and Old Testament*, Chicago.

Klengel, H. 1980. "Near Eastern Trade and the Emergence of Interaction with Crete in the Third Millennium BC," *SMEA* 24, 7–19.

Knapp, B. 1991. "Spices, Drugs, Grain and Grog: Organic Goods in Bronze Age East Mediterranean Trade," in *Bronze Age Trade in the Mediterranean* (*SIMA* 90), ed. N. Gale, Jonsered, 21–52.

Kober, A. 1949. "'Total' in Minoan (Linear Class B)," *ArchOrient* 17, 386–398.

Körte, G. and A. Körte 1904. *Gordion: Ergebnisse der Ausgrabung im Jahre 1900* (*Jährliches Ergänzungsheft* 5), Berlin.

Köhler, F. 1887. *Medizinal-Pflanzen*, Gera.

Kohler, E. 1962. "Ivory horse-trappings from Gordion – 1961," *AJA* 66, 198.

Koren, Z. 2005. "The First Optimal All-Murex All-Natural Purple Dyeing in the Eastern Mediterranean in a Millennium and a Half," *Dyes in History and Archaeology* 20, 136–149.

Kotz, S. 1997. *Dallas Museum of Art: A Guide to the Collection*, contributor Tom Jenkins. Dallas.

Krzyszkowska, O. 2005. *Aegean Seals: An Introduction*, London.

Kuniholm, P. 1988. "Dendrochronology and Radiocarbon Dates for Gordion and other Phrygian Sites," in *Phrygian Art and Archaeology* (*Source: Notes in the History of Art* 7), ed. O. Muscarella, New York, 3–4.

Lackenbacher, S. 2002. *Textes akkadiens d'Ugarit. Textes provenant des vingt-cinq premières campagnes*, Paris.

Landsberger, B. 1935. "Studien zu den Urkenden aus der Zeit des Ninurta-tukul-Assur," *AfO* 10, 140–159.

Laviosa, R. 1987. "The Minoan Thalassocracy, Iasos," in *Function of the Minoan Palace*, 183–185.

Lax, E. and T. Strasser 1992. "Early Holocene Extinctions on Crete: The Search for the Cause," *JMA* 5, 203–224.

Lejeune, M. 1957. "Les documents pyliens des series Ns, Ng, Nn," in *Études Mycéniénnes: Actes du Colloque International sur les Textes Mycéniens, Gif-sur-Yvette, 3–7 avril 1956*, ed. M. Lejeune, Paris, 137–165.

Lejeune, M. 1964. "Sur quelques termes du vocabulaire économique mycénien," in *Mycenaean Studies: Proceedings of the Third International Colloquium for Mycenaean Studies held at 'Wingspread' 4–8 September 1961*, ed. E. Bennett, Jr., Madison, 77–109.

Lejeune, M. 1969. "A propos de la titulaire de Midas," *Athenaeum* 47, 179–192.

Lejeune, M. 1970. "Les inscriptions de Gordion et l'alphabet phrygien," *Kadmos* 9, 51–74.

Lejeune, M. 1971. "Observations sur l'idéogramme 146," in *Mémoires de Philologie Mycénienne* (Deuxième Série 1958–1963), ed. M. Lejeune. Rome, 315–325.

Lillethun, A. 2003. "The Recreation of Aegean Cloth and Clothing," in *METRON*, 463–72.

Leukart, A. 1994. *Die frühgriechischen Nomina auf -tas und -as*, Vienna.

Levine, T. ed. 1992. *Inka Storage Systems*, Norman.

Liebhart, R. 1988. *Timber Roofing Spans in Greek and Near Eastern Monumental Architecture during the Early Iron Age*, Ph.D. diss., University of North Carolina, Chapel Hill.

Lindgren, M. 1973. *The People of Pylos: The Use of Personal Designations and their Interpretation* II, Uppsala.

Loftus, A. 1998–2000. "The Myth of Male Weaving: Textile production in Classical Athens," *Archaeological News* 23, 11–32.

MacDonald, C. and J. Driessen 1988. "The Drainage System of the Domestic Quarter in the Palace at Knossos," *BSA* 83, 235–258.

MacDonald, C. 2005. *Knossos*. London.

Maekawa, K. 1980. "Female weavers and their children in Lagash: Pre-Sargonic and Ur III," *Acta Sumerologica* 2, 82–125.

Mallory, J. 1989. *In Search of the Indo-Europeans*, New York.

Manning, S., B. Kromer, P. I. Kuniholm and M. Newton 2001. "Anatolian Tree Rings and a New Chronology for the East Mediterranean Bronze-Iron Ages," *Science* 294.5551, 2532–5.

Mansfield, J. 1985. *The Robe of Athena and the Panathenaic 'Peplos'*, Ph.D. diss., University of California, Berkeley.

Marcar, A. 2005. "Reconstructing Aegean Bronze Age Fashions," in *The Clothed Body in the Ancient World*, ed. L. Cleland, M. Harlow and L. Llewellyn-Jones, Oxford, 30–43.

Marcar, A. 2004. "Aegean Costume and the Dating of the Knossian Frescoes," in *Knossos: Palace, City, State*, 225–38.

Marinatos, S. 1951. "Ἀνασκαφὴ μεγάρου Βαθυπέτρου (Κρητης)," *Prakt.*, 258–72.

Marinatos, S. 1964. "Ἀνασκαφαι εν Πυλω," *Prakt.*, 78–95.

Marinatos, S. 1967. *Kleidung-Haar und Barttracht* (*Archaeologia Homerica* I), Göttingen.

Masson, O. 1991. "The Phrygian Language," *CAH* 3(2), 666–9.

McClellan, J. 1975. *The Iron Objects from Gordion, A Typological and Functional Analysis*, Ph.D. diss., University of Pennsylvania.

McCorriston, J. 1997. "The Fiber Revolution: Textile Extensification, Alienation, and Social Stratification in Ancient Mesopotamia," *CurrAnthr* 38(4), 517–49.

McDonald, W. and G. Rapp Jr. eds 1972. *Minnesota Messenia Expedition*, Minneapolis.

McGovern, P. and R. Michel 1984. "Royal Purple and the Pre-Phoenician Dye Industry of Lebanon," *MASCA Journal* 3, 67–70.

Melena, J. 1975. Studies on Some Mycenaean Inscriptions from Knossos Dealing with Textiles (*Minos* Supplement 5), Salamanca.

Melena, J. 1987. "On the Linear B Ideogrammatic Syllabogram ZE," in *Studies in Mycenaean and Classical Greek Presented to John Chadwick* (*Minos* 20–22), ed. J. Killen, J. Melena and J.-P. Olivier, Salamanca, 389–458.

Melena, J. and J.-P. Olivier 1991. *Tithemy: The Tablets and Nodules in Linear B from Tiryns, Thebes and Mycenae* (*Minos* Supplement 12), Salamanca.

Mellink, M. 1956. *A Hittite Cemetery at Gordion*, Philadelphia.

Mellink, M. 1965. "Mita, Mushki and Phrygians," *Anadolu Araştırma* 2, 317–25.

Mellink, M. 1979. "Midas in Tyana," in *Florilegium Anatolicum*, ed. E. Laroche, Paris, 249–57.

Mellink, M. 1991. "The Native Kingdoms of Anatolia," *CAH* 3(2), 619–643.

Michailidou, A. 1992–93. "'Ostrakon' with Linear A Script from Akrotiri (Thera): A Non-Bureaucratic Activity?" *Minos* 27–28, 7–24.

Michailidou, A. 1999. "Systems of Weight and Social Relations of 'Private' Production in the Late Bronze Age", in *From Minoan Farmers to Roman Traders*, ed. A. Chaniotis, Stuttgart, 87–113.

Michel, R. and P. McGovern 1990. "The chemical processing of royal purple dye: ancient descriptions as elucidated by modern science II," *Archaeomaterials* 4, 97–104.

Militello, P. 2007. "Textile Industry and Minoan Palaces," in *Ancient Textiles: Production, Craft, Society*, ed. C. Gillis and M.-L. Nosch, Oxford, 36–45.

Miller, N. 1993. "Plant Use at Gordion: Archaeobotanical Research from the 1988–1989 Seasons," *AJA* 97, 304.

Miller, N. 2006. "The Origins of Plant Cultivation in the Near East," in *The Origins of Agriculture: An International Perspective*, ed. C. W. Cowan and P. J. Watson, Tuscaloosa, 39–58 (2nd edition).

Minniti, C. 2005. "Shells at the Bronze Age Settlement of Coppa nevigata (Apulia, Italy)," in *Archaeolmalacology*, ed. D. Bar-Yosef Mayer. Oxford, 71–81.

Morgan, L. 1988. *The Miniature Wall Paintings of Thera: A Study in Aegean Culture and Iconography*, Cambridge.

Morris, C. 1974. "Reconstructing Patterns of Non-agricultural Production in the Inca Economy:

Archaeology and Documents in Institutional Analysis," in *Reconstructing Complex Societies: An Archaeological Colloquium* (*BASOR* Supplement 20), ed. C. Moore, Cambridge, 49–68.

Morris, H. 1986. *An Economic Model of the Late Mycenaean Kingdom of Pylos*, Ph.D. diss., University of Minnesota.

Morris, S. 1990. "Greece and the Levant," *JMA* 3(1), 57–66.

Morris, S. 1992. *Daidalos and the Origins of Greek Art*, Princeton.

Morrison, M. 1981. "Evidence for Herdsmen and Animal Husbandry in the Nuzi Documents," in *Studies on the Civilization and Culture of Nuzi and the Hurrians, in Honor of Ernest R. Lacheman on His Seventy-fifth Birthday, April 29, 1981,* ed. M. Morrison and D. Owen, Winona Lake, 257–296.

Morpurgo Davies, A. 1983. "Mycenaean and Greek Prepositions: *o-pi, e-pi* etc.," in *Res Mycenaeae: Akten des VII. Internationalen Mykenologischen Colloquiums,* 1981, ed. A. Heubeck and G. Neumann, Göttingen, 287–310.

Mountjoy, P. 2003. *Knossos: The South House* (*BSA* Supplement 34). London.

Muhly, J. 2008. "An Introduction to Minoan Archaeometallurgy," in *Aegean Metallurgy in the Bronze Age: proceedings of an international symposium held at the University of Crete, Rethymnon, Greece, on November 19–21, 2004*, ed. I. Tzachili, Athens, 35–41.

Murra, J. 1989. "Cloth and Its Function in the Inca State," in *Cloth and Human Experience,* ed. A. Weiner and J. Schneider, Washington, DC, 275–302.

Murra, J. and C. Morris 1976. "Dynastic Oral Tradition, Administrative Records and Archaeology in the Andes," *WorldArch* 7(3), 270–279.

Muscarella, O. 1967a. "Fibulae Representation in Sculpture," *JNES*, 82–6.

Muscarella, O. 1967b. *Phrygian Fibulae from Gordion*, London.

Muscarella, O. 1989. "King Midas of Phrygia and the Greeks," in *Anatolia and the Ancient Near East: Studies in Honor of T. Özgüç,* ed. K. Emre, M. Mellink, B. Hrouda and N. Özgüç, Ankara, 335–344.

Muscarella, O. 2003. "The Date of the Destruction of the Early Phrygian Period at Gordion," *Ancient West and East* 2, 225–252.

Μυλωνάς, G. 1973. Ο ταφικός κύκλος Β των Μυκηνών. Athens.

Nesbitt, M. 1995. "Plants and People in Ancient Anatolia," *Biblical Archaeologist* 58(2), 68–81.

Nikoloudis, S. 2008a. "Multiculturalism in the Mycenaean World," in *Anatolian Interfaces: Hittites, Greeks and their Neighbours*, ed. B. J. Collins, M. Bachvarova and I. Rutherford, Oxford, 45–66.

Nikoloudis, S. 2008b. "The Role of the *ra-wa-ke-ta*. Insights from PY Un 718," in *Colloquium Romanum: Atti del xii Colloquio Internazionale di Micenologia, 20–25 Febraio 2006*, ed. A. Sacconi, M. Del Freo, L. Godart, M. Negri, Rome, 587–94.

Niemeier, W. D. 1982. "Mycenaean Knossos and the Age of Linear B," *SMEA* 23, 219–287.

Niemeier, W. D. 1996. "A Linear A Inscription from Miletus (MIL Zb1)," *Kadmos* 35, 87–99.

Niemeier, W. D. 1997. "The Mycenaean Potter's Quarter at Miletos," in *TEXNH*, 347–352.

Niemeier, W. D. 1998. "Minoan Frescoes in the Eastern Mediterranean," in *The Aegean and the Orient in the Second Millennium. Proceedings of the 50th Anniversary Symposium Cincinnati, 18–20 April 1997*, (*Aegaeum* 18), ed. E. Cline and D. Harris-Cline, Liège, 69–97.

Niemeier, W. D. 2005a. "Minoans, Mycenaeans, Hittites and Ionians in Western Asia Minor: New Excavations in Bronze Age Miletus-Millawanda," in *The Greeks in the East* (*British Museum Research Publication* 157), ed. A. Villing, London, 1–36.

Niemeier, W. D. 2005b. "The Minoans and Mycenaeans in Western Asia Minor: Settlement, Emporia or Acculturation," in *Emporia*, 199–204.

Nosch, M.-L. 1999. "L'administration de textiles en Crète centrale, hors des series Lc/Le/Ln," *BCH* 122, 404–406.

Nosch, M.-L. 2000a. "Acquisition and Distribution: *ta-ra-si-ja* in the Mycenaean Textile Industry," in

Trade and Production in Premonetary Greece: Acquisition and Distribution (*SIMA Pocket-book* 154), ed. C. Gillis, C. Risberg and B. Sjöberg, Jonsered, 43–61.

Nosch, M.-L. 2000b. *The Organization of the Mycenaean Textile Industry*, Ph.D. diss., University of Salzburg.

Nosch, M.-L. 2001a. "The Geography of the ta-ra-si-ja," *Aegean Archaeology* 4, 27–44.

Nosch, M.-L. 2001b. "The Textile Industry at Thebes in the Light of the Textile Industries at Pylos and Knossos," in *Festschrift in Honour of A. Bartonek.* Studia Minora Facultatis Philosophica Universitatis Brunensis VI, 177–189.

Nosch, M.-L. 2003. "The Women at work in the Linear B Tablets," in *Gender, Cult, and Culture in the Ancient World from Mycenae to Byzantium* (*SIMA Pocket-book* 166), ed. A. Strömberg and L. Larsson Lovén, Sävedalen, 12–26.

Nosch, M.-L. 2004. "Red Coloured Textiles in the Linear B Inscriptions," in *Colour in the Ancient Mediterranean World* (*BAR International Series* 1267), ed. L. Cleland and K. Stears, Oxford, 32–39.

Nosch, M.-L. 2007. *The Od Tablets. Suggestions to a New Classification*, Österreichische Akademie der Wissenschaften, Mykenische Kommission. Vienna.

Nosch, M.-L. 2008. "Haute Couture in the Bronze Age: A History of Minoan Female Costumes from Thera," in *Dressing the Past*, ed. M. Gleba, C. Munkholt and M.-L. Nosch, Oxford, 1–12.

Nosch, M.-L. and M. Perna 2001. "Cloth in Cult," in POTNIA: Deities and Religion in the Aegean Bronze Age. Proceedings of the 8th International Aegean Conference, Göteborg University, 12–15 April 2000, (Aegaeum 22) ed. R. Laffineur and R. Hägg, Liège and Austin, 471–477.

Olivier, J.-P. 1967a. "La série Dn de Cnossos," *SMEA* 2, 71–93.

Olivier, J.-P. 1967b. "L'industrie textile dans la Grèce mycénienne," *SMEA* 4, 120–121.

Olivier, J.-P. 1984. "Administrations at Knossos and Pylos: What Differences?" in *Pylos Comes Alive,* ed. C. Shelmerdine and T. Palaima, New York, 11–18.

Olivier, J.-P. 1988. "KN: Da–Dg," in *Texts, Tablets and Scribes* (*Minos* Supplement 10), ed. J-P. Olivier and T. Palaima, Salamanca, 219–267.

Olivier, J.-P. 1996. "The Graffito," in "Minoan Graffito from Tel Haror (Negev, Israel)," E. Oren, *Cretan Studies* 5, 99–118.

Olivier, J.-P. and L. Godart 1996. *Corpus Hieroglyphicarum Inscriptionum Cretae* (CHIC). (*Études Crétoises* 31), Paris.

Oppenheim, L. 1967. "Essay on Overland Trade in the First Millennium BC," *Journal of Cuneiform Studies* 21, 236–254.

Palaima, T. 1984. "Inscribed Stirrup Jars and Regionalism in Linear B Crete," *SMEA* 25, 189–201.

Palaima, T. 1987. "Palatial Control of Economic Activity in Minoan and Mycenaean Crete," in *Function of the Minoan Palace*, 301–305.

Palaima, T. ed. 1990. Aegean Seals, Sealings and Administration, (Aegaeum 5), Liège.

Palaima, T. 1991. "Maritime Matters in the Linear B Tablets," in *Thalassa: L'Egée préhistorique et la mer*, (*Aegaeum* 7), ed. R. Laffineur and L. Basch, Liège, 273–310.

Palaima, T. 1997. "Potter and Fuller: The Royal Craftsmen," in *TEXNH*, 407–412.

Palmer, L. 1957. "Review of Documents in Mycenaean Greek," *Gnomon* 29, 569–570.

Palmer, L. 1963. *The Interpretation of Mycenaean Greek Texts*, Oxford.

Palmer, L. 1972. "Mycenaean Inscribed Vases II: The Mainland Finds," *Kadmos* 11, 27–46.

Panagiotakopulu, E., P. Buckland, P. Day, C. Doumas, A. Sarpaki and P. Skidmore 1997. "A lepidopterous cocoon from Thera and evidence for silk in the Aegean Bronze Age," *Antiquity* 71, 420–29.

Panagiotakopulu, E. 2000. *Archaeology and Entomology in the Eastern Mediterranean: Research into the History of Insect Synanthropy in Greece and Egypt.* Oxford, BAR, v. 836.

Panagiotopoulos, D. 2002. "Keftiu in Context: Theban Tomb-paintings as a historical Source," *Oxford Journal of Archaeology* 20.3, 263–83.

Parsons, M. 1972. "Spindle whorls from the Teotihuacan Valley, Mexico," in *Miscellaneous Studies in Mexican Prehistory,* ed. M. Spence, J. Parsons and M. Hrones Parsons, Ann Arbor, 45–79.

Parsons, M. 1975. "The Distribution of Late Postclassic Spindle Whorls in the Valley of Mexico," *AmerAnt* 40, 209–215.

Parsons, J. and M. Parsons 1990. *Maguey Utilization in Highland Central Mexico* (Anthropological Papers 82), Ann Arbor.

Payne, S. 1973. "Kill-off Patterns in Sheep and Goats," *AnatSt* 23, 281–303.

Pelon, O. 1966. "Maison d'Hagia Varvara et architecture domestique à Mallia," *BCH* 90, 552–585.

Payne, S. 1970. *Mallia: Exploration des maisons et quartiers d'habitation, 1963–1966* (*Études Crétoises* XVI), Paris.

Payne, S. 1983. "Fonction politique dans un palais minoen," in *Minoan Society: Proceedings of the Cambridge Colloquium 1981,* ed. O. Krzyszkowska and L. Nixon, Cambridge, 251–257.

Pendlebury, J. and M. Money-Coutts 1937–38. "Excavations in the Plain of Lasithi II," *BSA* 38, 1–56.

Perna, M. 2005. "La culture du lin en Grèce mycénienne et au Proche-Orient ancien," in *Emporia*, 805–813.

Petrie, F., Griffith and P. Newberry 1890. *Kahun, Gurob, and Hawara*, London.

Petrie, F, 1917. *Tools and Weapons Illustrated by the Egyptian Collection in University College London, and 2,000 Outlines from Other Sources*. London.

Petruso, K. 1986. "Wool-Evaluation at Knossos and Nuzi," *Kadmos* 25, 26–37.

Pini, I. 1990. "The Hieroglyphic Deposit and the Temple Repositories at Knossos," in *Aegean Seals, Sealings and Administration,* (*Aegaeum* 5), ed. T. Palaima, Liège, 33–60.

Pinnock, F. 1984. "Trade at Ebla," *Bulletin of the Society of Mesopotamian Studies* 7, 19–36.

Piteros, C., J.-P. Olivier and J. Melena 1990. "Les inscriptions en linéaire B des nodules de Thèbes (1982): la fouille, les documents, les possibilités d'interpretation," *BCH* 114, 103–184.

Platon, N. 1957. "Ἀνασκαφὴ Χονδροῦ Βιαννου," *Prakt.*, 136–45.

Platon, N. 1967. "Kato Zakros," in *Ancient Crete*, ed. L. Von Matt, Zurich, 163–196.

Platon, N. 1985. *Zakros: The Discovery of a Lost Palace of Ancient Crete*, Amsterdam.

Platon, L. 1997. "The Minoan 'Villa' in Eastern Crete," in *The Function of the Minoan 'Villa': Proceedings of the Eighth International Symposium at the Swedish Institute at Athens, 6–8 June, 1992*, ed. R. Hägg, Stockholm, 187–202.

Popham, M. 1976. "Mycenaean-Minoan relations between 1450 and 1400 BC," *BICS* 23, 119–121.

Popham, M., J. Betts, M. Cameron, H. Catling, E. Catling, D. Evely, R. Higgins and D. Smyth 1984. *The Minoan Unexplored Mansion* (*BSA* Supplement 17), Athens.

Popham, M. and H. Sackett 1972–1973. "The Unexplored Mansion at Knossos," *Archaeological Reports* 19, 50–71.

Poursat, J.-Cl. 1980. "Sceaux et empreintes de Sceaux," in *Fouilles Exécutées à Mallia. Le Quartier Mu II* (*Études Crétoises* XXVI), ed. B. Detournay, J-Cl. Poursat and F. Vandenabeele, Paris, 157–230.

Poursat, J.-Cl. 1990. "Hieroglyphic Documents and Sealings from Malia, Quartier Mu: a Functional Analysis," in *Aegean Seals, Sealings and Administration,* (*Aegaeum* 5), ed. T. Palaima, Liège, 25–33.

Προμπονᾶς, Ι. 1983. Ἀνθολογία Μυκηναϊκῶν Κειμένων. Athens.

Prayon, F. 1987. *Phrygische Plastik: die früheisenzeitliche Bildkunst Zentral-Anatoliens und ihre Beziehungen zu Griechenland und zum Alten Orient*, Tübingen.

Pritchard, J. 1985. *Tell es-Sa'idiyeh: Excavations on the Tell 1964–1967*, Philadelphia.

Pulak, C. 1988. "The Bronze Age Shipwreck at Ulu Burun, Turkey: 1985 Campaign," *AJA* 92, 1–37.

Rahmstorf, L. 2008. *Tiryns Forshungen und Berichte XVI: Kleinfunde aus Tiryns: Terrakotta, Stein, Bein und Glas/Fayence vornehmlich aus der Spätbronzezeit*, Wiesbaden.

Reese, D. 1979–1980. "Industrial Exploitation of Murex Shells: Purple-dye and Lime Production at Sidi Khrebish, Benghazi (Berenice)," *Libyan Studies* 11, 79–93.

Reese, D. 1987. "Palaikastro Shells and Bronze Age Purple-Dye Production in the Mediterranean Basin," *BSA* 82, 203–206.

Reese, D. 1995. "Muricacea," in *Kommos I: The Kommos Region and the Houses of the Minoan Town I-II*, ed. J. Shaw and M. Shaw, Princeton, 258–261.

Rehak, P. 1996. "Aegean Breechcloths, Kilts, and the Keftiu Paintings," *AJA* 100, 35–51.

Rehak, P. 1998. "Aegean Natives in the Theban Tomb Paintings: The Keftiu Revisited," in *The Aegean and the Orient in the Second Millennium. Proceedings of the 50th Anniversary Symposium Cincinnati, 18–20 April 1997*, (*Aegaeum* 18), ed. E. Cline and D. Harris-Cline, Liège, 39–44.

Rehak, P. and J. Younger 2001. "Review of Aegean Prehistory VI: The Neopalatial, Final Palatial and Post-Palatial Periods on Crete, of Aegean Prehistory VI," in *Aegean Prehistory: A Review* (*AJA* Supplement 1)*, ed. T. Cullen, 383–473.

Reinhold, M. 1970. *History of Purple as a Status Symbol in Antiquity* (Collection Latomus 116), Brussels.

Renfrew, C. 1972. *The Emergence of Civilization: The Cyclades and the Aegean in the Third Millennium BC*, London.

Renfrew, C. 1986. "Peer Polity Interaction and Socio-Political Change," in *Peer Polity Interaction and Socio-Political Change*, ed. C. Renfrew and J. Cherry, Cambridge, 1–18.

Renfrew, C. 1998. "Word of Minos: the Minoan Contribution to Mycenaean Greek and the Linguistic Geography of the Bronze Age Aegean," *CAJ* 8(2), 239–264.

Renfrew, C. 1999. "The Loom of Language and the Versailles Effect," in *Meletemata: Studies in Aegean Archaeology Presented to M. H. Wiener as he enters his 65th Year*, (*Aegaeum* 20), ed. P. Betancourt, V. Karageorghis, R. Laffineur and W. Niemeier, Liège-Austin, 711–720.

Ribichini, S. and P. Xella 1985. *La terminologia dei tessili nei testi di Ugarit* (Collezioni dei Studi Fenici 20), Rome.

Riis, P. J. 1948. *Hama, Fouilles et recherches 1931–1938, II 3: Les Cimitières à cremation*, Copenhagen.

Robkin, A. 1979. "The Agricultural Year, the Commodity SA and the Linen Industry of Mycenaean Pylos," *AJA* 83, 469–474.

Robkin, A. 1981. "The Endogram *WE* on Mycenaean Textiles *146 and *166+*WE*: A Proposed Identification," *AJA* 85, 213.

Rodenwaldt, G. 1912. *Tiryns* II: *Die Fresken des Palastes,* with R. Hackl and N. Heaton, Athens.

Roller, L. 1987. *Gordion Special Studies, Volume I: The Nonverbal Graffiti, Dipinti, and Stamps*, Philadelphia.

Roth, H. 1913. *Ancient Egyptian and Greek Looms*, Halifax.

Rougemont, F. 2001. "Some thoughts on the Identification of the 'Collectors' in the Linear B tablets," in *Economy and Politics in the Mycenaean Palace States* (*PCPS* Supplement 27), ed. S. Voutsaki and J. Killen, Cambridge, 1219–1238.

Rougemont, F. 2004. "The Administration of Mycenaean Sheep rearing (flocks, shepherds, 'collectors')," in *Pecus: Man and Animal in Antiquity*, ed. B. Frizell, Rome, 20–30.

Rougemont, F. 2007. "Flax and Linen in the Mycenaean Palatial Economy," in *Ancient Textiles: Production, Craft, Society*, ed. C. Gillis and M.-L. Nosch, Oxford, 46–49.

Runnels, C. and T. Van Andel 1988. "Trade and the Origins of Agriculture in the Eastern Mediterranean," *JMA* 1, 83–109.

Ruscillo, D. 1988. "Working Double Tides: The Marine Molluscs from Kommos, Crete," *AJA* 102, 392.

Ruscillo, D. 2005. "Reconstructing Murex Royal Purple and Biblical Blue in the Aegean," in *Archaeolmalacology: Molluscs in former Environments of Human Behaviour* ed. D. Bar-Yosef Mayer, Oxford, 99–106.

Ruscillo, D. 2006. "Chapter 6G: Faunal Remains from the Civic Buildings at Kommos," in *Kommos V: The Monumental Minoan Buildings at Kommos* ed. J. Shaw and M. Shaw, Princeton.

Ryder, M. 1969. "Changes in the Fleece of Sheep Following Domestication," in *The Domestication and Exploitation of Plants and Animals,* ed. P. Ucko and G. Dimbleby, Chicago, 495–521.

Ryder, M. 1983. *Sheep and Man*, London.

Ryder, M. 1993. "Sheep and Goat Industry with Particular Reference to Textile Fibre and Milk Production," *Bulletin on Sumerian Agriculture* 7, 9–32.

Sacconi, A. 1971. "A proposito dell'epiteto omerico λινοθώραξ", *ZA* 21, 49–54.

Saggs, H. 1958. "The Nimrud letters, 1952– part IV," *Iraq* 20, 182–212.

Sakellarakis, J. and E. Sapouna-Sakellaraki 1991. *Archanes,* Athens.

Salmon-Minotte, J. and R. Franck 2005. "Flax," in *Bast and Other Plant Fibres,* ed. R. Franck, Cambridge, 94–175.

Sams, G. K. 1977. "Beer in the City of Midas," *Archaeology* 30, 108–115.

Sams, G. K. 1993. "Gordion and the Near East in the Early Phrygian Period," in *Aspects of Art and Iconography: Anatolia and its Neighbors,* ed. M. Mellink, et al., Ankara, pp.549–555.

Sams, G. K. 1994. *The Gordion Excavations, 1950–1973: Final Reports IV, Early Phrygian Pottery,* Philadelphia.

Sams, G. K. 1995. "Midas of Gordion and the Anatolian Kingdom of Phrygia," in *CANE* 1147–1159.

Sapouna-Sakellaraki, E. 1971. *To Minoïkon Zoma,* Athens.

Schaeffer, F. 1952. *Enkomi-Alasia,* Paris.

Schibli, H. 1990. *Pherekydes of Syros*, Oxford.

Schick, T. 1988. "Cordage, Basketry, and Fabrics," *Atiquot* 18, 31–43.

Schirmer, W. 1993. "Die Bauanlagen auf dem Göllüdag in Kappadokien," *Architectura* 23, 121–131.

Schliemann, H. 1880a. *Mycenae,* New York.

Schliemann, H. 1880b. *Ilios: The City and Country of the Trojans*, New York.

Schliemann, H. 1886. *Tiryns. The Prehistoric Palace of the Kings of Tiryns*, London.

Schmidt, E. 1930. *The Alishar Hüyük, Season of 1927*, Chicago.

Schoenhammer, M. 1993. "Women and Textiles in Homer," *American Philological Association Abstracts*, 16.

Schoep, I. and K. Knappett 2004. "Dual Emergence: Evolving Heterarchy, Exploding Hierarchy," in *Emergence of Civilisation Revisited*, ed. J. Barrett and P. Halstead, Oxford, 21–37.

Schofield, E. 1996. "Wash and Brush-Up at the 'Travellers' Rest': The Caravanserai Reconsidered," in *Minotaur and Centaur: Studies in the Archaeology of Crete and Euboia Presented to Mervyn Popham* (*BAR International Series* 638), ed. D. Evely, I. Lemos and S. Sherratt, Oxford, 27–33.

Schofield, L. and R. Parkinson 1994. "Of Helmets and Heretics: A Possible Egyptian Representation of Mycenaean Warriors on a Papyrus from el-Amarna," *BSA* 89, 157–170.

Seager, R. 1908. "Excavations at Vasiliki," in *Gournia, Vasiliki and Other Prehistoric Sites on the Isthmus of Hierapetra, Crete,* ed. H. Hawes, B. Williams, R. Seager and E. Hall, Philadelphia, 49–50.

Shaw, M. 1997. "Aegean Sponsors and Artists: Reflections of their Roles in the Patterns of Distribution of Themes and Representational Conventions in the Murals," in *TEXNH*, 481–504.

Shaw, J. and M. Shaw 1993. "Excavations at Kommos (Crete) during 1986–1992," *Hesperia* 62, 161–188.

Shaw, J. and M. Shaw 1995. *Kommos I: The Kommos Region and the Houses of the Minoan Town I–II,* Princeton.

Shaw, J., A. Van de Moortel, P. Day and V. Kilikoglou 1997. "A LM IA Pottery Kiln at Kommos, Crete," in *TEXNH*, 323–331.

Shaw, T., P. Sinclair, B. Andah and A. Okpoko eds 1993. *The Archaeology of Africa: Food, Metals and Towns.* London.

Sheftel, P. 1974. *The Ivory, Bone and Shell Objects from Gordion from the Campaigns of 1950 through 1973*, Ph.D. diss., University of Pennsylvania.

Shelmerdine, C. 1973. "The Pylos MA Tablets Reconsidered," *AJA* 77, 261–275.

Shelmerdine, C. 1981. "Nichoria in Context: a major town in the Pylos kingdom," *AJA* 85, 324–388.

Shelmerdine, C. 1985. *The Perfume Industry of Mycenaean Pylos* (Studies in Mediterranean Archaeology and Literature), Göteborg.

Shelmerdine, C. 1987a. "Industrial Activity at Pylos," in *Tractata Mycenaea: Proceedings of the VIIIth International Colloquium on Mycenaean Studies, held in Ohrid, 15–20 September 1985*, ed. P. Ilievski and L. Crepajac, Skopje, 333–342.

Shelmerdine, C. 1987b. "Architectural Change and Economic Decline at Pylos," in *Studies in Mycenaean and Classical Greek Presented to John Chadwick* (*Minos* 20–22), ed. J. T. Killen, J. L. Melena and J.-P. Olivier, Salamanca, 557–568.

Shelmerdine, C. 1992. "Historical and Economic Considerations in Interpreting Mycenaean Texts," in *Mykenaïka: Actes du IXe Colloque international sur les textes mycéniens et* (*BCH Supplément* XXV), ed. J.-P. Olivier, Paris, 569–590.

Shelmerdine, C. 1995. "Shining and Fragrant Cloth in Homeric Epic," in *The Ages of Homer: A Tribute to Emily Townsend Vermeule,* ed. J. Carter and S. Morris, Austin, 99–107.

Shelmerdine, C. 1997. "Workshops and Record Keeping in the Mycenaean World," in *TEXNH*, 387–396.

Shelmerdine, C. 1999a. "The Southwestern Department at Pylos," in *A-NA-QO-TA: Studies Presented to J. T. Killen* (*Minos* 33–34), ed. J. Bennet and J. Driessen, Salamanca, 309–337.

Shelmerdine, C. 1999b. "A Comparative Look at Mycenaean Administration(s)," in *Floreant Studia Mycenaea*, 555–576.

Shelmerdine, C. 2001. "Review of Aegean Prehistory VI: The Palatial Bronze Age of the Southern and Central Greek Mainland," in *Aegean Prehistory: A Review* (*AJA* Supplement 1), ed. T. Cullen, 329–82.

Shelmerdine, C. 2008. "Mycenaean Society," in *A Companion to Linear B: Mycenaean Greek Texts and their World*, ed. Y. Duhoux and A. Morpurgo Davies, Leuven, 115–158.

Shelmerdine, C. ed. 2008. *The Cambridge Companion to the Aegean Bronze Age*. Cambridge.

Shelmerdine, C. and J. Bennet 2008. "Mycenaean States: Economy and Administration," in *The Cambridge Companion to the Aegean Bronze Age*, ed. C. Shelmerdine, Cambridge, 289–309.

Shelmerdine, C. and T. Palaima eds 1984. *Pylos Comes Alive,* New York.

Sherratt, A. 1983. "The Secondary Products Revolution of Animals in the Old World," *WorldArch* 15, 90–104.

Sherratt, A. and S. Sherratt 1991. "From Luxuries to Commodities: The Nature of Mediterranean Bronze Age Trading Systems," in *Bronze Age Trade in the Mediterranean* (*SIMA* 90), ed. N. Gale, Jonsered, 351–380.

Smith, J. 1995. *Seals for Sealing in the Late Cypriot Period,* Ph. D. dissertation, Bryn Mawr Collge.

Smith, M. and K. Hirth 1988. "The Development of Prehispanic Cotton-Spinning Technology in Western Morelos, Mexico," *JFA* 15, 349–358.

Singer, I. 2008. "Purple-dyers in Lazpa," in *Anatolian Interfaces: Hittites, Greeks and their Neighbours*, ed. B. J. Collins, M. Bachvarova, and I. Rutherford, Oxford, 21–44.

Snodgrass, A. 1967. *Arms and Armour of the Greeks*, London.

Soles, J., J. Bending and C. Davaras 2004. *Mochlos IC: Period III,* Philadelphia.

Sollberger, E. 1986. *Administrative Texts Chiefly Concerning Textiles* (L. 2752), Rome.

Spanier, E. and N. Karmon 1987. "Muricid Snails and the Ancient Dye Industry," in *The Royal Purple and The Biblical Blue: Argaman and Tekhelet,* ed. E. Spanier, Jerusalem, 179–196.

Speiser, E. 1936. *One Hundred New Selected Nuzi Texts* (ASOR 16), New Haven.

Spyropoulos, T. and J. Chadwick 1975. *The Thebes Tablets II* (*Minos* Supplement 4), Salamanca.

Stein, G. and M. Blackman 1993. "Specialized Craft Production in Mesopotamia," in *Economic Aspects of Water Management in the Prehispanic New World,* ed. V. Scarborough and B. Isaac, Greenwich, Connecticut, 29–59.

Strasser, T. 1992. *Neolithic Settlement and Land Use on Crete*, Ph.D. diss., Indiana University.

Summers, G. 1990, "Grey Ware and The Eastern Limits of Phrygia", Anadolu Demir Çağları Sempozyumu Bildiriler 3, 241–252.

Sundwall, J. 1936. "Altkretische Urkundenstudien," *Acta Academiae Aboensis Humaniora* 10(2), 1–45.

Svenbro, J. and J. Scheid 1996. *The Craft of Zeus: Myths of Weaving and Fabric.* Cambridge.

Szarzynska, K. 1988. "Records of Garments and Cloth in Archaic Uruk/Warka," *Altorientalische Forschungen* 15(2), 220–230.

Thomé, O. 1885. *Flora von Deutschland, Österreich und der Schweiz*, Gera, Germany.

Thompson, W. 1982. "Weaving, a Man's Work," *Classical World* 75, 217–23.

Tiboni, F. 2005. "Weaving and Ancient Sails: Structural Changes to Ships as a Consequence of New Weaving Technology in the Mediterranean Late Bronze Age," *Nautical Archaeology* 34.1, 127–130.

Tomkins, P., P. Day and V. Kilikoglou 2004. "Knossos and the earlier Neolithic landscape of the Herakleion Basin," in *Knossos: Palace, City, State*, 51–59.

Tomkins, P. 2004. "Filling in the 'Neolithic Background'," in *Emergence of Civilisation Revisited*, ed. J. Barrett and P. Halstead, Oxford, 38–63.

Tournavitou, I. 1995. *The 'Ivory Houses' at Mycenae*, London.

Trnka, E. 1998. *Tracht und Textilproduktion in der Ägäischen Bronzezeit*, Ph.D. diss., University of Vienna.

Tsipopoulou, M. and E. Hallager 1996. "Inscriptions with Hieroglyphs and Linear A from Petras," *SMEA* 37, 7–46.

Tsipopoulou, M. and A. Papacostopoulou 1997. "'Villa' and Villages in the Hinterland of Petras, Siteia," in *The Function of the Minoan 'Villa': Proceedings of the Eighth International Symposium at the Swedish Institute at Athens, 6–8 June, 1992*, ed. R. Hägg, Stockholm, 211–14.

Tsountas, C. and J. Manatt 1897. *The Mycenaean Age: A study of the monuments and culture of pre-Homeric Greece.* Boston/New York.

Tzachili, I. 1990. "All Important yet Elusive: Looking for Evidence of Cloth-Making at Akrotiri," in *Thera and the Aegean World* III, ed. D. Hardy, C. Doumas, J. Sakellarakis and P. Warren, London, 380–389.

Tzachili, I. 2007. "Weaving at Akrotiri, Thera: Defining Cloth-Making Activities as Social Process in a Late Bronze Age Aegean Town," in *Ancient Textiles: Production, Craft, Society,* ed. C. Gillis and M.-L. Nosch, Oxford, 190–196.

Τζαχίλη, Ι. 1998. Υφαντική και Υφάντρες στο Προϊστορικό Αιγαίο 2000–1000 π.Χ

Van de Mieroop, M. 1997. *The Ancient Mesopotamian City*, Oxford.

Van Soldt, W. 1990. "Fabrics and Dyes in Ugarit," *Ugarit-Forschungen* 22, 321–57.

Van Soldt, W. 1997. "Kassite Textiles for Enlil–Nērāru's Messenger," *Altorientalische Forschungen* 24, 97–104.

Van Zeist, W. and J. Bakker-Heeres 1975. "Evidence for Linseed Cultivation Before 6000 BC," *JAS* 2, 215–220.

Vassileva, M. 2006. "Phrygian Literacy in Cult and Religion," in *Pluralismus und Wandel in den Religionen im vorhellenistischen Anatolien,* ed. M. Hutter and S. Hutter-Braunsar, Münster, 225–239.

Ventris, M. and J. Chadwick 1956. *Documents in Mycenaean Greek*, Cambridge.

Ventris, M. and J. Chadwick 1973. *Documents in Mycenaean Greek*, 2nd ed., Cambridge.

Vercoutter, J. 1956. *L'Égypte et le monde égéen préhellenique*, Cairo.

Vlasaki, M. and E. Hallager 1995. "Evidence for Seal Use in Pre-Palatial Western Crete," in *Sceaux Minoens et Mycéniens* (*CMS Beiheft* 5), ed. W. Müller, Berlin, 251–270.

Voigt, M. 1994. "Excavations at Gordion 1988–89: The Yassıhöyük Stratigraphic Sequence," in *Anatolian Iron Ages 3: The Proceedings of the Third Anatolian Iron Ages Colloquium,* ed. A. Çilingiroğlu and D. French, London, 265–293.

Völling, E. 2008. *Textiltechnik im Alten Orient: Rohstoffe und Herstellung*, Würzburg.

Völling, T. 1998. "Ein phrygischer gürtel aus Olympia," *AA*, 243–52.

Von der Osten, H. 1937. *The Alishar Hüyük, Seasons of 1930–1932* (OIP 30), Chicago.

Wace, A. 1948. "Weaving or Embroidery?" *AJA* 52, 51–55.

Waetzoldt, H. 1972. *Untersuchungen zur Neusumerischen Textilindustrie,* Studi Economici e Tecnologici 1, Rome.

Waetzoldt, H. 2007. "The Use of Wool for the Production of Strings, Ropes, Braided Mats, and Similar Fabrics," in *Ancient Textiles: Production, Craft, Society,* ed. C. Gillis and M.-L. Nosch, Oxford, 112–21.

Wachsmann, S. 1987. *Aegeans in the Thebans Tombs* (*OLA* 20), Leuven.

Walters, H. 1892–1893. "Odysseus and Kirke on a Boeotian Vase," *JHS* 13, 77–87.

Warren, P. 1968. "A Textile Town 4500 Years Ago?" *Illustrated London News* 252, 25–27.

Warren, P. 1972. *Myrtos. An Early Bronze Age Settlement in Crete* (*BSA* Supplement 7), Oxford.

Warren, P. 1980–1981. "Knossos: Stratigraphical Museum Excavations, 1978–1980," *Archaeological Reports* 27, 73–92.

Warren, P. 1987. "The Genesis of the Minoan Palace," in *Function of the Minoan Palace*, 47–64.

Warren, P. and I. Tzedakis 1974. "Debla. An Early Minoan Settlement in Western Crete," *BSA* 69, 299–342.

Watrous, L. V. 1984 "Ayia Triada: A New Perspective on the Minoan Villa," *AJA* 88, 123–134.

Watrous, L. V. 1987. "The Role of the Near East in the Rise of the Cretan Palaces," in *Function of the Minoan Palace*, 65–70.

Watrous, L. V. 2001. "Review of Aegean Prehistory III: Crete from Earliest Prehistory through the Protopalatial Period," in *Aegean Prehistory: A Review* (*AJA* Supplement 1), ed. T. Cullen, 157–223.

Watrous, L. V. and H. Blitzer 1982. *Lasithi: A History of Settlement on a Highland Plain in Crete.* (*Hesperia Supplement* Vol. 18).

Watrous, L. V., D. Hadzi-Vallianou and H. Blitzer 2005. *The Plain of Phaistos: Cycles of Social Complexity in the Mesara Region of Crete.* (UCLA Monographs 23). Los Angeles.

Weingarten, J. 1990. "Three Upheavals in Minoan Sealing Administration: Evidence for Radical Change," in *Aegean Seals, Sealings and Administration,* (*Aegaeum* 5), ed. T. Palaima, Liège, 105–120.

Weingarten, J. 2000. "Some Stamped Weights from Eastern Crete," in Πεπραγμενα Η' Διεθνους Κρητολογικου Συνεδριου 1996 Τομος Α.3 Herakleion, 485–95.

Wetterstrom, W. 1993. "Foraging and Farming in Egypt: the transition from hunting and gathering to horticulture in the Nile Valley," in *The Archaeology of Africa: Food, Metals and Towns,* ed. T. Shaw, P. Sinclair, B. Andah and A. Okpoko, London, 165–26.

Whitelaw, T. 1983. "The Settlement at Fournou Korifi Myrtos and Aspects of Early Minoan Social Organization," in *Minoan Society: Proceedings of the Cambridge Colloquium 1981,* ed. O. Krzyszkowska and L. Nixon, Cambridge, 323–345.

Whitelaw, T. 1992. "Lost in the Labyrinth? Comments on Broodbank's 'Social change at Knossos before the Bronze Age'," *JMA* 5(2), 225–232.

Whitelaw, T. 2001. "Reading Between the Tablets: Assessing Mycenaean Palatial Involvement in Ceramic Production and Consumption," in *Economy and Politics in the Mycenaean Palace States* (*PCPS* Supplement 27), ed. S. Voutsaki and J. Killen, Cambridge, 51–79.

Whitelaw, T. 2004. "Alternative Pathways to Complexity in the Southern Aegean," in *Emergence of Civilisation Revisited* ed. J. Barrett and P. Halstead, Oxford, 232–56.

Whitelaw, T., P. Day, E. Kiriatzi, V. Kilikoglou and D. Wilson 1997. "Ceramic Traditions at EM IIB Myrtos, Fournou Korifi," in *TEXNH*, 265–274.

Wiener, M. 1987. "Trade and Rule in Palatial Crete," in *Function of the Minoan Palace*, 261–265.

Wilson, D. 1984. *The Early Minoan II A West Court Houses at Knossos*, Ph.D. diss., University of Cincinnati.

Wilson, D. 1994. "Knossos Before the Palaces: an Overview of the Early Bronze Age (EM I–EM II)," in *Knossos: A Labyrinth of History*, ed. D. Evely, H. Hughes-Brock and N. Momigliano, London, 23–44.

Wilson, D. 2008. "Early Prepalatial Crete," in *The Cambridge Companion to the Aegean Bronze Age*, ed. C. Shelmerdine, Cambridge, 77–104.

Xanthoudides, S. 1924. *The Vaulted Tombs of the Messará*, Liverpool.

Xenaki-Sakellariou, A. 1958. *Les cachet minoens de la collection Giamalakis* (*Études Crétoises* 10), Paris.

Young, D. 1965. "Some puzzles about Minoan Woolgathering," *Kadmos* 4, 111–122.

Young, R. 1955. "Gordion Preliminary Report – 1953," *AJA* 59, 1–18.

Young, R. 1956. "The Campaign of 1955 at Gordion," *AJA* 60, 249–266.

Young, R. 1957. "Gordion 1956: Preliminary Report," *AJA* 61, 319–331.

Young, R. 1958. "The Gordion Campaign of 1957," *AJA* 62, 139–154.

Young, R. 1960. "Gordion Campaign of 1959," *AJA* 64, 227–244.

Young, R. 1962. "The 1961 Campaign at Gordion," *AJA* 66, 153–168.

Young, R. 1964. "The 1963 Campaign at Gordion," *AJA* 68, 279–292.

Young, R. 1965. "Early Mosaics at Gordion," *Expedition* 7, 4–13.

Young, R. 1966. "The Gordion Campaign of 1965," *AJA* 70, 267–278.

Young, R. 1968. "The Gordion Campaign of 1967," *AJA* 72, 231–242.

Young, R. 1969. "Old Phrygian Inscriptions from Gordion: Toward a History of the Phrygian Alphabet," *Hesperia* 38, 270–275.

Young, R., K. DeVries and E. Kohler 1981. *Gordion Excavation Reports I: Three Great Early Tumuli (P, MM, W)*, Philadelphia.

Younger, J. 1988. "Review of P. Yule, Early Cretan Seals," *Göttingische Gelehrte Anzeigen* 240(3–4), 201–203.

Younger, J. 1995. "Aegean Seals and other Minoan-Mycenaean Art Forms," *CMS Beiheft* 5, 336–339.

Yule, P. 1980. *Early Cretan Seals: A Study of Chronology* (*Marburger Studien zur Vor- und Frühgeschichte* 4, Mainz am Rhein.

Zagarell, A. 1986. "Trade, Women, Class, and Society in Ancient Western Asia," *CurrAnthr* 27(5), 415–430.

Zohary, D. and M. Hopf 2000. *Domestication of Plants in the Old World: the origin and spread of cultivated plants in West Asia, Europe and the Nile Valley*, Oxford (3rd edition).

Zois, A. 1995. "Ανασκαφη Βασιλική Ιεραπετρά," *Prakt.*, 231–243.

INDEX